Cleveland

– Continuing the Renaissance –

Towery Publishing, Inc.

Cleveland
— Continuing the Renaissance —

By Fred Griffith and Barney Taxel

Profiles in Excellence and Captions by Larry Budd

Art Direction by Sandra Carter

URBAN
TAPESTRY
SERIES
TOWERY
PUBLISHING, INC.

LIBRARY OF CONGRESS CATALOGING-IN-PUBLICATION DATA
Griffith, Fred.
    Cleveland—continuing the renaissance / by Fred Griffith and
Barney Taxel ; profiles in excellence and captions by Larry Budd.
      p.   cm. — (Urban tapestry series)
    Includes index.
    ISBN 1-881096-42-4 (alk. paper)
    1. Cleveland (Ohio)—Civilization.   2. Cleveland (Ohio)—Pictorial
works.   3. Business enterprises—Ohio—Cleveland.   I. Taxel,
 Barney, 1949-   . II. Budd, Larry, 1958-   . III. Title.
 IV. Series.
 F499.C65G75   1997
 977.1'32—dc21
                                                97-16307
                                                  CIP

Towery Publishing, Inc., 1835 Union Avenue, Memphis, TN 38104

PUBLISHER: J. Robert Towery
EXECUTIVE PUBLISHER: Jenny McDowell
NATIONAL SALES MANAGER: Stephen Hung
MARKETING DIRECTOR: Carol Culpepper
PROJECT DIRECTORS: Dawn Park, Jim Tomlinson

EXECUTIVE EDITOR: David B. Dawson
MANAGING EDITOR: Michael C. James
SENIOR EDITORS: Lynn Conlee, Carlisle Hacker
EDITORS: Mary Jane Adams, Lori Bond, Jana Files
ASSISTANT EDITOR: Jennifer C. Pyron
EDITORIAL CONTRIBUTORS: Christopher Johnston, Alex Koleszar, Raizel
    Michelow, Cindy Walker

CREATIVE DIRECTOR: Brian Groppe
PROFILE DESIGNERS: Jennifer Baugher, Laurie Lewis, Ann Ward
TECHNICAL DIRECTOR: William H. Towery
PRODUCTION MANAGER: Brenda Pattat
PRODUCTION ASSISTANTS: Jeff McDonald, Robin McGehee
PRINT COORDINATOR: Beverly Thompson

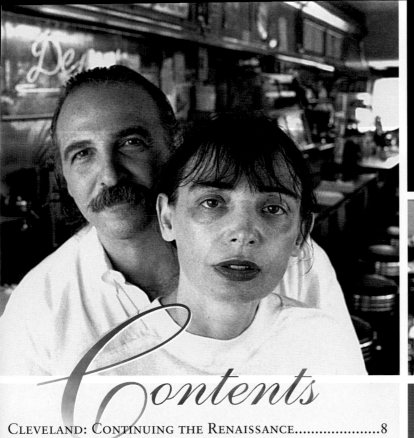

Contents

"Even though parts of Cleveland may seem pastoral and distant, when you view the city from the air, you see the awe-inspiring urban sprawl. The freeways keep taking people farther and farther out, and no boundaries seem large enough."

A look at the corporations, businesses, professional groups, and community service organizations that have made this book possible.

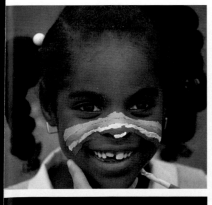

By Fred Griffith

*S*ome things take you by surprise. In my case, it was when I discovered that I was ready for an affair with Cleveland before I ever even saw the city.

It started back in the early 1950s when I was in college in West Virginia. My professors often talked about Cleveland as one of the country's most progressive cities. It had been so ever since the turn of the century, they said, and economic progress and urban growth were among Cleveland's hallmarks. Along with this growth and progress, however, had come the seemingly inevitable consequences of too rapid development: poverty, sickness, pollution, poor public schools,

*V*INTAGE PHOTOGRAPHS reveal Cleveland's rich heritage. A 1950 snapshot depicts the apothecary of yesterday as he fills prescriptions at John A. Jarmuzeski Drugs, while an image transfer captures two Polish girls who smile hopefully at the thought of their new hometown, revitalized for the 21st century.

THE WESTERN RESERVE HISTORICAL SOCIETY

inadequate public services. Every big city suffered from such problems, but it was Cleveland, nearly 100 years ago, that had forged a reputation as a reform-minded community, a place of tolerance and racial harmony, a true melting pot, a real working system of connected neighborhoods, a place where people cared about each other. It was a city where problems were addressed and solved.

FOUNDED IN 1915, THE
Cleveland Play House is
America's oldest continuously pro-
ducing theatrical company. The
Euclid Avenue complex also houses
the Cleveland Center for Contem-
porary Art and the Cleveland
Signstage Theatre.

Big Cleveland entrepreneurs had grown unbelievably rich, said my teachers,

on the bounty of the region and on the labor of the people who toiled for them.

They built lavish mansions on Euclid Avenue, but understood that with their

success came major obligations. They endowed the big cultural institutions like

the Cleveland Museum of Art and the Cleveland Orchestra, as well as colleges,

universities, and major hospitals. And they backed smaller but more daring

enterprises like Karamu House, where black and white actors and musicians

working together attracted a nation's attention. The idea for the Community

Chest was born here. And the Cleveland Foundation became a prototype for the

nation; it showed the wealthy how they could get the maximum social good out

of their financial support of important causes.

Knowing all that, I decided that Cleveland was what a big city ought to be.

It sounded, in short, like utopia.

$\mathcal{S}$INCE ITS FORMATIVE YEARS in the 1940s, the Karamu House has grown into an internationally recognized venue. Rooted in African-American cultural heritage, the center promotes multicultural understanding through a full array of community services.

ROGER MASTROIANNI ▶

◆ BARNEY TAXEL

THE CERAMIC TILES OF THE Unity Walk at Settlers Landing (TOP) and Billie Lawless' *The Politician: A Toy* on Chester Avenue near University Circle (BOTTOM LEFT) make distinctive statements through outdoor sculpture. Inside Severance Hall, musicians and other performers have been making their own artistic statements for the better part of a century (BOTTOM RIGHT).

▲ B. MOLNAR

▲ B. MOLNAR

So, when one of my friends began his graduate studies in Cleveland, I decided I had to visit. He was at Western Reserve University, in the middle of the most glorious arts and education complex I could have ever imagined. On the walls of the museum, I saw for the first time in my life the work of the world's greatest artists. I was astonished by the intelligence and liveliness of the graduate students I met. I loved the colorful student hangouts. I heard great jazz. And once, I even got standing room at Severance Hall to hear George Szell conduct Beethoven's Ninth Symphony.

And that's where the surprise came in. Even though I thought I would enjoy Cleveland, I had no idea how much.

Nonetheless, I returned to West Virginia, where I got married, found a job doing news on the radio, started a family, and spent a little time in the air force. But by the late 1950s, I had reached the limit of what I could do for my family as a radio newsman in the Appalachians. I needed a "bigger market," as they say in broadcasting, and when I went looking for another job, I thought first, foremost, and only of Cleveland.

I sent out letters to the city's radio stations, and in October 1959, one offered me a job doing the morning news. I jumped at the chance, moved to Cleveland, and have been here ever since.

OPENED IN 1916, THE CLEVE-land Museum of Art features a world-renowned collection of some 30,000 works covering 5,000 years. The building's grand architectural design accentuates the artistic ambience that pervades University Circle.

▶ B. MOLNAR

THE CITY OF BRIDGES, Cleveland is known for its series of iron spans. Here, the Conrail Bridge is brightened by the luster of fireworks during the bicentennial celebration in 1996 (BELOW). The events surrounding the city's 200th birthday saw many festive displays over the Cuyahoga River (PAGES 16 AND 17).

Also lighting the way, the Marblehead Lighthouse guides boats off the Marblehead Peninsula, west of Cleveland.

*A*s everyone in northern Ohio knows, Cleveland recently celebrated its bicentennial. On July 22, 1796, General Moses Cleaveland started it all when he landed on the "north coast" of Lake Erie to explore the Connecticut Western Reserve, 3 million acres that the state of Connecticut had sold to a group of investors. Cleaveland's assignment was akin to that of Lewis and Clark in conjunction with the Louisiana Purchase some decades later: to nose around, draw a few maps, and check out the potential of this vast stretch of land.

Cleaveland laid out a little town plan where our city (sans the extra *a*) now stands. And over the next quarter of a century, people from the east arrived and went to work, mostly clearing land and starting farms. Then came the modest services that a farming community needs. None of those early Clevelanders could have guessed what this place would be like by the end of the century.

Natural resources were abundant. Lake Erie made shipping easy. Iron ore and coal came together on the banks of the Cuyahoga in the early foundries. A canal system tied navigable rivers together. Railroads were built. Oil was brought in from nearby fields and turned into usable fuel, something that was essential for the coming motor culture of 20th-century America.

The word went out that there were jobs here—jobs with a future. There was opportunity. People responded from across the country and around the world.

The Irish were among the first to come, followed closely by other groups of emigrants from northern and western Europe. In the 20th century, people flocked to Cleveland from places all over eastern Europe, and then Puerto Rico, and then Asia, and then the former Soviet bloc. In the post-World War II years, African-Americans moved here from the South. And people from the Appalachians came by the thousands, fleeing the poverty of marginal farms and the perils of digging coal. All were looking for a chance to work and prosper, and, for the most part, they found it in Cleveland.

▲ ADAM MISZTAL

HROUGHOUT THE 20TH century, Cleveland has drawn immigrants from all over the world. While the various groups have assimilated into the city's ethnic tapestry, each has maintained its own identity, celebrating its cultural heritage year-round. With diversity comes contrast. Here, nature lends its unmistakable beauty to a local industrial site.

s often as not, the dreams I developed in college turned out to be true. Although it wasn't utopia, Cleveland seemed to be the next best thing. Cleveland was still a hot town when I arrived, a place where stacks poured out the smoke and steam of metalworking and chemical and paint factories. And people were coming from all over just for the opportunity to be a part of it.

At the time, the city had a population of close to 1 million. Yet almost every neighborhood was unique and could be characterized by the nationality of the people who had been living there since they (or their forebears) had first arrived—Czech, Ukrainian, Hungarian, African-American, Chinese. In these communities there were retail strips with mom-and-pop businesses. People could walk a block or two from their houses to the grocery stores and butcher shops and beauty parlors. There were bars, pool halls, restaurants, churches, and music studios. Residents owned small, neat houses near the factories that supported them. People could walk to work or grab a quick ride on the trolley. The schools were good, and they were close enough that most kids could come home for a hot lunch.

Not many of us knew it then, but our nuts-and-bolts economy was changing. The decline of the heavy industry that supported the northeastern economy was under way. And major manufacturing companies were starting to move their operations south—or overseas—in search of lower labor costs. The labor unions lost their power. The Rust Belt was born.

*M*ORE THAN 200 YEARS ago, Moses Cleaveland set foot on the desolate shores of what is now downtown Cleveland. Today, the city stands tall and vibrant as it begins its third century of growth.

◆ ADAM MISZTAL

Cleveland's wonderful old neighborhoods began to decay, while the development of the suburbs and the freeways that would take us to them started to accelerate. As factories closed, urban workers fled to Parma, Euclid, and Willoughby, where jobs in the growing service sector and in the new high-tech factories were said to be plentiful. For more affluent citizens, developers built (or expanded) Shaker Heights, Bay Village, Rocky River, and Beachwood. While all of this was going on, Cleveland just sort of faded economically without anyone really noticing.

The urban riots of the mid- and late 1960s were a wake-up call. And we started to realize that things needed fixing.

By then, I was working as a television newsman, and one of my assignments was to cover the election of Carl B. Stokes, who, after the Hough riots of 1966, became the first African-American mayor of a major U.S. city. "He'll fix things,"

First settled in 1799, the east-side neighborhood of Hough exploded in seven days of violent riots in 1966. Today, the community is being revitalized, thanks to the Hough Area Partners in Progress.

we thought. "He understands what's happening." But the problems were bigger than Stokes or any of us suspected. The Glenville riots in 1968, and others across the country, served notice that the nation's cities were still in trouble and that economic failings were at the heart of the crisis.

After Stokes, Clevelanders elected Ralph Perk, and although the riots ended, the economic slide continued. Perk was followed by the 32-year-old Dennis Kucinich, who dramatized the crisis in his short term when he confronted the banks and precipitated a financial default. Then, George Voinovich, a Republican in a Democratic town, came to city hall. And after him, Michael White. In their own ways, these mayors were able to build coalitions of all kinds of interests and people. Things started to happen, the climate began slowly improving, and by the early 1980s, Cleveland's recovery was under way.

VIEWED FROM A LOFTY VANtage point south of downtown, the skyline and connecting roadways glimmer with energy.

Today, we seem to have returned somewhat to the utopia I fell in love with. I live just 12 minutes from the downtown television station where I work, and although I am close to the skyscrapers, I can still see deer nibbling at my neighbors' hostas. They amble in through the network of green parks, what we call the "emerald necklace." Within a five-minute walk of my house, the Shaker Lakes that separate Cleveland Heights from Shaker Heights are a rich broth of wildlife: I have seen snapping turtles that look like they came from the Galapagos Islands, as well as muskrats, rabbits, squirrels, skunks, opossums, raccoons, chipmunks, owls, three kinds of heron, ducks, geese, and a kingfisher. Once, I spied a group of swans that stopped for a rest, and on one cool fall day, I even spotted an eagle from one of the Lake Erie preserves resting in a tall tree. And there are ravens everywhere—raucous creatures that we have come to hate, ever since the Football Team Formerly Known as the Browns was packed off to Baltimore.

Still, even though parts of Cleveland may seem pastoral and distant, when you view the city from the air, you see the awe-inspiring urban sprawl. The freeways keep taking people farther and farther out, and no boundaries seem large enough. Most of the new houses and neighborhoods being developed, no matter what the price range, are slated for completion in the next county. Cleveland is growing once again.

𝒩 OT FAR FROM THE HUSTLE and bustle of downtown, Clevelanders can enjoy nature in the city's parks, suburbs, and natural sanctuaries. In nearby Lake County, a beach pea blooms at Headlands Dunes State Nature Preserve, one of the last sand dune communities remaining along Lake Erie's south shore (OPPOSITE).

SQUIRREL AND RABBIT: DAVID DVORAK JR.

FROM THE QUAINT TO THE ultramodern, Cleveland has it all. Old neighborhoods like Little Italy continue to prosper, while downtown boasts its share of new skyscrapers. The 57-story Key Tower—home to financial services giant KeyCorp, as well as a luxury hotel and other professional offices—stands highest on the city's skyline.
ROGER MASTROIANNI ▼

Cleveland has always been kaleidoscopic, polyglot, varied. In the 1970s, when my son Wally was a child, he'd say, "Dad, let's get lost." He wanted to see where everyone lived, what their neighborhoods looked like. And almost every week, we would set off in the car for some part of the city we had never seen before. We went to Hough Avenue and Mt. Pleasant, Fleet Avenue and Buckeye Road, Slavic Village, Tremont, and Ohio City. We visited fire stations and outdoor markets. We watched the big cranes unload the ore carriers and later marveled at the fire of the blast furnaces.

As my son and I moved around the city, we heard people speaking in all kinds of accents and, in some cases, foreign tongues. Nonetheless, no matter where we "got lost," we heard folks displaying our distinctive Clevelandspeak.

All right, maybe we can't compete with the people in Minnesota or the Deep South when it comes to twang or drawl, but we do have some characteristics that stand out. Watch out for our *a*'s. We put a special twist on them. For example, "dee-add"—that's your father. If he is old enough, he'll need some reading "glee-asses." The guy who comes down our chimneys at Christmas is "See-yan-ta." And the place you go to get educated is the "skoo-uhl," making Cleveland perhaps the only place in America where it has two syllables. I knew a film editor who said "youse guys." Was he from Brooklyn? Well, yes. But not Brooklyn, New York. Brooklyn, *Ohio*. And the crooked Cuyahoga River that dissects the city as it snakes its way to Lake Erie? Forget the phonetically sensible "Ky-uh-hoe-guh." For most of us here, it's "Ka-HOG-uh."

his isn't Walt Disney World quite yet. Or San Francisco or New York City. But lately Cleveland has become a big-time tourist destination.

As you drive from the airport, you will pass the Cleveland Metroparks Zoo on the south and the MetroHealth System complex, like two giant glass silos, on the north. Then, as you go across the Flats and the river on the high interstate bridge, downtown rises before you, a physical reminder of Cleveland's heritage and its renaissance.

If it's your first visit, and it's summer, try to get some tickets to a baseball game. Home of the Cleveland Indians, the gorgeous Jacobs Field hasn't had an empty seat in the few years it's been open. The stadium forces you to embrace the cityscape: Through the gap in center field you can see the biggest buildings of downtown, bringing city and stadium into a seamless blend of work and play. Jacobs Field is by no means the only place to enjoy professional sports. The tall guys (the Cavaliers) play hoops at the Gund Arena at Gateway next door, a three-minute walk from Public Square, which houses the Terminal Tower and

GREAT SHIPS WERE ONCE BUILT along Cleveland's industrial lakefront. Today, such tourist venues as the Great Lakes Science Center adorn the North Coast Harbor.

Tower City Center. And a new facility is being built on the lakefront to replace the cavernous and ancient Municipal Stadium and to provide a home for the new Browns (when they finally get here).

Speaking of the lakefront, it is yet another tangible symbol of Cleveland's rich past and its glowing future. Long dedicated to industry—complete with docks, piers, an eight-lane expressway, railroads, and an airport—the lakefront has become a place for people. A glistening extension of our rapid transit line now carries riders from the Terminal Tower to the Flats and the lakefront, to the Rock and Roll Hall of Fame and Museum, to the Great Lakes Science Center, and eventually to the new stadium.

Cleveland is also a city where public art has become important again. After producing a flurry of monumental art early in the century, we lagged until Noguchi's *Portal* was erected in front of the Cleveland Justice Center. At first, we thought it looked like a pretzel made of four-foot pipe, but now we love it. And then there is Coosje van Bruggen's and Claes Oldenberg's *Free Stamp*, intended to stand on a pedestal in front of Sohio's new skyscraper. The sculpture looks like one of those stamps that you use to mark something paid, except that it says "free" instead. The piece was rejected when BP took over Standard Oil. Something about the symbolism. But now, with some irony, *Free Stamp* has been placed down by city hall. Irony or no, it's still controversial: One of our *Plain Dealer* editorial writers wants to send it to Baltimore, the city that nabbed our football team.

*L*OCATED ON EITHER SIDE OF the Cuyahoga River, the Flats district draws impressive crowds with its multitude of entertainment options. The neighborhood also provides inspiration to local artists. Here, painter Ron Joranko captures one of the many bridges that dot the riverfront (OPPOSITE).

The Flats down by the Cuyahoga, near where Moses Cleaveland first came ashore, is another area of the city that is alive again. In the last century and for most of this one, the Cuyahoga was lined with factories and refineries, warehouses and wholesalers, union halls and beer joints. But now buildings that were merely relics of an earlier age are sparkling with new life, occupied by hip advertising agencies, slick restaurants, glossy nightclubs, progressive art galleries, popular microbreweries, and upscale stores. And there's an open-air stage on the west bank where big acts play.

A must-see for newcomers and tourists alike is Severance Hall. It's small, with barely 2,000 seats, yet there is no greater place in the world to listen to the classics. And where is there a finer serious music organization than the Cleveland Orchestra? In the summer, the renowned orchestra takes the stage at the Blossom Music Center, an airy venue located between Cleveland and Akron that most consider to be better than Wolf Trap or Tanglewood or Ravinia.

As rich as Cleveland is in culture, it is equally great in cultural contrasts. This is a place where "rap meisters" mingle with mavens of jazz and rock-and-roll superstars. Disc jockey Alan Freed, who gave rock and roll its name, toiled in radio here. Cleveland is where George Szell, the man who led the Cleveland Orchestra to its international reputation, made recordings of Beethoven symphonies in the 1960s that are still regarded as definitive performances. This was once the

▼ SCOTT MARLON SYKES

polka capital of the world, and Frankie Yankovich was the king. He and Szell were contemporaries and, while we don't know if they listened to each other, folks in Cleveland are certain that they should have.

Szell, a Czech, often ate Italian food at Guarino's, located a few minutes from Severance Hall. (His autographed photo is still on the wall.) But he had plenty of other options, and so do we. Within a 30-minute drive of University Circle, you can have a dinner of kielbasa, pot stickers, plantains, pita, pizza, pierogi, polenta, pasties, bratwurst, paprikash (Cleveland has the largest concentration of Hungarians in the United States), moussaka, gyros, schnitzel, samosas, bigos, huevos rancheros, stuffed cabbage, stuffed grape leaves, kibbeh, pork hocks with turnip greens, vushka, and sushi. And for dessert, you'll find strudel, baklava, spumoni, or good old deep-dish apple pie.

JENNIE JONES

*M*USICIANS KEEP THE BEAT nightly in Cleveland, the town where rock and roll got its name. Tourists can learn this and other interesting facts at the Rock and Roll Hall of Fame and Museum, within walking distance of the Great Lakes Science Center at North Coast Harbor.

he 1996 bicentennial celebration helped remind us of Cleveland's countless assets, which make our city such a special place in which to live and work. However, even as we swirled in the euphoria that came with the Rock and Roll Hall of Fame, the winning Indians, an exciting bicentennial celebration, reams of positive national press, and a significant economic revival, we still took time to talk about problems we have yet to solve. While we were busy patting ourselves on the back, the Citizens League did a major study and reminded us that there are a number of areas for improvement—from education to the arts, from urban sprawl to air quality. The kinds of problems being faced by big, successful cities across the country, but problems nonetheless.

CLEVELAND INDIANS FANS crowd Jacobs Field, the city's new baseball stadium. The home team is so popular that the facility hasn't had an empty seat in the few years it's been open.

Now, our job is to take care of our assets and do everything we can to attract more of them. Lately, we've been doing a pretty good job of just that. We still build steel and cars, but now we do it in state-of-the-art facilities. Cleveland is also a growing center for the next generation of high-tech manufacturing, and promising research is going on in universities and corporations that will lead to further economic development. Much of our recovery has been driven by the fast-growing and competitive service sector. The city has become a regional center for health care, law, education, communications, accounting, banking, and insurance.

Indeed, there is a cohesiveness here now, a progressive spirit that my college professors first told me of, and that I first experienced when I visited Cleveland more than four decades ago. Perhaps we lost it for a brief time, but having paid attention to such things through the years, I'm happy to report that the spirit is now back. Our troubles have, in the end, tended to make us more whole, more determined to understand our problems, and better able do something about them.

A renaissance really is unfolding before us every day. My affair with this city—the one that started more than 40 years ago—continues. And, looking back at my time in Cleveland, some things really come as no surprise at all. ■

CLEVELAND'S FUTURE WILL BE painted according to the ambitions of its children, while its past is remembered through such monuments as the War Memorial Fountain, completed in 1962 by Marshall Fredericks.

▲ JANET CENTURY

*T*HE BEAUTY OF THE CLEVE-
land skyline stands out,
whether it's illuminated by fireworks
exploding over the North Coast Harbor or by bolts of lightning courtesy
of Mother Nature.

BRIDGES OVER THE CUYAHOGA River connect Cleveland's Flats and other downtown districts. The spans, permanently lit as part of the city's bicentennial celebration in 1996, also support motorists traveling above the river valley.

ONCE DARKNESS SETTLES OVER the city, light emanating from building windows and decorative displays welcomes visitors to Cleveland's revitalized downtown.

CARS CRUISE ALONG OLD RIVER Road as boats taxi down the Cuyahoga River, which separates the two sides of the sprawling Flats entertainment district (TOP). While much of the draw to the area comes from numerous regular attractions, such special events as a vintage car show at Playhouse Square (BOTTOM) supplement the energy of the city at night.

$\mathcal{A}$T NIGHT, THE ENTER-
tainment options run the
gamut—from strolling along a misty
downtown avenue to pouring drinks
for thirsty customers to raising a
glass to a new, albeit unusual, friend.

F RANK L. JIROUCH's 1928 bronze statue *Night Passing the Earth to Day*, which stands at the south end of the lagoon outside the Cleveland Museum of Art (OPPOSITE), seems to provide inspiration to the city's residents. Here, children push an oversized globe during the Cuyahoga Valley Heritage Festival, an annual summer celebration of folk art and music (TOP), while these "boulder rollers" guide fiberglass rocks, sculpted to represent the five original members of the Rolling Stones, during the grand opening parade of the Rock and Roll Hall of Fame and Museum (BOTTOM).

*M*USIC FILLS THE AIR DURING the Feast of the Assumption, a festival held each summer in the east side neighborhood of Little Italy. Commemorating the return of the Virgin Mary to heaven, the event features music from around the world, as well as plenty of traditional Italian foods and wines.

▲ JANET CENTURY

CLEVELANDERS DON'T NEED much excuse to take to the streets and dance, as a giant puppet performing during the city's bicentennial birthday party in 1996 demonstrates (LEFT). Unique, human-powered floats mark Parade the Circle, an annual celebration presented by the Cleveland Museum of Art (TOP RIGHT AND OPPOSITE, TOP LEFT).

▶ JANET CENTURY

𝓛OCALS FOUND COUNTLESS ways to celebrate the opening of the Rock and Roll Hall of Fame. Trends from throughout the history of popular music were represented in the festivities, from tie-dyed Dead Heads (RIGHT) to poodle-skirted bobby-soxers (BOTTOM LEFT) to peace-loving Woodstockers (OPPOSITE, BOTTOM RIGHT).

*A*t the Dancing in the Streets celebration, people embracing all walks of life gather for food, music, and, of course, dancing (OPPOSITE). The Gay Pride Parade, held in the summer, also brings together diverse segments of the city's populace (THIS PAGE).

IN 1796, SURVEYOR MOSES Cleaveland set the stage for the aggregation of a melting pot of humanity when he first came ashore near the mouth of the Cuyahoga River. Today, through a string of celebrations, Cleveland continues to nurture the uniqueness of that rich ethnic tradition.

ALTHOUGH THESE CHILDREN are several generations removed from their ancestors' home-lands, they are able to get a taste of old-world charm at this Hungarian festival.

*T*HERE IS NO BETTER WAY TO experience an ethnic culture than by donning its traditional garb and observing its customs, even while holding the state flag of Ohio.

OR DECADES, AUDIENCES
have marveled at the brilliance of local performing arts organizations, including the Karamu House, the nation's oldest African-American cultural institution (TOP), and the Great Lakes Theater Festival, which combined theater, music, and dance in a production of *The Bakkhai* (BOTTOM). Here, two dancers from the Cleveland Ballet grace the aisles of St. John's Cathedral, the headquarters of the Catholic Diocese of Cleveland (OPPOSITE).

*A*LL ACROSS GREATER Cleveland, religious ceremonies and festivities are of central importance. A magnificent organ accompanies services at the Pilgrim Congregational Church (OPPOSITE), while, each summer, celebrants of all ages gather for the Feast of the Assumption on Murray Hill in Little Italy (THIS PAGE). As part of the festivities, participants adorn a statue of the Virgin Mary with a monetary offering that is later used to support the church and care for the poor.

N 1996, THE LOCAL UKRAI-
nian community commemo-
rated the 10th anniversary of the
Chernobyl nuclear disaster with a
candlelight vigil.

*C*LEVELANDERS WHO DIED defending their country are remembered through parades, reenactments, and cemetery services.

▲ DENNIS L. ANDERSON

𝒱ETERANS ARE HONORED through various area monuments, including the Vietnam War Memorial at Lake View Cemetery (BOTTOM RIGHT) and Public Square's Soldiers' and Sailors' Monument, which pays tribute to fallen Civil War soldiers (BOTTOM LEFT).

*I*N 1991, THE 48-FOOT *Free Stamp* by Claes Oldenburg and Coosje van Bruggen was installed in Willard Park, at Lakeside Avenue near East 9th Street. Com-missioned by the Standard Oil Company, the sculpture was donated to the city after the company became part of British Petroleum.

CLEVELAND

Statues and monuments decorate public places around the city. Chester A. Beach's *Sun* punctuates the Fine Arts Garden outside the Cleveland Museum of Art (OPPOSITE), and the Soldiers' and Sailors' Monument, completed by Levi T. Scofield in 1894, adds to the beauty of Public Square (ABOVE). This historic memorial features a 100-foot esplanade that supports a granite and sandstone tablet room, as well as four bronze statues to depict the infantry, cavalry, artillery, and navy.

*L*IFE IMITATING ART: A WOMAN rehearsing for a modern dance performance unknowingly mirrors a sculpture in downtown Cleveland.

$\mathcal{R}$ESTING ON A LANDING OUTSIDE the Cleveland Museum of Art, this enlargement of *The Thinker* by Auguste Rodin serves as a reader's backdrop (TOP LEFT). Malvina Hoffman's *Bacchanale*, also called *Russian Dancers*, was first lent to the museum in 1917 and later became part of the permanent collection (BOTTOM LEFT). Sculptor Henry Hering's *Progress in Transportation* (1932) adorns the Lorain-Carnegie Bridge in the Flats (RIGHT), while his *Energy in Respose* (1923) decorates the Federal Reserve Bank at East 6th and Superior (OPPOSITE).

MELLOTT / THE IMAGE FINDERS

JIM BARON / THE IMAGE FINDERS

C LEVELAND OFFERS NUMEROUS locations for solitary contemplation—whether you're inside one of the city's many churches or outside in the Metroparks, viewing Mother Nature's murals.

CONTINUING THE RENAISSANCE

79

*A*RT LOVERS CAN ENJOY A
diverse mix of painting
styles at the Cleveland Institute of
Art (ABOVE) and the Museum of Art
(OPPOSITE).

A WOMAN PAUSES FOR A longer look at this work of art near East 70th Street and Carnegie Avenue (PAGES 82 AND 83). Although the mural no longer covers this wall, others can be found throughout the city.

The TERMINAL TOWER looms behind *Last*, a massive arch fabricated of hollow steel that spans 75 feet across and rises 35 feet high (TOP). Completed in 1979 by Tony Smith, the sculpture sits outside the Ohio State Office Building at West 6th Street and Superior Avenue. Another outdoor sculpture, *Three for One* by Dennis L. Jones, twists and turns on the grounds of the Crile Building, an outpatient facility of the Cleveland Clinic Foundation (BOTTOM).

*T*HE *Hart Crane Memorial*, located in a park of the same name, stands in tribute to the well-known American poet, who was born in nearby Garrettsville. The park and its sculpture, designed by local artist Gene Kangas, are nestled beneath the Columbus Road lift bridge in the Flats.

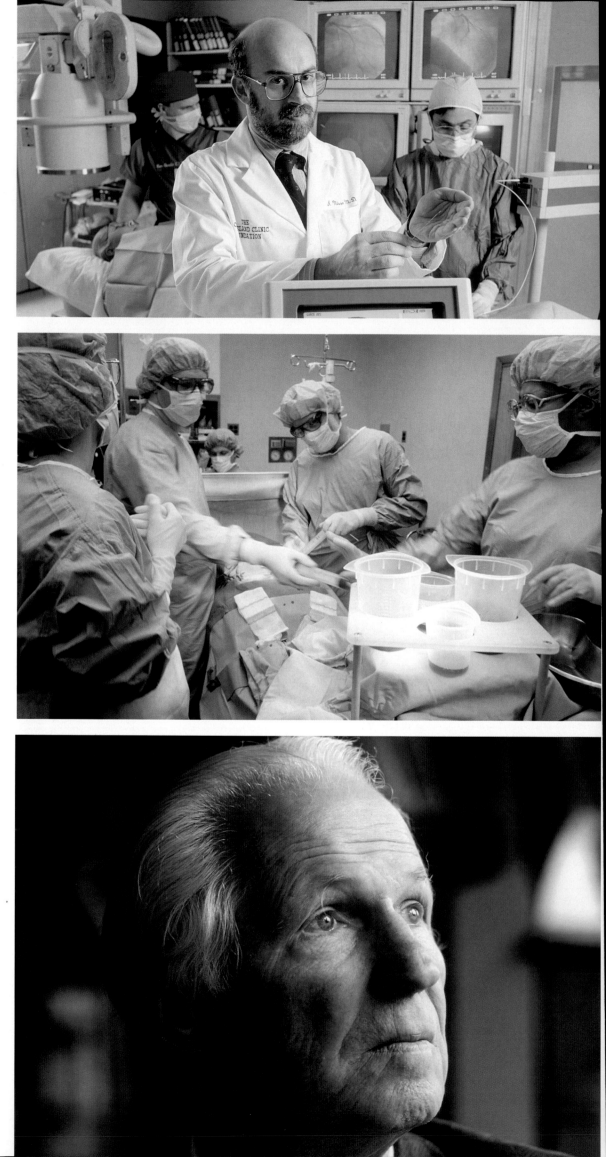

$\mathcal{L}$ ONG A TRENDSETTER IN THE medical field, the Cleveland Clinic boasts state-of-the-art facilities and procedures. The world-renowned health care organization was founded by Dr. George W. Crile Sr. in 1921. The late Dr. George W. Crile Jr. continued in his father's tradition, becoming one of the industry's most influential surgeons (BOTTOM).

WITH TWO OF THE NATION'S top 25 medical institutions, according to *U.S. News & World Report*, Cleveland has established an enviable reputation for health care. The acclaimed University Hospitals of Cleveland campus includes the 10-story Alfred and Norma Lerner Tower (BOTTOM).

$\mathcal{S}$UCH EDUCATORS AS INEZ
Boone Powell (TOP) and
Wanda Jean Green (BOTTOM) help
prepare local youngsters for a bright
future.

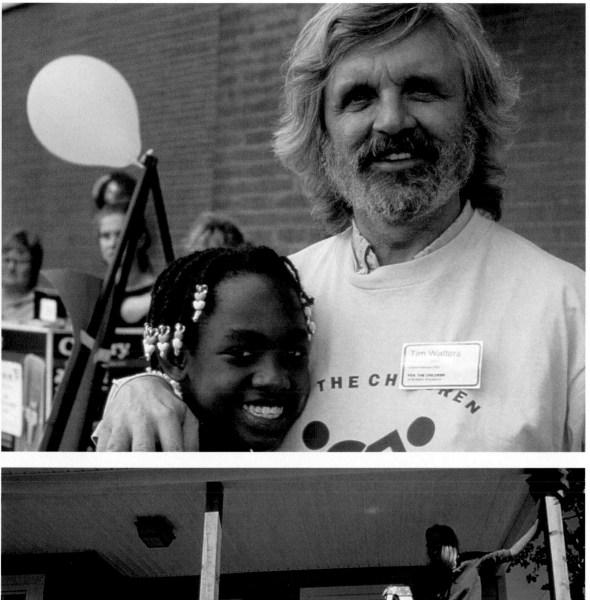

*T*HROUGH THE WORK OF such organizations as For the Children and Habitat for Humanity, residents of the city's poorer neighborhoods gain hope and opportunity.

HROUGH COMMUNITY
policing and other innovative
programs, Cleveland's men and
women in blue develop rapport, even
friendship, with the city's residents.

ONTINUING THE RENAISSANCE

HETHER YOU'RE ON THE job or enjoying time off, a pair of shades and a motorcycle give the promise of an adventure.

ALTHOUGH THE TRANSIT may not be especially rapid, bicycles are a good way to get around Cleveland and its suburbs.

ROM WHEELCHAIRS AND dogsleds to bicycles and race cars, Clevelanders match skills and wits in contests staged throughout the year. The city is also the site of several marathons, as well as the Krazy Kraft boat race on the Cuyahoga River.

$\mathcal{F}$ ROM RACES AT THISTLE-
down to polo matches and
numerous other equestrian events,
horses are a popular mode of con-
veyance for Clevelanders.

*W*HETHER YOU'RE TRAVEL-
ing on land or by air, the
faster the speed, the better.

OCALS TEST THEIR ATHLETIC prowess—and their bravery—through such exhilarating activities as ice climbing, hot air ballooning, dirt biking, parasailing, and flying a biplane.

CASEY BATULE

PECTACULAR MULTICOLORED
kites, sometimes flown in
perfect formation, thrill the crowds
at Edgewater Park.

▲ CARL J. SKALAK JR.

PARADE OF BRIGHT COLORS
and tall masts glides across
the surface of Lake Erie. Each year,
the sailing season is highlighted by
a week of races and good times at
Put-in-Bay.

ARGE CROWDS OPT FOR THE passive approach to nautical life aboard such magnificent paddle wheelers and cruise ships as *Star of Nautica*. During the warm months, boaters can take a break from the water and enjoy the clubs and restaurants along the Cuyahoga River in the Flats.

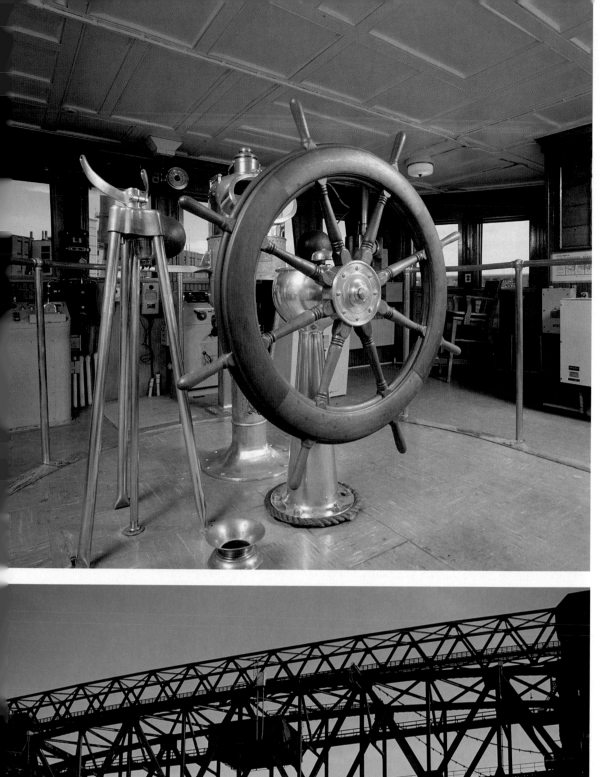

THE FREIGHTER *William G. Mather* (TOP AND OPPOSITE TOP) never leaves the North Coast Harbor. Instead, it serves as a museum of the storied maritime industry that has long flourished on the Great Lakes. Other freighters, such as *American Republic*, continue to carry tons of iron ore and other commodities into the Port of Cleveland, occasionally with assistance from tugboats.

*S*UNSETS ILLUMINATING THE
downtown skyline, river-
front, and North Coast Harbor
reveal the diverse beauty of the city.

HE END OF THE DAY IS
sealed by the setting sun over
Lake Erie (THIS PAGE), while the on-
set of morning is signaled by a sun-
rise off the Marblehead Peninsula
(OPPOSITE). The peninsula is home
to Marblehead Lighthouse, the oldest
continuously operating lighthouse on
the Great Lakes.

C LEVELAND-AREA BEACHES
provide for serene contemplation, long sandy walks, and excellent
views.

OUTSIDE THE CITY, BIRD-watchers find ample opportunity to enjoy the sights, from a graceful gull in flight to a brightly colored goldfinch at rest. Nature lovers can also get their fill in nearby Kirtland at the Holden Arboretum, the largest venue of its kind in the United States (OPPOSITE).

$\mathcal{T}$HE ARTISTRY OF NATURE can be found in many forms— in a peacock's majestic plumage or in the wings of colorful luna and polyphemus moths.

CONTINUING THE RENAISSANCE

W HETHER IN A BOAT, ON the shore, or knee-deep in an area lake, anglers enjoy their solitary sport. In fact, walleye fishing is a major tourist draw to northern Ohio and the Great Lakes area.

THE SEVENTH-OLDEST ZOO in the United States, the Cleveland Metroparks Zoo features a collection of interesting animals from across the globe, from orangutans and macaroni penguins to African lions and grizzly bears (PAGES 126 AND 127).

$\mathcal{I}$N GREATER CLEVELAND,
nature finds striking ways
to mimic itself. A fawn rests quietly
on the forest floor (ABOVE), while
this skunk cabbage curls in its own
unusual way (OPPOSITE).

T HE CUYAHOGA VALLEY National Recreation Area, located south of downtown Cleveland, comprises 33,000 acres along 22 miles of the Cuyahoga River.

When visitors find themselves amid the beauty of Blue Hen Falls and other natural wonders, the hustle and bustle of the city seems far away (PAGES 130 AND 131).

PAGES 130 AND 131: DALE DONG

SCENES OF NATURAL BEAUTY, such as Buttermilk Falls in the Cleveland Metroparks North Chagrin Reservation (TOP), Brandywine Falls in the Cuyahoga Valley National Recreation Area (BOTTOM), and a bridge near Blue Hen Falls (OPPOSITE) await those who explore the area's hiking trails.

$\mathcal{A}$LTHOUGH GENERALLY considered to be part of the region's past, covered bridges can still be found throughout Greater Cleveland. While these spans, designed for buggies, are no longer of practical use, their utility is in the picturesque scenes they create.

W INTER PUTS A WHOLE NEW face on the local landscape, blanketing the covered bridge at Warner's Hollow in Ashtabula County (OPPOSITE), as well as the shore of the Rocky River in Olmsted Falls (CENTER). Sometimes, beach and lakefront become almost indistinguishable.

𝒩O MATTER THE SEASON, locals flock to area lakes for all kinds of activities. Ice-skaters race across frozen surfaces on bright days, while in warmer weather, a boat is the preferred mode of transportation. Here, a kayaker paddles off Headlands Beach State Park, located east of the city.

A NEW DAY SHEDS ITS LIGHT
on the Cuyahoga Valley
National Recreation Area (OPPO-
SITE), while the shoreline at Perkins
Beach in Cleveland Lakefront State
Park glows from the last rays before
sunset (ABOVE).

JIM BARON / THE IMAGE FINDERS

DARRYL POLK

*A*LTHOUGH ANY OLD SUN-glasses will do on a bright, clear day, just the right pair can make a fashion statement.

CLEVELANDERS PUT THEIR best "face" forward, whether it's as a participant in the Cuyahoga Valley Heritage Festival (RIGHT), a mime practicing his art (OPPOSITE LEFT), or the brave souls behind home plate at an Indians game (OPPOSITE, TOP RIGHT). Local modernist architect Richard Fleischman (OPPOSITE, BOTTOM RIGHT), who has designed many area schools, churches, and other institutions, also knows the importance of putting up the right facade.

CARL J. SKALAK JR.

ℰSTABLISHED IN CLEVELAND in time for the 1970-1971 NBA season, the Cavaliers have drawn a strong local following. Coach Mike Fratello and the team's loyal fans anxiously watch the fast-paced play on the home court at Gund Arena. During time-outs, the CAVS Dance Team takes to the floor and adds to the excitement.

▼ CARL J. SKALAK JR.

INNERS OF THE AMERICAN League Championship in 1995, the Cleveland Indians continue to field contenders, evoking ever heightening levels of fan hysteria at Jacobs Field.

As the city where rock and roll got its name, Cleveland was a logical choice for the Hall of Fame, a unique, I.M. Pei-designed structure that houses exciting exhibits on the musical genre and those who have shaped it, including such superstars as Eric Clapton (TOP). Jane Scott has displayed her affection for rock and roll for decades as a music reviewer for the *Plain Dealer* (OPPOSITE).

ONE OF THE LARGEST PER-
forming arts centers in the
United States, Playhouse Square was
saved from the wrecking ball in
1971, thanks in part to the late
Homer Wadsworth, who was also
the director of the Cleveland Foundation (OPPOSITE). Among the stars
to have graced the stages of Playhouse Square's four historic theaters
are (CLOCKWISE FROM TOP) Jack
Klugman and Tony Randall, Hal
Holbrook, and Jerry Seinfeld.

THE PLAIN DEALER

AFTER THE DEMISE OF the *Cleveland Press*, Dick Feagler, a popular and sometimes controversial commentator/columnist (OPPOSITE), moved over to the *Plain Dealer*. With a circulation of just under 400,000, the daily paper supplies Clevelanders with all the latest news.

LEVELAND'S HOST OF FINE
restaurateurs and caterers are
bent on adding something unique to
the food they serve. Visiting chef
Paul Bocuse and Sans Souci chef
Claude Rodier delight patrons with
their French cuisine (OPPOSITE TOP);
Harlan Diamond, owner of Executive Caterers, has pleased people's
palates for more than 35 years (TOP);
and Maury Feren shares his extensive
knowledge of vinegars and wines on
his radio show *Maury's Market*
(BOTTOM).

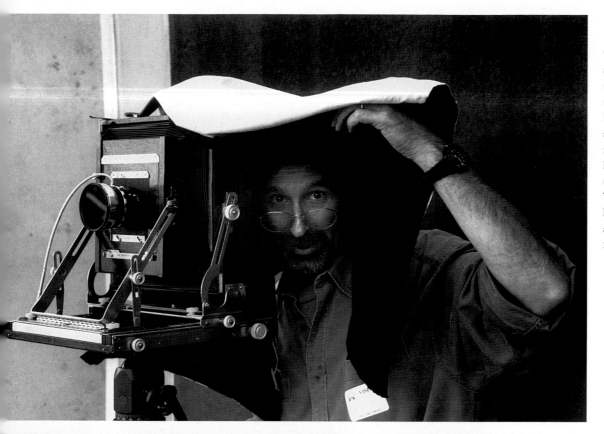

$\mathcal{P}$ROOF POSITIVE THAT A picture is worth a thousand words, such local photographers as Roger and Steven Mastroianni (OPPOSITE TOP) and Barney Taxel (TOP) work to capture their beloved hometown on film, while salesman Joseph Downey and the folks at Nelson's Photography have made portraits their business (BOTTOM). Lifelong Clevelander Tony Tomsic has made a name for himself both locally and nationally as a sports photographer (OPPOSITE BOTTOM).

𝒦 NOWN FOR THEIR CRE-
ative flair, hairdressers
learn to stay on top of the latest
styles. But if volcanoes and palm
trees aren't your bag of tricks,
there's always a removable
alternative.

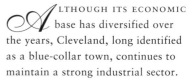LTHOUGH ITS ECONOMIC base has diversified over the years, Cleveland, long identified as a blue-collar town, continues to maintain a strong industrial sector.

N RECENT DECADES, WOMEN have made a name for themselves in all areas of Cleveland's workforce, including those occupations traditionally filled by men.

AST NETWORKS OF PIPES
connect the systems that support the city and its industrial base.

THE SPRAWLING COMPOUND
of LTV Steel Company, the
third-largest integrated steel producer in the United States, is visible
from the highways approaching the
city (ABOVE AND OPPOSITE). LTV is
located in the Flats district, which is
home to numerous factories and
warehouses (PAGES 172 AND 173).

PAGES 172 AND 173: STEVEN MASTROIANNI

T HE TECHNIQUES OF ART and industry can be surprisingly similar. Intense heat is used in firing a piece of *raku* (OPPOSITE) and in coaxing molten metal into different shapes and alloys (LEFT).

THE TOWERS OF INDUSTRY
and religion rise dramatically before a brilliant Cleveland
sunset.

▲ MELLOTT / THE IMAGE FINDERS

*T*HE MAGNIFICENCE OF area towers, including those of St. Theodosius Orthodox Cathedral (LEFT) and the clock tower in West Side Market (OPPOSITE), is mirrored in the century-old monument to President James A. Garfield at Lake View Cemetery (RIGHT). Similarly, the patterns on the ceiling at 820 Superior Avenue downtown (PAGE 180) seem to take their cues from a windmill near Oberlin (PAGE 181).

OOKING DOWN ON A STAIR-
case at General Electric's Nela
Park complex (OPPOSITE) or the rock
steps below Blue Hen Falls in the
Cuyahoga Valley National Recreation Area (LEFT) can be a dizzying
experience.

A TOWERING PILE OF SCRAP glass stands ready for recycling at the Whiskey Island Marina in the Flats, while finished glass dominates the sleek exterior of the North Point Building at East 9th Street and Lakeside downtown.

KYLIT DOMES, NUMEROUS restaurants, movie theaters, and upscale stores draw crowds to Tower City Center, a shopping, entertainment, and commercial complex in Public Square that once housed the Cleveland Union Terminal (OPPOSITE). The 52-story Terminal Tower, mirrored here in a nearby office building, is the anchor for Tower City Center and is the city's second-tallest structure (ABOVE).

N O MATTER YOUR PER-
spective, a variety of
architectural periods and styles are
represented in structures across
the city.

T HANKS TO THE CAREFUL renovation of many of its historic buildings, Cleveland's Warehouse District has retained a distinctive 19th-century look.

T HE CLEVELAND METRO-
parks system, often called the
Emerald Necklace because it circles
the city with a band of green space,
boasts a network of streams and
bridges that enhance the area's
natural beauty.

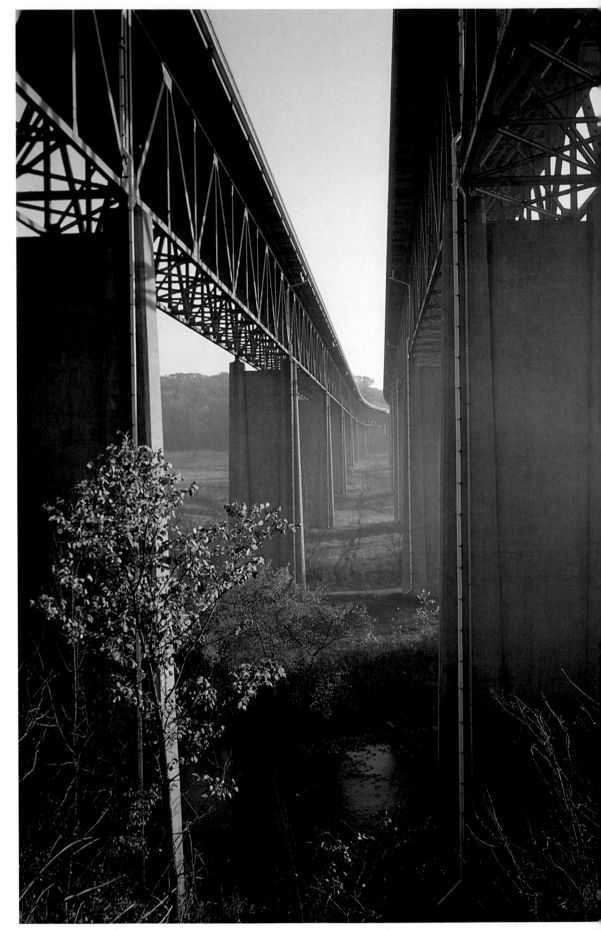

RUNNING FROM EAST TO WEST across the state, the James W. Shocknessy Ohio Turnpike affords picturesque views when it traverses the Cuyahoga Valley National Recreation Area.

SERGIO'S DELI

RONWORK SUPPORTS DECO-rative lighting and railings at the Arcade (OPPOSITE), while forbidding entrance to this historic mansion in the Lyme Township in Huron County, west of Cleveland (LEFT).

$\mathscr{S}$EVERAL AREA STRUCTURES from the early to mid-1800s have become popular sites for leisure time activities. The Hale Farm and Village, located in nearby Bath, re-creates farm life in the old Western Reserve.

T HE QUAINTNESS OF BYGONE eras is recalled by Cleveland's historic homes and quiet neighborhoods.

$\mathcal{I}$N 1996, A JOINT EFFORT between the City of Cleveland, Habitat for Humanity, National City Bank, and Cleveland Clinic created the Bicentennial Village in honor of the city's 200th birthday. Located in the Fairfax District, the village features 40 new homes and 150 rehabilitated residences.

WHETHER THEY'RE GROWING wild in the Cuyahoga Valley National Recreation Area (OPPOSITE) or being cultivated at the Cleveland Botanical Garden (TOP), flowers abound during the spring and summer. Although the real thing fades with the changing seasons, this metalwork variety, which adorned the former Silver Grille restaurant in the Higbee Building, has managed to stand the test of time (BOTTOM).

HE AREA S
rhododendro
asters, roses, purple
bloodroots, mayapp
orchids, tiger lilies,

LOWERS OF THE WORLD are on display at various local venues, including the two-level RainForest at the Cleveland Metroparks Zoo (OPPOSITE TOP), the four-acre Rockefeller Park Greenhouses (TOP AND OPPOSITE BOTTOM), and the Cleveland Garden Center in Wade Park (BOTTOM).

AST LAWN CEMETERY IN Portage County pays homage to citizens of the past (OPPOSITE). Lake View Cemetery (THIS PAGE) is home to numerous historic grave sites as well as a towering monument to industrialist and financier John D. Rockefeller Sr. (TOP).

T. WILLIAMS / THE IMAGE FINDERS

IF I HAVE DONE WELL, THOU KNOWEST IT

GEORGE C. JULIER
DEC. 27, 1836 — DEC. 2, 1896

MOTHER
DOROTHEA STOER CHANDLER
1905 — 1955

*T*HE MYSTICAL SIDE OF Cleveland is captured by Coventry Elementary School students during a field trip to Lake View Cemetery.

PAGES 220 AND 221: BARBARA BREEN

A Reason- able Fac- simile

JIM BARON / THE IMAGE FINDERS

CLEVELANDERS REMEMBER THE past in numerous ways. Fife players and knights recall the merriment and chivalry of the Renaissance, while two youngsters dress the part of fierce dragons for Halloween. Squire's Castle in North Chagrin Reservation re-creates the architecture of the medieval period. Designed to serve as a gatehouse and caretaker's quarters, the castle and its grounds are a favorite destination for picnickers.

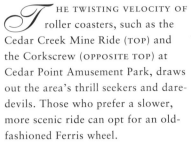

THE TWISTING VELOCITY OF roller coasters, such as the Cedar Creek Mine Ride (TOP) and the Corkscrew (OPPOSITE TOP) at Cedar Point Amusement Park, draws out the area's thrill seekers and daredevils. Those who prefer a slower, more scenic ride can opt for an old-fashioned Ferris wheel.

BARBARA DURHAM

RAIN TRACKS THROUGHOUT northeastern Ohio still see plenty of activity. The Cuyahoga Valley Scenic Railroad (THIS PAGE) is a steam-driven line that transports passengers through the Cuyahoga Valley National Recreation Area and along sections of the Ohio and Erie Canal.

Once a means by which locals traveled to and from work, Cleveland's Rapid Transit Authority (RTA) today also carries patrons who are out for a good time. The RTA Waterfront Line, which runs between Tower City, Settler's Landing in the Flats, and the Rock and Roll Hall of Fame and Museum, is the latest addition to the city's existing service (TOP AND OPPOSITE BOTTOM). Designed by architect Robert Madison (BOTTOM), the train will soon transport fans to Cleveland's new waterfront football stadium.

THE REGION'S ROLE IN THE development of the auto industry is celebrated through classic car shows. Today, several automakers continue to have a manufacturing presence in northeast Ohio.

*C*LEVELANDERS TAKE RESPITE
from their busy schedules at
area coffeehouses and cafeterias.

Profiles in

A LOOK AT THE CORPORATIONS, BUSINESSES, PROFESSIONAL GROUPS, AND COMMUNITY SERVICE ORGANIZATIONS THAT HAVE MADE THIS BOOK POSSIBLE. THEIR STORIES—OFFERING AN INFORMAL CHRONICLE OF THE LOCAL BUSINESS COMMUNITY—ARE ARRANGED ACCORDING TO THE DATE THEY WERE ESTABLISHED IN GREATER CLEVELAND.

Allen Telecom Inc. • AlliedSignal Truck Brake Systems Co. • Associated Estates Realty Corporation • Babcock & Wilcox • Bacik, Karpinski Associates Inc. • Bank One • CCF Health Care Ventures, Inc. • Centerior Energy Corporation • Central Cadillac • Central Reserve Life Insurance Company • Charter One Bank/Charter One Financial, Inc. • Chase Financial Corporation • Christian & Timbers Inc. • City Architecture • Clarion Hotel and Conference Center • City of Cleveland, Division of Water • Cleveland-Cliffs • The Cleveland Clinic Foundation • Cleveland-Cuyahoga County Port Authority • Cleveland Department of Port Control • Cleveland Energy Resources • Cleveland Health Network • Cleveland Public Power • Cleveland State University • Cole National Corporation • CSM Industries • Cuyahoga Community College • Developers Diversified Realty Corp. • The Diocese of Cleveland • Elsag Bailey Process Automation • Embassy Suites Hotel/Cleveland Downtown • Energizer • Equitable/EQ Financial Consultants, Inc. • Fabri-Centers of America, Inc. • Ferro Corporation • Finast Friendly Markets • Forest City Enterprises, Inc. • Garland Floor Co. • Greater Cleveland Regional Transit Authority • Health o meter, Inc./Mr. Coffee Inc. • HKM Direct Market Communications, Inc. • The Huntington National Bank • Invacare Corporation • Kaiser Permanente • A.T. Kearney, Inc. • Kent State University • KeyCorp • Kichler Lighting Group •

1845

IAN ADAMS

1886
ENERGIZER

1890
SQUIRE, SANDERS & DEMPSEY L.L.P.

1892
THE OSBORN ENGINEERING COMPANY

1895
THE LINCOLN ELECTRIC COMPANY

1897
KPMG PEAT MARWICK LLP

1898
EQUITABLE/EQ FINANCIAL CONSULTANTS, INC.

1901
PENTON PUBLISHING

1905
ROYAL APPLIANCE MFG. CO.

1906
BABCOCK & WILCOX

1906
CLEVELAND ENERGY RESOURCES

1906
CLEVELAND PUBLIC POWER

1908
ULMER & BERNE LLP

1908

THE CATHEDRAL OF ST. JOHN THE EVANGELIST ANCHORS THE corner at East 9th Street and Superior Avenue, the virtual center of the city of Cleveland. For 150 years, this majestic place of worship has also served as the spiritual center of the city for almost 1 million

Catholics living within the eight counties comprising the Diocese of Cleveland.

A century and a half ago, when Bishop Louis Amadeus Rappe decided to build the cathedral, its tower dominated the rural streets below. Today, the building is overshadowed in physical terms by the skyscrapers that mark Cleveland's renaissance, but it remains no less vital to the diocese in shepherding northeastern Ohio into the 21st century.

From the sprawling complex surrounding the cathedral, officials direct the 10th-largest diocese in the nation. It covers 236 parishes, including not only Cleveland and all of Cuyahoga County but the communities within Ashland, Geauga, Lake, Lorain, Medina, Summit, and Wayne counties. The organization's educational network extends to 144 elementary schools, 23 high schools, and two seminaries, as well as a number of universities and colleges. Through Catholic Charities, the diocese annually manages and directs more than $83 million in health and human services, coordinates the efforts of more than 150,000 volunteers, and helps to support other social service programs.

HEALTH AND HUMAN SERVICES TO THE COMMUNITY

Since 1912, Catholic Charities of the Diocese of Cleveland has consistently broken new ground in the delivery of health and human services to the community. The organization operates the largest Catholic Charities system in the United States. To support such a comprehensive system, over the past 30 years more than $100 million has been raised through the organization's Annual Appeal. The money is well spent, providing services annually to nearly 600,000 children and families, older adults, persons with disabilities, and individuals in need of emergency assistance.

More than 80 cents of every dollar goes directly to health and human services. To deal with expanding needs, Catholic Charities has been implementing a reorganization and long-range plan, modernizing its fund-raising program,

"CHARITY IS THE WORK OF THE CHURCH," SAYS BISHOP ANTHONY PILLA (LEFT). "CHARITY IS THE HEART AND SOUL OF WHAT WE PRACTICE, PREACH, AND TEACH AS CATHOLICS AND CHRISTIANS."

EACH YEAR, CATHOLIC CHARITIES PROVIDES SERVICES TO NEARLY 600,000 CHILDREN AND FAMILIES, OLDER ADULTS, PERSONS WITH DISABILITIES, AND INDIVIDUALS IN NEED OF EMERGENCY ASSISTANCE (RIGHT).

treamlining its service delivery ystem, and updating its facilities.

"There's a simple reason why our system of charity is so important to me, and should be to you as well: Charity is the work of the Church," says Bishop Anthony Pilla. "Charity is the heart and soul of what we practice, preach, and teach as Catholics and Christians."

"Catholic Charities must maintain its position at the table of health and human services providers. We must do this at a time of rapidly changing public policy and at a time when persons who use our services need them more than ever," says Secretary for Social Concerns/President and CEO of Catholic Charities Services Corporation J. Thomas Mullen.

DUCATING THE COMMUNITY

For more than 160 years, Catholic educators have been teaching the skills needed to prepare young people for society. Today, nearly 70,000 students are enrolled in Catholic schools within the Diocese of Cleveland, comprising the sixth-largest Catholic school system in the country. More than 140 elementary and 23 secondary schools are scattered throughout the eight-county area, as well as 16 Head Start programs, which provide lower-income parents with preschool facilities.

Although heavily populated by Catholics, the school system is open to children of all denominations, as well as all races. Twelve percent of the system's students are non-Catholic, and approximately 13 percent are minorities. All students, regardless of their background, learn lessons that will prepare them for adult Christian lives and will equip them with the knowledge needed to prosper and contribute to the community.

While serving a diverse student body, including those otherwise unable to afford quality schooling, the diocese has always provided

the highest quality of education. Fifteen of its schools have been given the U.S. Department of Education's prestigious Blue Ribbon Schools of Excellence Award since 1984. During the 1995-96 school year, local diocesan schools produced 41 National Merit finalists and 34 National Merit semifinalists. The diocese's sports teams consistently warrant national recognition, and many players have gone on to professional careers.

To support its school system, the Diocese of Cleveland depends on contributions to the Inner City School Fund and the Catholic Education Endowment Trust. "All our efforts are directed toward ensuring that Catholic schools remain available and vital for all those who desire a quality education grounded in faith," says Sister Carol Anne Smith, secretary for education/superintendent.

In 1994, the Diocese of Cleveland launched Catholic Schools Futuring, an eight-step, school-centered planning process that guides school communities in continuous improvement planning while helping them achieve accreditation through the Ohio Catholic School Accrediting Association.

PROMULGATING THE FAITH

In 1991, Pilla established the Center for Pastoral Leadership. Consisting of Borromeo Seminary, the Pastoral Ministry Office, the Permanent Diaconate Program, Saint Mary Seminary and Graduate School of Theology, and the Office of Continuing Education and Formation of Priests, the center is located on a 56-acre campus east of Cleveland in Wickliffe.

Educating its own is among the oldest traditions of the Diocese of Cleveland. Indeed, the organization remains one of the few still operating its own seminaries: Saint Mary, the graduate school of theology, and Borromeo, the college-level program. In this

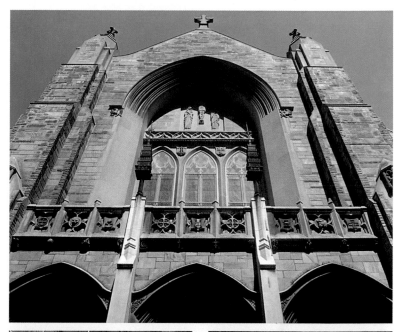

way, the diocese can ensure a steady stream of newly ordained priests, emphasizing Catholic ideals from leadership positions throughout the community. Today, about 400 graduates serve as priests in Cleveland-area parishes.

Such an elaborate developmental web is necessary to carry on the primary work of the Diocese of Cleveland: the promulgation of the Christian faith. Every day, from Painesville to Lorain and from Wooster to downtown Cleveland, the work of the diocese goes on in churches, schools, and the Cathedral of St. John the Evangelist, the heart of it all.

FOR 150 YEARS, THE CATHEDRAL OF ST. JOHN THE EVANGELIST HAS SERVED AS THE SPIRITUAL CENTER OF THE CITY FOR ALMOST 1 MILLION CATHOLICS LIVING WITHIN THE EIGHT COUNTIES COMPRISING THE DIOCESE OF CLEVELAND.

For more than 150 years, Clevelanders have been turning to National City Bank for a lending hand. "We have grown by investing in and supporting the Greater Cleveland area," says Chairman, President, and CEO William E. MacDonald III.

NATIONAL CITY CENTER IN DOWN-TOWN CLEVELAND IS HOME TO THE BANK'S PARENT COMPANY, NATIONAL CITY CORPORATION (LEFT).

THE BANK REMAINS COMMITTED TO THE PRINCIPALS OF INTEGRITY AND SERVICE TO CUSTOMERS, STOCK-HOLDERS, EMPLOYEES, AND THE COMMUNITY (RIGHT).

The lead bank of Cleveland-based National City Corporation—a $51 billion diversified financial services company that maintains subsidiaries in Ohio, Kentucky, Indiana, and Pennsylvania—it is an active member of the local community.

"National City Bank is one of Cleveland's premier financial institutions. For more than 150 years, the bank has kept pace with Greater Cleveland's rapid growth,

providing its customers with quality advice, information, and services," says Mayor Michael R. White.

COMMITTED TO CLEVELAND

The organization was established as City Bank in 1845 on the principles of integrity and service to its customers, stockholders, communities, and employees. The first institution chartered under the Ohio Bank Act of 1845, the bank intended to set the standard for the industry. It became National City Bank in 1865, when it received a national charter that included the right to print U.S. currency. In the 1930s,

recognizing a need for customer- and cost-focused service, National City opened its doors to retail customers.

Over the years, the bank has been a responsive partner to numerous major Cleveland-based corporations. It encourages business borrowing by developing convenient and easy-to-use programs and terms, and has been recognized as a leading Small Business Administration lender. Today, National City has 95 branch offices in the Cleveland area.

National City believes in making opportunities available to everyone. To that end, the bank strongly supports the Community Reinvestment Act.

In 1982, National City was one of the first banks in the United States to form a for-profit organization, known as the National City Community Development Corporation (NCCDC), to make equity investments to revitalize low- and moderate-income neighborhoods. The corporation has invested nearly $70 million in affordable housing since 1983. From these efforts emerged the Bicentennial Village, Beacon Place, and Glenville Commons, among other urban developments. NCCDC also offers a low-interest National City housing assistance mortgage on any project in which NCCDC makes an investment.

National City takes an active interest in cultural institutions and civic organizations as well, boasting a lengthy list of contributions. It was the sponsor of the 1997 National City® Cleveland Home and Garden Show, and supports the Cleveland Museum of Art, Cleveland Orchestra, and other cultural institutions. National City also supports Harvest for Hunger, the third-largest food drive of its type in the nation, as well as the College Fund/United Negro College Fund Walkathon, a leading fund-raiser to support a consortium of 41 private, historically African-American colleges and universities.

The bank's vision for the future includes broadening its horizons through technology and a diverse workplace. This translates into superior service and value for National City customers and shareholders. Its tradition of lending a hand to the people and communities of Greater Cleveland will remain at the foundation of the bank's mission.

atCity Investments, Inc. is a full-service, regional investment, banking, and brokerage firm headquartered in Cleveland. The firm, a subsidiary of National City Corporation, has offices throughout Indiana, Ohio, Kentucky, and western Pennsylvania. It is known for

its personalized approach with clients when advising them on investment opportunities and financial solutions to their concerns.

In July 1995, National City Corporation acquired the business assets of Raffensperger, Hughes & Co., a firm founded in Indianapolis in 1937 and regarded as a predominant player in the investment arena. Today, NatCity Investments combines independent thinking and institutional strength, making it one of the Midwest's leading investment houses. The company's long history of excellence in the municipal and corporate markets, coupled with its extensive knowledge of both local and publicly owned companies, has made NatCity's commitment to personalized client services unsurpassed.

REGIONAL FOCUS

The "small company" approach to service, combined with a "big company" performance, is truly the best of both worlds for NatCity's clients. "We have the same capabilities as Wall Street, but we provide these services at the regional level," says Chairman and CEO Herbert R. Martens Jr.

NatCity Investments is noted for having an independent, regional focus with a midwestern philosophy. The firm has comprehensive research that specifically targets companies based in the midwestern states. It is among the largest independent market makers of equity securities in the region. Specializing in more than [...] stocks, NatCity has managed or comanaged major syndication and marketing efforts for many

midwestern companies. The firm is a major underwriter of municipal bonds, ranking among the top managers in the country for bank-qualified issues.

NatCity Investments is prominent in the business community, providing capital to municipalities, school districts, and cities for roads and other infrastructure projects. The company's performance in the areas of public and corporate finance is competitive with investment firms throughout the United States. NatCity is a growing organization, and with that growth, expects to see an increase in the services it provides to its clients.

PERSONALIZED SERVICE AND ACCESSIBILITY

In addition to its commitment to regional markets, the company focuses on building long-term relationships with clients and places the utmost importance on maintaining integrity in all its business dealings. Martens says that emphasis on highly personalized services, including

client access to senior executives, is a key reason the firm maintains its position in the marketplace. Clients as well as employees know that if there is ever a need to speak with any member of the senior staff, accessibility is the policy.

Providing insight and guidance unavailable elsewhere, NatCity's exclusive research on local and regional companies is virtually unmatched. "Serving our clients with the highest degree of professionalism and utmost respect is the standard within our firm," says Senior Vice President and Retail Managing Director David W. Dunning.

NatCity Investments employs exceptionally experienced, highly disciplined professionals who are supported by state-of-the-art automated systems and technologies. The firm's commitment to maintaining the highest degree of integrity and investing in long-term client relationships places it among the premier firms to service the investment needs of the Midwest.

HERBERT MARTENS (LEFT), CHAIRMAN AND CEO OF NATCITY INVESTMENTS, INC., AND DAVE DABERKO, CHAIRMAN AND CEO OF NATIONAL CITY CORPORATION, NATCITY'S PARENT COMPANY

NATIONAL SALES MANAGER DAVID DUNNING (SEATED, FAR LEFT) AND VICE CHAIRMAN GENE TANNER (STANDING) OFFER FINANCIAL ADVICE TO CLIENTS.

*W*HEN THE NEW YORK LIFE INSURANCE COMPANY SET UP SHOP IN Cleveland in 1845, Israel S. Converse, a 40-year-old Clevelander, bought a $10,000 policy—the first in Ohio. In its formative days, the company also insured famous Ohioans, including former President

James A. Garfield. At that time, Cleveland was still a part of the western frontier. In fact, several of New York Life's first claims involved people who had been felled by arrows.

But as the city has grown, so have the fortunes of New York Life. In 1995, the company celebrated its 150th anniversary, while Cleveland commemorated its own bicentennial.

urb of Seven Hills. From here, the company administers life insurance policies worth more than $7.3 billion. More than 75,000 families rely on this office for insurance to protect their financial futures in uncertain economic times.

Eric Campbell, managing partner of the Northern Ohio Agency, oversees more than 100 full-time career agents from the

New York Life currently represents individuals, as well as the area's largest companies, in their quest to secure a prosperous financial future. Managing life insurance valued at more than $449 billion, the company paid its policyholders dividends of $1.12 billion in 1995, more than any other year in history and $45 million more than in 1994. In addition, living policyholders were paid a total of $9.5 billion, while beneficiaries received $1.1 billion.

PRESENCE IN NORTHERN OHIO

*N*ew York Life's Northern Ohio Agency is located in the southwestern sub-

Seven Hills office. Collectively, his staff boasts more than 200 years of experience. Other northern Ohio locations include the Boardman office, the Beachwood office, the NYLCare sales office in Independence, and the Cleveland Service Center in Lakewood. In addition, five of the company's leading agents have come from Greater Cleveland, including the late Ben Feldman of East Liverpool, one of the leading insurance agents in the world. In 1995, the Northern Ohio Agency was ranked second in the nation in first-year commissions.

New York Life believes that the sharing of knowledge and financial strategies readies agents

to help people recognize the importance of life insurance in achieving and maintaining financial security, while building family fortunes. To demonstrate this philosophy, Campbell asks, "If you had a goose that was laying golden eggs, would you insure the goose or the eggs? Most of us are guilty of insuring eggs—i.e., car, house, or other property—when in fact you really should insure the goose."

To that end, New York Life provides customers with products meeting the full range of their needs and expectations. Through these products, customers prepare for retirement and the expense of college tuition, ensure continuing incomes and mortgage-free homes and receive health insurance benefits in the event of disability.

The Cleveland Service Center in Lakewood employs 172 people serving approximately 2 million policyholders in 11 northeastern states. The Service Center also houses a nationwide incoming call center and provides underwriting services to 2,500 agents.

NEW YORK LIFE'S CIVIC COMMITMENT

*T*oday, New York Life continues its tradition of reinvesting a major portion of its assets in the community. Currently, 11 loans worth more than $95 million are outstanding on commercial projects, including $5.8 million on Embassy Corporate Park in Bath, near Akron; $13.9 million on the East Ohio Gas Building; and $56 million on National City Center. New York Life also financed the Diamond Shamrock Building and the Ohio Savings Plaza.

WHEN ABUNDANT DEPOSITS OF IRON WERE DISCOVERED IN MICHIGAN'S Upper Peninsula in the 1840s, a giant iron and steel industry was born in Cleveland. Local businessmen, including Samuel L. Mather, organized to mine and market the rich deposits. ❖ Soon, the industrial development of the Great Lakes region began fueling the progress of the entire nation. Early pioneers in the iron mining industry made significant contributions to the development of vital transportation links between the mines and steel mills. By the early 1900s, steel and steel-related products, such as ore vessels and machinery, had become Cleveland's number one industry.

A MATHER LEGACY

Mather and his associates founded the Cleveland Iron Company, which later became The Cleveland-Cliffs Iron Company following an 1891 merger with the Iron Cliffs Company. Under Mather's leadership, Cleveland-Cliffs acquired vast iron ore reserves and built schools, churches, and hospitals in the communities near its mines to provide for its growing workforce. The Mather family took a well-chronicled leadership role in establishing Cleveland's cultural and community life through many institutions that are still prominent.

William G. Mather continued the family legacy when he took the helm of Cleveland-Cliffs upon his father's retirement. By 1929, Cleveland-Cliffs was the largest independent producer of iron ore in the United States. Together, the father-son executive team managed Cleveland-Cliffs' successful and growing operations until 1933. The Great Depression almost sank the company, but William oversaw its rescue without sacrificing its ore reserves. William continued to work in his Cleveland-Cliffs office until his death in 1951 at age 91.

THE PELLETIZING ERA

Periods of high iron ore production during the first half of the 20th century, particularly during the war years, depleted most of the high-grade direct-shipping ores. Cleveland-Cliffs was a leader in developing the technology required to beneficiate and pelletize the huge quantities of low-grade ores in Michigan and Minnesota. The iron and steel industry spent many billions of dollars on new plants and transportation facilities from the 1950s through the 1970s.

For 25 years, there was unprecedented prosperity for the industry, Cleveland-Cliffs, its employees, and the mining communities. But in the early 1980s, near depression-level conditions sent the iron and steel industry into a tailspin. A number of steel companies declared bankruptcy, and by 1986, Cleveland-Cliffs itself was in danger of going under. But the company set a new course of strategic repositioning and renewed growth, which resulted in record earnings, sales, and production.

Its actions included divestiture of non-iron-ore assets, restructuring of mine partnerships, and acquisitions of competitors Pickands Mather & Co. and Northshore Mining Company.

Today, Cleveland-Cliffs is world renowned as the leading supplier of high-quality iron ore pellets in North America. It manages six mines in the United States and Canada, selling and trading ores, and leasing ore reserves. Nearly all integrated steel companies in North America are mine partners or customers of Cleveland-Cliffs.

THE FUTURE

Celebrating its sesqui centennial in 1997, Cleveland-Cliffs—under the leadership of M. Thomas Moore, chief executive officer since 1987—aims to capitalize on its expertise in iron ore mining, processing, and marketing by nurturing its existing operations, broadening its recent entry into the growing reduced-iron business, and expanding its international focus.

CELEBRATING ITS SESQUICENTENNIAL IN 1997, CLEVELAND-CLIFFS IS WORLD RENOWNED AS THE LEADING SUPPLIER OF HIGH-QUALITY IRON ORE PELLETS IN NORTH AMERICA.

Hᴇɴ Sᴀᴍᴜᴇʟ G. Mᴀᴛʜᴇʀ ᴀɴᴅ sᴇᴠᴇʀᴀʟ ᴘʀᴏᴍɪɴᴇɴᴛ Cʟᴇᴠᴇʟᴀɴᴅ businessmen founded Society for Savings in a one-room office in 1849, they could hardly have predicted their bank's potential for growth. Today, its descendant, KeyCorp, is a significant national

financial services company, with some $67 billion in assets, a presence from coast to coast, and bold plans for transforming itself to meet the needs of the future.

COMMITMENT TO THE NORTH COAST

Mirroring the growth of Cleveland, Mather's Society for Savings grew into Society National Bank a century later and eventually expanded to become Society Corporation. In 1994, Society merged with New York-based KeyCorp, with a vision of becoming a truly national bank and America's first choice for world-class financial products and services. Sharing that vision across the United States are more than 25,000 employees, who proudly wear the distinctive key lapel pin as a symbol of commitment and innovation.

KeyCorp has nurtured its roots throughout its expansion. The company is today headquartered in Cleveland's Public Square, the site of the original Society for

Savings. The majestic Key Tower, reaching 57 stories, is the city's tallest building and a recent distinctive addition to the Cleveland skyline.

COMMITMENT TO CUSTOMERS

Key serves a wide range of customers in the Cleveland market and across the country, providing innovative financial services for individuals, families, small-business owners, and corporate clients. Key's pro-

▼ JOE GLICK

fessional relationship managers specialize in the diverse financial needs of the people in each community—not just savings, checking, credit, mortgage, and small-business needs, but also investments, financial planning, and wealth management for today and tomorrow.

Key reaches throughout the United States under its KeyBank USA national consumer finance organization, ranking among the top in the country in education

lending, marine and recreational vehicle financing, auto financing, credit cards, and mortgage/home equity business.

By working closely as a trusted adviser to its corporate clients, Key ranks among the nation's top overall corporate lenders and is prominent in commercial real estate lending, bank-affiliated equipment leasing, and agricultural lending.

COMMITMENT TO CONVENIENCE

Because of consumers' changing lifestyles and needs, the future of banking will rely less on traditional branch locations and more on convenient alternatives, such as banking by phone, home computer, and ATMs (automatic teller machines).

Key is a national leader in bringing customers around-the-clock access to financial services. Its 1-800-KEY2YOU 24-hour telephone banking service logs some 3.5 million calls each month, and electronic interactions are quickly outpacing paper-based transactions.

Key's ATM network is growing rapidly as well, with installations in grocery stores, retail stores, and other high-traffic areas. Not all of Key's ATMs look alike, however. Bobbie, the nation's first cash-dispensing robot, brings science, technology, and banking together at the Great Lakes Science Center, and Key installed the nation's first jukebox ATM at the Rock and Roll Hall of Fame and Museum.

KeyCenters in the Cleveland area and throughout the country are being updated to provide better, more efficient customer service. While customers can perform transactions at any KeyCenter, some locations are specializing in service for specific client groups, such as small-business owners, mature customers, and the emerging affluent, whose unique needs

are met by the right mix of technology and trained Key employees. Traditional bank brochures available in the KeyCenters have been replaced by attractive magazines, published in partnership with Time Inc.

COMMITMENT TO ITS COMMUNITY

Through both corporate and personal commitment, Key employees truly make a difference in Cleveland and throughout the country. On Key's annual Neighbors Make the Dif-

ference national volunteer day in September 1996, teams of employees labored together to construct a Habitat for Humanity home on Cleveland's East 87th Street, while others performed volunteer work at social service agencies, schools, and other public facilities.

Robert W. Gillespie, Key's chairman and chief executive officer, is personally committed to the city, having served in 1996 as cochair of Cleveland's bicentennial celebration and the previous year as chair of United Way's annual fund campaign. He is also a member of the Civic Vision steering committee, a task force of community leaders focusing on downtown development beyond the year 2000.

Since 1992, Key has partnered with the City of Cleveland for a landmark neighborhood reinvest-

ment agreement. Between 1996 and 1999, Key has set a lending goal of nearly $325 million to assist with financing, including home and small-business lending, rehab lines of credit, church financing, and community development. More than one-third of the financial goal is expected to be loaned in African-American and Hispanic neighborhoods.

COMMITMENT TO PROGRESS

Samuel Mather's one-room Society for Savings has become a leading national financial services provider, the first choice for Clevelanders and other Key customers from coast to coast. As the company grows across the country, KeyCorp is still proud to be right at home in Cleveland.

ROBERT W. GILLESPIE IS KEYCORP'S CHAIRMAN AND CHIEF EXECUTIVE OFFICER (LEFT).

KEY TOWER, ADJOINING THE ORIGINAL SOCIETY FOR SAVINGS SITE ON PUBLIC SQUARE, TOPS THE CLEVELAND SKYLINE (RIGHT).

FOR MORE THAN 130 YEARS, THE HUNTINGTON NATIONAL BANK HAS been a leading provider of financial services to Ohio residents. Through a mixture of innovative banking services and products—complemented by support for civic and cultural life in Cleveland—the bank has played an integral part in the city's economic and spiritual rebirth.

The Huntington, which is the principal subsidiary of Huntington Bancshares Inc., founded in 1866 by Pelatiah Huntington, entered the Cleveland market in 1982 with the acquisition of Union Commerce Bank, a local institution since 1853. From headquarters in Columbus, its leadership manages 419 offices in 12 states. Offering banking, mortgage, trust, investment banking, and automobile financing services, the institution has combined assets of more than $20 billion.

Located in Cleveland at East Ninth Street and Euclid Avenue, The Huntington's main offices, which feature the world's largest banking lobby, are a majestic architectural accomplishment. The lobby's restoration in the 1970s earned the bank a number of awards, including the President's Award from the National Trust for Historic Preservation.

A BRIDGE TO THE 21ST CENTURY

During a time of technological innovation and heightened competition, The Huntington has unveiled a variety of services to meet the needs of individual customers, borrowers, and businesses preparing for the 21st century. The bank offers a mix of commercial and consumer banking services, ranging from checking accounts and personal credit lines to investments and cash management. In addition, it provides convenient 24-hour access to its services, as well as lobby hours for those still favoring a personal touch. The bank will continue to expand its number of remote locations, while introducing new products to meet changing needs.

The Huntington has long displayed a commitment to customer service. In 1972, for example, it became the first bank in the country to open a fully automated, 24-hour Handy Bank. And in 1984, through the Relationship Banking program, it was able to offer business customers all of its resources

THE HUNTINGTON OFFERS ITS CUSTOMERS ROUND-THE-CLOCK ACCESS TO PERSONAL BANKERS THROUGH HUNTINGTON DIRECT.

through a single bank contact. Two years later, The Huntington unveiled the Personal Banker program, delivering this same level of service to individuals by providing them with their own personal banker.

Since 1986, The Huntington has worked to provide quality service to customers from all facets of life, offering them a full spectrum of choices to use in selecting the mix of banking services that suit their individual needs. While meeting traditional expectations, the bank continually diversifies, offering the financial services, products, and information sought by its customers.

Since 1992, through Huntington Direct, the bank has offered round-the-clock access to personal bankers. Ahead of the rest of the industry, the bank has allowed customers to open accounts, apply for loans, discuss investment alternatives, or complete noncash banking transactions by calling 800-480-BANK. Since 1994, through Huntington Personal Touch machines, customers have been able to communicate with Huntington Direct personal bankers through a two-way interactive video network.

In October 1994, The Huntington opened the world's first virtual bank in Columbus, combining Personal Touch access with high-tech automatic teller machines that print statements and cash checks, as well as fulfill traditional services. Such offices will become a larger part of the bank's network in coming years.

The Huntington and Security First Network Bank began offering banking services via the Internet in June 1996. While having access to traditional services, Internet customers enjoy the convenience of interactive work sheets that allow them to test investment strategies or compare rates of return. The Huntington's Web Bank was one of the first on the World Wide Web that allowed customers to initiate transactions.

In addition to high-tech access anywhere and anytime, customers can enjoy convenient checking accounts, check cards that are accepted worldwide by 10 million merchants, direct payment of bills via the telephone, and answers to loan inquiries in 10 minutes or less. In the fall of 1996, The Huntington began offering Smart Cards through a joint venture with Batelle Research Center and Cybermark. Smart Cards afford customers a plethora of options, from securing business premises to purchasing goods via debits from a bank account or a digital cash transaction.

A VALUABLE MEMBER OF THE COMMUNITY

*O*ur bank has to offer customers relationships that provide them with value," says George S. Brookes, president, Northern Ohio Region. "We are not going after a share of the market as much as a share of customers' hearts. To win a share of the heart, you have to provide services that delight customers. Otherwise, you just become another commodity."

The Huntington demonstrates that same level of energy and commitment to community projects. Through local churches, the Community Centered Banking program provides retail services, business and church lending, seminars, and workshops. The bank also participates in the Adopt-a-School program, Junior Achievement, and the Cleveland Initiative for Education, while sponsoring mortgage workshops and community lending programs. The Playhouse Square, Cleveland Orchestra, Cleveland Playhouse, and Blossom Music Center are additional beneficiaries of the bank's support.

The Huntington will continue to invest in the community and its people, while responding to new customer needs stimulated by changes in lifestyle and technological advancements. In this way, the bank stands ready to provide unparalleled service to customers and shareholders, as well as to secure its place in the 21st century.

THE BANK'S MAGNIFICENT OFFICE IN THE HUNTINGTON BUILDING CONTAINS THE LARGEST BANKING LOBBY IN THE WORLD.

ONE SUMMER DAY IN 1996, WHEN TWO ELDERLY WOMEN FOUND themselves trapped inside a car teetering over the edge of the Rocky River Bridge, three members of a pipe repair crew from the City of Cleveland, Division of Water came to their rescue. Merely inves-

THE ROCK AND ROLL HALL OF FAME AND MUSEUM ILLUMINATES THE LAKE ERIE SHORELINE IN CLEVELAND, THE ONLY U.S. DESTINATION RATED AS ONE OF THE WORLD'S 10 HOT SPOTS FOR 1997 TRAVELERS, ACCORDING TO THE DECEMBER 1996 ISSUE OF *Travel & Leisure* MAGAZINE. THE DIVISION OF WATER AND CLEVELAND PUBLIC POWER SUPPLY THE WATER AND ELECTRIC POWER FOR THE MUSEUM.

tigating a leak, Dave Rado, Joseph Kives, and Barret Dorsey found themselves transformed instantly into heroes, as a television crew filmed the event for the evening news. The men also received the Looking Out for You Award, given to city employees who go to extraordinary lengths to help members of the community.

Such stories are not uncommon with the City of Cleveland, Division of Water. All 1,200 employees strive to bring similar levels of commitment to their ev-

eryday routines, resulting in the processing and delivery of approximately 300 million gallons of water a day for use by more than 420,000 customers in Cleveland and 69 outlying communities.

"Water naturally is one of the world's most important resources," Mayor Michael R. White says. "The Division of Water is a major asset to the continued growth of Cleveland."

SERVING GREATER CLEVELAND

For approximately 150 years, the Division of Water has supplied water to Greater Cleveland. Today, it is the nation's eighth-largest public water supply agency, distributing its product to customers within a 640-square-mile area.

The division also makes direct contributions to the local economy: In 1996, it awarded approximately $83 million in capital improvement contracts and spent more than $69 million on expansion and improvements to preserve the system's high-quality service. The bulk of expenditures went to upgrading the division's facilities: five plants and 34 stations serving businesses, home owners, and institutions in Cleveland and 69 other communities from Twinsburg and North Olmsted to Middleburg Heights and Bratenahl.

"In 1996, we reached the midway point in a $750 million capital improvement program— the most ambitious in the division's history," says Cleveland Public Utilities Director Michael G. Konicek. "With this investment, we will continue to provide the highest-quality water that meets or exceeds every Environmental Protection Agency standard, as

well as ensure continued reliability. We are able to do this while maintaining water rates among the lowest in the country."

COMMITTED TO CUSTOMER SERVICE

The Division of Water is constantly involved in expanding, repairing, upgrading, and replacing the pipelines that carry water from its plants and secondary stations to customers all over Cuyahoga County and adjoining communities.

Before water leaves the plant, samples are tested with a sensitive gas chromatograph mass spectrophotometer—the latest in clean-water technology—to ensure that even the smallest amounts of contaminants have been removed. Each plant also employs an analyzer to detect tiny pieces of floating matter in water samples. In hopes of controlling lead contamination caused by aged household plumbing, the city is testing the effectiveness of phosphates in combating this hazardous leachate. Eventually, the entire system will benefit from the program, which is critical in overcoming the potential presence of lead in the local water supply.

The division's base of distribution operations, the Harvard Yard Maintenance Facility, is currently undergoing a $30 million renovation. From here, a new, automated system is being used to read some meters by radio frequency, completing the task from remote locations in a fraction of the time required by traditional methods. The system, already in place at LTV Steel Company, will soon be in use on converted meters in Cleveland and Twinsburg. The

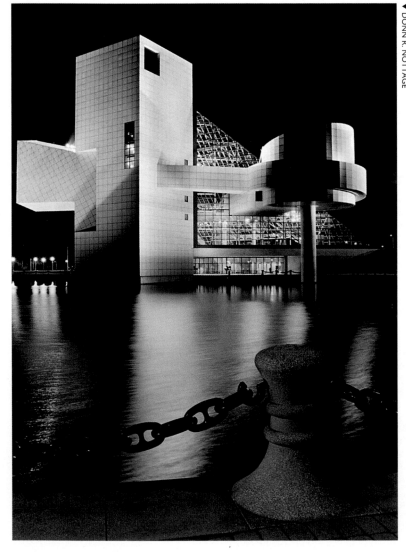

DONN R. NOTTAGE

STATE-OF-THE-ART EQUIPMENT CON-
TROLS THE FILTRATION PROCESS IN
THE DIVISION OF WATER'S GARRETT
MORGAN WATERWORKS PLANT,
REBUILT IN THE 1980S AND REDEDI-
CATED IN HONOR OF MORGAN,
INVENTOR OF THE GAS MASK AND
THE TRAFFIC SIGNAL.

division also spends $10 million year cleaning and lining main pipelines—some of which are more than 100 years old. In addition, all aboveground fire hydrants are frost proofed through an electronically controlled steam system, while other hydrants and all water mains are installed safely below the frost line.

From 1993 to 1996, the Division of Water's Engineering Section oversaw the installation of an 800-megahertz radio dispatch system that allows all city departments to communicate on a single frequency. Division engineers have also concentrated on programs related to water quality. For example, cathodic protection is applied to existing main pipelines and included in newly installed pipes, preventing external corrosion that could otherwise result in the collapse of these essential underground arteries. The division's supervisory Control and Data

▶ DONN R. NOTTAGE

Acquisition system—a network of computers, electronic sensors, radio transmitters, and phone lines—monitors operations at all remote locations and operates an essential system of pumps and valves.

Beyond its plants and general operations, the Division of Water

maintains a large customer service operation that answers questions, responds to service calls, reads meters, and generates bills for more than 420,000 customers. Through the expansion of service hours and the continued education and training of customer representatives, the rate of customer complaints has dropped significantly in recent years. To further bolster positive relations and community awareness, the division holds plant tours and makes speeches to schools and other groups throughout the area.

Whether rescuing people from danger or responding to a customer's call for repairs, the Division of Water is committed to serving Greater Cleveland in its rebirth. As White says, "Our municipal water system is the foundation upon which we can continue to grow our businesses and community."

COMPLIANCE LAB ASSISTANT TERESA
FARILEY ANALYZES A WATER SAMPLE
AS PART OF THE DIVISION OF WATER'S
CONTINUOUS TESTING TO ENSURE THE
HIGHEST LEVEL OF DRINKING WATER
QUALITY.

NATIONAL LEADER IN MEDICAL CARE, RESEARCH, AND EDUCATION University Hospitals of Cleveland provides an array of advanced technologies, and exceptional hospitals and outpatient facilities. A medical staff of 1,300 physicians, representing more than 60

specialties, provides superior patient care and stays at the forefront of medicine by pioneering research into the causes and cures of disease and by teaching the medical leaders of tomorrow.

With a strong collaboration between basic science and patient care, University Hospitals of Cleveland and its academic counterpart, Case Western Reserve University (CWRU), form the largest biomedical research center in Ohio. Because of University Hospitals' unique role as an academic medical center, and as the primary affiliate of the CWRU School of Medicine, patients at University Hospitals are among the first in the nation to benefit from the new discoveries and therapies this research yields. And it is also

this approach of patient-centered research and treatment that has earned University Hospitals the highest patient satisfaction rating of any hospital in Greater Cleveland, in keeping with its position as the city's premier medical center.

FOUNDED IN 1866

The history of University Hospitals of Cleveland can be traced back to the Civil War era when the Ladies Aid Society of the First Presbyterian Church, now known as the Old Stone Church, operated the Home for the Friendless to help people displaced by the Civil War. Seeing the need for a hospital to provide medical care for Cleveland's underserved, a group of civic leaders

worked with the church members to form the Cleveland City Hospital Society in 1866. That same year, the society opened its first hospital in a small frame house on Wilson Street, but by 1875, it had outgrown its humble beginnings and was relocated to the former Marine Hospital facility on Cleveland's Lakeside Avenue. In 1888, the name of the Wilson Street Hospital was changed to Lakeside Hospital.

Today, University Hospitals of Cleveland comprises six major facilities and numerous centers of excellence—all of which are located on a 25-acre campus in the heart of Cleveland's University Circle. The hospitals include Alfred and Norma Lerner Tower, Samuel Mather Pavilion, and Lakeside

UNIVERSITY HOSPITALS OF CLEVELAND, LOCATED ON A 25-ACRE CAMPUS IN THE HEART OF UNIVERSITY CIRCLE, IS OHIO'S LEADING CENTER FOR MEDICAL RESEARCH.

ospital for adult medical and surgical care; Rainbow Babies and Childrens Hospital; MacDonald Womens Hospital; and the Psychiatric Center at Hanna Pavilion. Multidisciplinary centers of excellence include the Musculoskeletal Institute, Spine Institute, Elder-Health Services, Center for Human Genetics, Center for Stroke, Rainbow's Cystic Fibrosis Treatment Center, and the Ireland Cancer Center, among others.

PIONEERS OF MEDICINE

Throughout its distinguished history, University Hospitals of Cleveland has been at the forefront of medical breakthroughs. In the 1930s, physicians performed pioneering work in surgical treatment of coronary artery disease. And in 1947, University Hospitals was the site of the first successful defibrillation of the human heart, which led to the development of cardiopulmonary resuscitation in the 1950s.

In the 1980s, psychobiology experts codeveloped Clozapine—the first successful drug for the treatment for schizophrenia in two decades. In 1991, physicians performed the nation's first triple-organ transplant (liver, kidney, and pancreas). In 1995, pediatric specialists performed the region's first marrow transplant with umbilical cord blood to treat a young leukemia patient. And in 1996, University Hospitals cardiologists were the first in Ohio to implant an experimental atrial defibrillator, a device that electrically stimulates the heart's upper chambers to stop painful and life-threatening irregular heart rhythms.

While the 1990s ushered in exciting breakthroughs in medical care, major changes were taking place in the health care market. Businesses and patients demanded that hospitals find ways to reduce costs, while simultaneously finding ways to improve patient care. Large academic medical centers with an

emphasis on clinical research, high-tech equipment, and education—factors that drive costs up—were particularly vulnerable in this shifting market. Through a team approach to patient care that included physicians, nursing staff, and other medical and support personnel, University Hospitals developed significant new standards of care that not only helped to reduce overall costs but, more important, improved patient outcomes.

For example, University Hospitals orthopedists devised an innovative procedure for the surgical treatment of herniated disks. Physicians used a minimally invasive arthroscopic technique to treat this painful, disabling condition on an outpatient basis. Now, a patient who would have previously faced lengthy, complex surgery and rehabilitation can undergo a less invasive, less risky, and more cost-effective treatment.

University Hospitals physicians have also made important strides in treating and reversing the effects of a stroke—long considered an irreversible medical event that resulted in devastating impairments or death. Physicians found that emergency use of thrombolytic agents, or clot-dissolving drugs, could effectively halt the process of brain cell death that occurs during a stroke, allowing patients to retain vision, speech, and major motor functions. For patients, the findings resulted in a second chance at an improved quality of life. For patients' families and health care payers, the findings yielded a secondary benefit—an enormous cost savings—since patients were three times less likely to be admitted to such extended-care facilities as a nursing home.

Finding new ways to use existing technologies and techniques has also greatly influenced cancer

THE 10-STORY ALFRED AND NORMA LERNER TOWER FEATURES 210 PRIVATE ROOMS. THE ADJOINING SAMUEL MATHER PAVILION CONTAINS STATE-OF-THE-ART OPERATING ROOMS, INTENSIVE CARE BEDS, AND SUPERIOR DIAGNOSTIC AND TREATMENT CENTERS FOR OUTPATIENT CARE.

treatment. For example, using a combination of magnetic resonance imaging and a technology called radio-frequency ablation, physicians developed a nonsurgical procedure for the treatment of localized malignancies of the liver, kidney, and abdomen. This minimally invasive approach has the potential to replace conventional cancer treatments, including surgery and radiation for certain tumors, and offers new hope to patients for whom standard measures have failed.

Cancer treatment and research are among University Hospitals' greatest strengths. At the Ireland Cancer Center, research efforts are concentrated in developmental therapeutics—the rapid "translation" of laboratory research findings into clinical practice, providing patients with early access to investigational drugs that have shown promising results. In basic research, the physicians and scientists of University Hospitals Ireland Cancer Center join forces with CWRU to form a comprehensive biomedical research program. The CWRU/University Hospitals Ireland Cancer Center is northern Ohio's only cancer program to earn the National Cancer Institute designation as a Clinical Cancer Center.

This partnership between basic research and clinical care has already provided new hope for patients. Recently, physicians discovered a genetic defect that

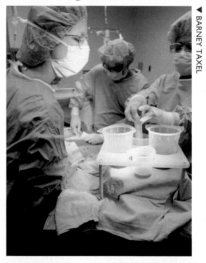

◄ BARNEY TAXEL

factors in the development of colon cancer. Their findings will lead to the development of a simp blood test for early diagnosis and screening, and in the design of new treatments for this second-leading cause of cancer-related deaths.

University Hospitals of Clev land is recognized nationally in women's health and children's health. Its MacDonald Womens Hospital is Ohio's only comprehensive hospital that provides ser vices to meet the health care nee of women of all ages. Specialized services include programs for gynecologic and surgical needs, the Breast Center for detection and treatment of breast diseases, a nationally recognized in vitro fertilization program, and service for women in midlife. The hospit has also been rated among the nation's top 10 maternity hospitals, and is recognized throughou the United States for its expertise in the management of high-risk pregnancies.

IN 1977, UNIVERSITY HOSPITALS IRELAND CANCER CENTER OPENED OHIO'S FIRST MAJOR BONE MARROW TRANSPLANT PROGRAM (TOP).

SPECIALISTS IN NEUROLOGICAL SURGERY, NEURORADIOLOGY, NEUROLOGY, AND EMERGENCY MEDICINE HAVE POOLED THEIR EXPERTISE AND DEVELOPED A COMPREHENSIVE TREATMENT PROTOCOL FOR PATIENTS WHO ARE ADMITTED TO UNIVERSITY HOSPITALS WITH SYMPTOMS SIGNIFYING A STROKE (BOTTOM).

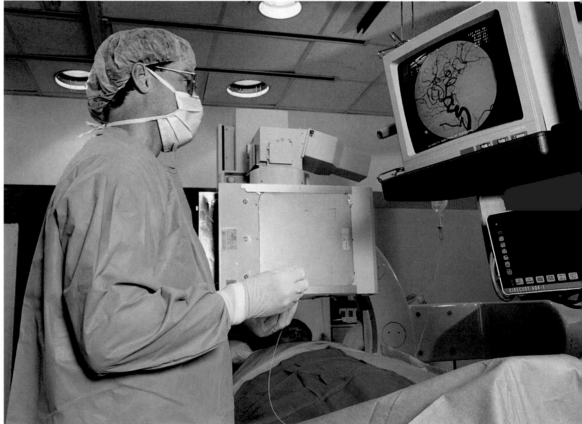

CLEVELAN

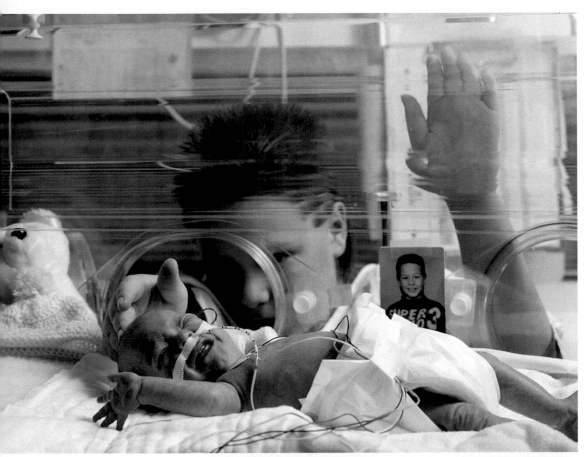

TOGETHER, MACDONALD WOMENS
HOSPITAL AND RAINBOW BABIES AND
CHILDRENS HOSPITAL PROVIDE CARE
FOR MORE AT-RISK NEWBORNS THAN
ANY OTHER FACILITY IN GREATER
CLEVELAND.

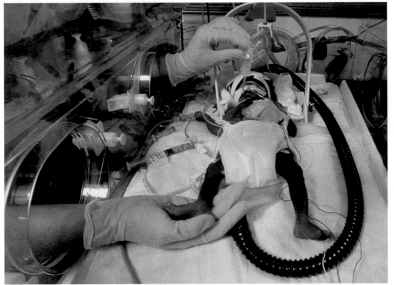

One of Cleveland's greatest treasures is Rainbow Babies and Childrens Hospital, the only hospital in Cleveland dedicated solely to the comprehensive care of children. Serving as a principal pediatric referral center for Ohio and bordering states, Rainbow provides health care to thousands of children in Greater Cleveland and is the primary pediatric teaching hospital of Case Western Reserve University. Rainbow is a national leader in the treatment of children with cancer, heart disease, cystic fibrosis, sickle-cell disease, pulmonary disorders, and endocrine disorders. In 1997, Rainbow opened the eight-story, 90-bed Leonard and Joan Horvitz Tower, the nation's most advanced family-centered pediatric facility.

For newborns at risk, Rainbow's 38-bed neonatal intensive care unit (NICU) serves as the primary source of expert care for the most critically ill infants. The NICU is designated as a level III

unit—the highest classification available—and is one of only 12 units in the nation designated by the National Institutes of Health as a neonatal research center. Rainbow's survival rate for high-risk newborns is among the highest in the country.

For more than 130 years, University Hospitals of Cleveland

has provided the highest-quality and most compassionate care to people in need. Its mission—"To Heal. To Teach. To Discover."— has enriched the well-being of the people of Cleveland in the past, and will continue to be at the heart of its success and its service to Greater Cleveland in the next century.

THE NEONATAL INTENSIVE CARE UNIT
AT RAINBOW BABIES AND CHILDRENS
HOSPITAL IS ONE OF 12 UNITS IN
THE NATION DESIGNATED BY THE
NATIONAL INSTITUTES OF HEALTH
AS A NEONATAL RESEARCH CENTER.

FUNDAMENTAL CHANGES ARE TAKING PLACE IN THE HEALTH CAR industry. To improve the quality and reduce the cost of medical car a national movement is focusing not on the business of hospitals, b on the business of health care. To effectively respond to this shifti

market, providers must focus on managing the total health care needs of large groups of people through a continuum of services.

Recognizing the impending changes in health care delivery, a regional, fully integrated health system with a core foundation of primary and community-based care was developed. Called University Hospitals Health System (UHHS), it focuses the delivery of health care away from expensive, inpatient hospital services and facilities, and instead moves toward the physician-driven approach of community-based physician offices and ambulatory and diagnostic centers. The goal is to provide the most convenient and cost-effective patient care in northern Ohio.

Today, University Hospitals Health System is the region's leading health care system and boasts the region's largest network of primary care providers. With more than 10,000 health care professionals and support staff, UHHS logs more than 2 million outpatient visits and 50,000 hospitalizations each year. As of the first quarter of 1997, UHHS services could be found at more than 80 locations in 40 communities. These numbers continue to grow.

A STRONG NETWORK

The full services that UHHS provides fall into five general areas: primary and specialty care physician practices, ambulatory and urgent care centers, hospitals, ancillary services, and managed care.

The backbone of UHHS is quality care provided through its diverse physician groups. The UHHS physician network, more than 2,000 strong, includes many of th nation's top academic physicians at University Hospitals of Clevelar and a broad range of well-respecte community-based physicians, including the newly created University Primary Care Physician Practices and the multi-specialty practices of University MEDNET and University Suburban Health Center. This physician-based focus reflects the demands of patients and their providers for quality, cost-effectiveness, service and accessibility, allowing UHHS to attract the area's largest insurance and managed care contracts—today's primary source of busines.

To complement its physician practices, UHHS has established numerous multispecialty outpatie centers throughout Greater Cleveland, providing a comprehensive range of adult and pediatric outpatient services. In mid-1996, UHHS opened a major multispecialty center on Cleveland's west side: University Hospitals Medical and Surgical Center at Westlake. This facility marked an important expansion of the organization's presence in the western suburbs of Cleveland. Future plans call for the establish ment of additional outpatient cer ters, as well as an even broader range of specialty services at existing centers.

UHHS has also formed selective partnerships with several well-positioned and well-respecte hospitals to provide patients acut and ambulatory care in a convenient, cost-effective community setting. As of the beginning of 1997, UHHS community hospita included Bedford Medical Center in Cuyahoga County, Geauga

TO COMPLEMENT ITS PHYSICIAN PRACTICES, UHHS HAS ESTABLISHED MAJOR, MULTISPECIALTY OUTPATIENT CENTERS THROUGHOUT GREATER CLEVELAND, PROVIDING A COMPREHENSIVE RANGE OF ADULT AND PEDIATRIC SERVICES.

Regional Hospital in Geauga County, Memorial Hospital of Geneva in Ashtabula County, and Laurelwood Hospital in Lake County. These hospitals offer patients throughout northeastern Ohio easy access to UHHS and, when tertiary care is necessary, seamless access to University Hospitals of Cleveland. Another advantage for patients is that University Hospitals of Cleveland and the system's community hospitals share research breakthroughs, innovations in patient care, and cost efficiencies.

CONTINUUM OF CARE

*A*s the length of hospital stays continues to be shortened, providing patients a continuum of care becomes increasingly important. The system's Home Care Services division provides more than 125,000 home visits each year to adult and pediatric patients. And the Hanna House Skilled Nursing Center, located on the main campus of University Hospitals of Cleveland, provides care for patients who need intensive, short-term rehabilitation and daily skilled nursing, such as a joint replacement patient. A separate, 20-bed inpatient rehabilitation center, also at the Hanna House facility, allows for an even more comprehensive range of care specific to patients' needs.

UHHS reaches beyond traditional health care services. One of the most innovative aspects of the system is QualChoice, its managed care plan. QualChoice is one of the nation's first health plans created by a hospital system. As such, the philosophy behind the program is understandably unique: provide physicians and enrollees as much freedom as possible, while ensuring that costs are kept in check and that quality is not compromised. Just four years after its inception, QualChoice ranked first in patient satisfaction among 33

▶ JOE GLICK PHOTOGRAPHY

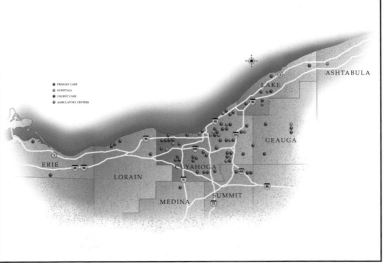

managed care plans nationwide. UHHS also offers University Comp-Care, a workers' compensation managed care program, one of a select group certified by the State Bureau of Workers' Compensation.

As UHHS looks to the future, it will continue to build upon its

strengths: uncompromised quality coupled with innovative health care delivery. It is these very strengths that make UHHS a health care leader today, and position it to carry on well into the 21st century.

A KEY TO UNIVERSITY HOSPITALS HEALTH SYSTEM'S EMERGENCE AS THE REGION'S LEADING HEALTH CARE DELIVERY SYSTEM IS A PHYSICIAN-BASED FOCUS THAT REFLECTS THE DEMANDS OF PATIENTS AND THEIR PROVIDERS FOR QUALITY, COST EFFECTIVENESS, SERVICE, AND ACCESSIBILITY. AS OF EARLY 1997, THE SYSTEM PROVIDED CARE AT MORE THAN 80 LOCATIONS IN 40 COMMUNITIES (TOP).

UHHS LINKS PATIENTS THROUGHOUT NORTHEAST OHIO TO EVERY ESSENTIAL HEALTH CARE SERVICE AND ENSURES THAT THEY RECEIVE VALUE, CONSIDERATION, AND THE NATION'S MOST ADVANCED MEDICINE (BOTTOM).

IN THE WORLD ACCORDING TO SHERWIN-WILLIAMS, CLEVELAND SITS at the top of the globe, the company's products flowing downward from the city and beautifying most of the structures of the earth. This symbolic vision, developed in 1893 as the Sherwin-Williams trademark, may still take many years to obtain, but in the meantime, the company's effects on trends in American life have been far reaching indeed.

SHERWIN PAINTS HIS FUTURE

In 1866, a young Henry Sherwin chose to join his fortune with those of Edward Williams and Alanson Osborn to form a firm "importing and jobbing . . . Zincs, Oils, Colors, Varnishes, and Window Glass." The company soon added Sereno Peck Fenn, longtime treasurer, and its formative leadership was established.

"It seems to have been one of those opportunities that arise early in life, and I am free to say that I did not realize what it would lead to," Sherwin recalled.

In 1880, the company unveiled the first ready-mix paint, ending the time-consuming tradition of mixing ingredients at job sites and simplifying the process for the painter. It also developed and began producing the industry's first tin paint cans. These developments totally changed the concept and structure of the paint industry.

In 1941, America entered World War II. With solvents and other chemical ingredients committed to the war effort, Sherwin-Williams introduced Kem-Tone®, the first commercially successful water-based paint, requiring only a single coat and water clean-up. This new product, along with Sherwin-Williams' invention of the Roller-Koater™ applicator, spurred the World War II development and expansion of do-it-yourself painting. The innovative technology that made Kem-Tone® paint a success permanently changed the architectural painting habits and products of the United States. In 1996, the American Chemical Society awarded Sherwin-Williams its National Historical Chemical Landmarks designation in recognition of this breakthrough.

Early on, the company also employed innovation in its marketing approach. In addition to selling its products through dealers and franchisers, in 1890, Sherwin-Williams opened its first retail store. The company has expanded its market share through the sale of Sherwin-Williams products through its own stores and the sale of other well-known, branded products through retail and specialized distribution channels.

While such foresight has had worldwide implications, the company itself has moved less than a mile since its founding, relocating in 1931 from its original facility on Canal Road along the Cuyahoga River in Cleveland's Flats area to headquarters in the Landmark Office Towers in the Tower City complex. The Sherwin-Williams laboratory today stands on the site of the original plant, an early example of the company's commitment to the renaissance of this now-vibrant area of Cleveland.

The company operates more than 2,150 stores and has manufacturing plants and automotive branches across the United States, Canada, Mexico, and South America. At the same time, Sherwin-Williams continues to strive to "cover the earth," acquiring brand names such as Dutch Boy®, Martin-Senour®, Krylon®, Pratt & Lambert®, Thompson's®, and Minwax® that strengthen its position as the largest producer of paints, varnishes, and specialty coatings in the United States and the second largest in the world.

CLOCKWISE FROM TOP: THE INTRODUCTION OF KEM-TONE® WATER-BASED PAINT, ALONG WITH SHERWIN-WILLIAMS' INVENTION OF THE ROLLER-KOATER™ APPLICATOR, SPURRED THE WORLD WAR II DEVELOPMENT AND EXPANSION OF DO-IT-YOURSELF PAINTING.

IN THE WORLD ACCORDING TO SHERWIN-WILLIAMS, CLEVELAND SITS AT THE TOP OF THE GLOBE, THE COMPANY'S PRODUCTS FLOWING DOWNWARD FROM THE CITY AND BEAUTIFYING MOST OF THE STRUCTURES OF THE EARTH.

PARTICIPANTS IN THE 1898 ANNUAL CONVENTION NO DOUBT TOOK PRIDE IN THE COMPANY'S INNOVATIVE PRODUCTS, WHICH CHANGED THE CONCEPT AND STRUCTURE OF THE PAINT INDUSTRY.

IN 1898, MARTIN A. MARKS WAS TAPPED TO HEAD CLEVELAND'S first general agency of The Equitable Life Assurance Society of the United States, which was founded in 1859. Marks' appointment began a long and gratifying relationship between Equitable and Cleveland,

with Marks and his successors becoming increasingly involved in the civic, cultural, and charitable affairs of the city.

More than a century later, Cleveland is a sophisticated, modern metropolis providing an outstanding environment for home and work life, and Equitable likewise has dramatically grown and flourished in its services to individuals and corporations. The firm today is much more than a life insurance company; it is a diversified financial services organization offering its clients the expert guidance they need to plan for the security of their families and businesses.

Given the tradition of civic commitment established by Marks, it is little wonder Equitable and the city have matured so well together. In 1903, Marks was a founder of the Jewish Welfare Federation and later of the Cleveland Federation for Charity and Philanthropy, the forerunner of the Welfare Federation of Cleveland and the model for today's United Way. His devotion to the city has been echoed in the activities of subsequent Cleveland Equitable agency managers, whose involvement over the years has included such groups as the Rotary Club, Citizens League, Better Business Bureau, Big Brothers of Greater Cleveland, and Greater Cleveland Growth Association.

Since May 1995, Ronald L. Hart has served as Equitable's agency manager for Cleveland and surrounding satellite offices. Hart came to northeast Ohio from Milwaukee, where he enjoyed a distinguished career at Equitable and won numerous company and industry awards for both

AL FUCHS

production and leadership.

As he looks forward to celebrating the Cleveland agency's centennial in 1998, Hart also can look with pride and satisfaction on the remarkable progress of Equitable in northeast Ohio. Today, the firm is one of the fastest-growing financial services institutions in Greater Cleveland. Equitable has more than 100 full- and part-time employees at its North Point headquarters in downtown Cleveland, and revenues locally are growing annually by 20 percent.

This local strength has global support. Together with its partner, AXA of France, Equitable is one of the world's largest and most influential insurance, investment management, and financial services organizations.

The Equitable Life Assurance Society, one of the nation's largest life insurers, and EQ Financial Consultants, Inc., a wholly owned investment advisory subsidiary and broker-dealer, serve millions of individuals as well as many of the world's largest corporations and institutions.

Equitable, including its subsidiaries, is ranked as one

Equitable's northeast Ohio leadership team includes (from left) Ralph J. Voracek, Thomas J. Chase, Michael A. Rufo, Raymond N. Sussel, Agency Manager Ronald L. Hart, Christine A. Weaver, and Michael W. Peterson. Not pictured are Peter Mooney and David Szafranski.

AL FUCHS

of the largest money managers and among the top pension fund managers in the United States. EQ Financial Consultants provides comprehensive financial programs, bolstered by the products and services of prominent investment firms and insurers.

In Greater Cleveland, Equitable's impact also rests in its strong and vital bond with the city. Through continued commitment to the Make-A-Wish Foundation and the French-American Chamber of Commerce, among others, Equitable intends to flourish with the community—charting mutual progress long into the 21st century.

Ronald L. Hart has successfully led the growth for Equitable as its agency manager in northeast Ohio since 1995.

ITTLE DID JAMES VAN DORN KNOW BACK IN THE EARLY 1870s that the iron fence he had built for his new home in Akron would be the foundation for what is today one of the world's largest manufacturers of injection molding machinery. The fence had caught his neighbors'

attention, and soon Van Dorn was manufacturing fences for a growing market of customers. In 1878, he moved his operation to Cleveland where, after noting that jails were nothing more than fences built indoors, he grew the company into the largest jail manufacturer in the world.

The Van Dorn Iron Works Co., as it became known, manufactured an increasingly large inventory of products in response to the needs of evolving markets. At various times, the company produced parts for streetcars, switchboards, bicycles, fabricated steel cases, map drawers, and office furniture. In 1945, the company began producing plastic injection molding machinery, and a year later, it took part in

the first National Plastics Exhibition in New York City.

Van Dorn Plastic Machinery Co., now known as Van Dorn Demag Corporation, quickly attained a leadership position in the injection molding field through product innovation, quality assurance, reliability, and attention to customer service. The company today enjoys 50 years of continued

success since plastic has become the material of choice in more and more lines of business.

In April 1993, Van Dorn was acquired by Mannesmann Demag AG of Germany. The Cleveland company was merged with Mannesmann Demag's plastic machinery operation to form today's Van Dorn Demag Corporation.

VAN DORN DEMAG CORPORATION TODAY ENJOYS 50 YEARS OF CONTINUED SUCCESS SINCE PLASTIC HAS BECOME THE MATERIAL OF CHOICE IN MORE AND MORE LINES OF BUSINESS (TOP).

THE COMPANY'S PLASTIC INJECTION MOLDING MACHINES ARE PRODUCING HOUSEWARES, CONTAINERS, AND COMPONENTS USED IN HIGH-PRECISION ELECTRONICS, MEDICAL, AND AUTOMOTIVE APPLICATIONS (BOTTOM).

LOCAL PRESENCE, GLOBAL INFLUENCE

Based in Strongsville, Ohio, Van Dorn Demag has produced more than 20,000 machines running on shop floors across North America—more than any other U.S. company. According to President Jerry Pryor, there are several reasons why Van Dorn Demag's midwestern location makes sense. Ohio leads the nation in plastics production, and the company's Greater Cleveland operations are located near numerous plastics processors. In addition, the company depends on the region's advanced roadway and other transportation systems, exceptional utilities support, pro-business environment, and a skilled workforce accustomed to complex machine assembly.

"Our location puts us close to our largest market since there is more molding done in Ohio than just about anywhere else," says Pryor. "We appreciate that the region is committed to the growth and development of the plastics industry through the advancement of academic and economic resources of the Polymer Valley. Northeast Ohio is an excellent source for the talented and capable people we need to manufacture technical products."

Van Dorn Demag employs more than 800 people at five highly efficient production facilities as well as two demonstration and distribution centers. The company recently opened a plant at 4600 West 160th Street, where employees manufacture vertical injection molding machines and operate a modification and integration operation as well as parts and service departments.

As a result of the merger, Van Dorn Demag has improved its position in the international market. Van Dorn has taken advantage of Mannesmann Demag's recognized position in the global marketplace, its international sales and service networks, and its established worldwide distribution network. Conversely, Mannesmann Demag has entered the U.S. market with the help of 65 Van Dorn Demag sales representatives and the company's proven distribution system and reputation.

PLASTICS FOR THE 21ST CENTURY

Today, Van Dorn Demag's plastic injection molding machines are producing housewares, containers, and components used in high-precision electronics,

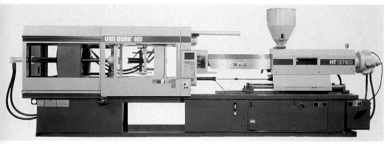

medical, and automotive applications. In addition to its commanding position in North America, the company's machines are used in Ireland, England, the Philippines, Brazil, Mexico, China, Australia, and the Netherlands. "We have grown through the globalization of the marketplace. We're doing business in the four corners of the world as these regions express strong interest in American technology," Pryor says.

Responding to the development of ever larger parts, Van Dorn Demag produces the Van Dorn HP series, hydraulic machines ranging from 275 to 4,400 tons. The Van Dorn HT series of toggle machines ranging from 85 to 650 tons and the ET series of small tonnage machines ranging from 25 to 110 tons are used for small and moderate-sized components. The company also distributes the ERGOtech line of high-performance toggle injection machines for precision, high-speed, and specialty applications.

In April 1996, Van Dorn Demag purchased Newbury Industries, which specializes in the design and manufacture of vertical injection machines. By acquiring Newbury, which had sold more than 12,000 machines in the previous 40 years, Van Dorn Demag improved the versatility of solutions it can offer companies involved in injection molding. Today, the expanded company serves markets from sporting goods to appliances, from kitchen storage containers to computers, and from toys to electronics.

"In our 50-plus years of service to the plastics industry, we have seen this marketplace do nothing but grow," Pryor says. "The development of new engineered resins has led to never-ending applications of plastics for a range of end markets."

With ties in Cleveland, across the United States, and abroad, and injection molding machines for virtually every application, Van Dorn Demag is well positioned to meet the multitude of needs for plastics in the 21st century.

VAN DORN DEMAG HAS PRODUCED AND DISTRIBUTED MORE THAN 20,000 MACHINES RUNNING ON SHOP FLOORS ACROSS NORTH AMERICA—MORE THAN ANY OTHER U.S. COMPANY.

A s CLEVELAND AND NORTHEAST OHIO GEAR UP FOR THE EXCITING challenges of the 21st century, Centerior Energy Corporation has positioned itself to remain a key contributor to the region's renaissance. In 1996, the company announced that it had signed a

definitive agreement to merge with Ohio Edison Company in a tax-free, stock-for-stock transaction resulting in a new holding company named FirstEnergy Corp.

Currently headquartered in Independence, Ohio, Centerior Energy is the holding company for the Cleveland Electric Illuminating Company (CEI) and the Toledo Edison Company, which together serve more than 1 million customers within 4,200 square miles of northern Ohio. The Ohio Edison Company, headquartered in Akron, and Pennsylvania Power Company, its subsidiary headquartered in New Castle, Pennsylvania, serve 1.1 million customers within 9,000 square miles of northeastern and central Ohio and western Pennsylvania.

The merger of Centerior Energy and Ohio Edison will create the nation's 11th-largest investor-owned electric system, based on annual electric sales of 64 billion kilowatt-hours. FirstEnergy will serve 2.1 million customers within 13,200 square miles of northern and central Ohio and western Pennsylvania. As of

June 30, 1996, the combined assets of Ohio Edison and Centerior Energy were nearly $20 billion and annual revenues totaled $5 billion. The new holding company will have an equity value of $4.8 billion.

A WINNING PROPOSITION

Under the terms of the merger, FirstEnergy Corp. will be a holding company of Ohio Edison, CEI, and Toledo

Edison, but Pennsylvania Power Company will remain a wholly owned subsidiary of Ohio Edison. The corporate headquarters of FirstEnergy will be located in Akron, while the principal offices of the operating companies will remain at their current locations.

Willard R. Holland, president and chief executive officer of Ohio Edison and chairman of Pennsylvania Power, says, "This merger creates a larger enterprise with more resources to enhance near-term and long-term value for shareholders, provide better service at lower prices to customers, and offer more career opportunities to employees than if the companies had remained separate. By sharing our employees' skills and each company's best practices, the combination will also enable us to realize substantial economic synergies that will further enhance our cash flow and our efforts to accelerate debt reduction."

Robert J. Farling, chairman and chief executive officer of Centerior Energy, adds, "This is

THE MERGER OF CENTERIOR ENERGY CORPORATION AND OHIO EDISON COMPANY WILL CREATE THE NATION'S 11TH-LARGEST INVESTOR-OWNED ELECTRIC SYSTEM (TOP).

MAINTENANCE PROGRAMS IMPROVE SERVICE TO CUSTOMERS (BOTTOM).

a win-win situation for our companies, our customers, and our shareholders. Together, we form a larger, stronger competitor, which is essential to our success as our industry continues to evolve. Our alliance will provide our customers and shareholders with more value and our employees with more opportunities than would be possible if we did not join forces."

By uniting these substantial resources, FirstEnergy will be able to provide customers with a wide range of energy services and enhanced service-restoration capabilities—key advantages as the power industry becomes more competitive. In addition, the holding company plans to extend to CEI and Toledo Edison customers a rate reduction program that would freeze rates through 2005; effect a rate reduction of $300 million, or approximately 15 percent, in 2006; and result in the accelerated depreciation of $2 billion in fixed costs during that period.

"Our merger also gives us increased flexibility to maximize the operating efficiency of the generating units in which our companies share ownership through the CAPCO arrangements," Holland says, referring to the Central Area Power Coordination Group, which is comprised of the merging companies and Duquesne Light Company. He continues, "This flexibility, along with the synergies we expect from the merger and our intended rate plan, will help us reduce financial risks related to stranded investments in a more competitive electric industry."

The merger is conditioned, among other things, upon the approval of each company's shareholders and various regulatory agencies, including the Federal Energy Regulatory Commission, the Nuclear Regulatory Commission, and the Securities and Ex-

change Commission. Actions in Ohio and Pennsylvania that may be needed to complete the transaction will also be undertaken. The companies are hopeful that the merger can be completed by the end of 1997. Holland will become FirstEnergy's chairman of the board, president, and chief executive officer; Farling will become vice chairman; and the new board of directors will be designated by Ohio Edison's existing board.

IN THE MIDDLE OF THE ACTION

*T*he combination of contiguous service areas located within a 500-mile radius of half of the U.S. population creates a significant advantage for FirstEnergy, which also serves several areas that, in recent years, have been listed by site selection experts as among the nation's most successful for attracting manufacturing operations and expansions. This strength enables communities to attract jobs over a wider and more diverse region, which is served by an extensive infrastructure that includes 10

major airports, portions of all major interstate highways in Ohio, multiple free-trade zones, abundant water supplies, and a highly integrated network of electrical facilities.

"FirstEnergy will continue the strong traditions of both companies by supporting their local communities through financial contributions and through the extensive volunteerism of their employees," Farling says. "In addition, our alliance will make us Ohio's largest taxpayer, with some $516 million in annual payments, as well as one of the state's largest employers."

As a result of the merger, the companies expect to save at least $1 billion over the first 10 years. The savings will come from the elimination of duplicative activities, improved operating efficiencies, lower capital costs, and the combination of the companies' workforces. In addition to efforts that are already under way to achieve appropriate staffing levels, the companies expect to reduce their collective workforce of ap-

OPERATIONAL EFFICIENCIES PRODUCE VALUE FOR CUSTOMERS, INVESTORS, AND THE COMMUNITY.

ELECTRICITY CONTINUES TO BE A
SAFE, RELIABLE SOURCE OF POWER
(TOP).

THE MISSION OF CENTERIOR
ENERGY AND ITS NEW PARTNERS IN
FIRSTENERGY CORP. IS TO PROVIDE
ELECTRICITY WHERE IT'S NEEDED,
WHEN IT'S NEEDED (BOTTOM).

proximately 11,000 by some 900
positions. FirstEnergy will seek to
minimize the effect of these reductions by implementing hiring limits and separation programs, and
by taking advantage of natural
attrition.

In addition, the companies'
ongoing cost reduction and efficiency improvement initiatives will
be available for implementation
throughout the new organization.
Through such programs—along
with reductions in new capital
requirements and lower overheads
resulting from the combination of
operations—FirstEnergy expects
to set an aggressive goal of reducing debt by $2.5 billion through
the year 2000.

A PART OF CLEVELAND'S HISTORY AND FUTURE

*I*n addition to today's
advancement of tech-
nology and the promise of future
growth, Centerior Energy remains

proud of its illustrious past and its
history of contributions to the
Cleveland community. The company traces the beginnings of
its rich history to one evening in

1879—six months prior to Thomas
Edison's invention of the incandes-
cent lightbulb—when inventor
Charles F. Brush astonished a sizable crowd of spectators by illuminating Cleveland's Public Square
with arc lights. Two years later,
Brush brought Edison's revolutionary invention to Clevelanders
through his Brush Electric Light
and Power Company, the ancestor
of the Cleveland Electric Illuminating Company.

After 1879, a new era began
in northeast Ohio, during which
convenience and comfort were
well matched with progress and
growth for the whole region. By
1881, line crews had strung the
first service lines across the roof-
tops of downtown Cleveland,
which was then only three-quarters of a square mile in size. At
that time, the town had 160,000
residents and 88 street lamps in
service.

In 1893, Brush's company
merged with the Cleveland General Electric Company, which had
approximately 400 customers, and
was renamed the Cleveland Electric Illuminating Company. By the
turn of the century, CEI already
served 1,900 of the city's 381,000

residents and was still growing strong. Cleveland industry had come to depend on electricity as a safe and reliable source of power, and by 1914, some 30,000 residents throughout Bratenahl, East Cleveland, Euclid, Cleveland Heights, Lakewood, and Rocky River were enjoying its benefits for a mere three cents per kilowatt-hour, as compared to 12.5 cents in 1881.

CEI continued to expand and unveil new innovations for the region, including powering the first all-electric homes in 1921 and producing a moving picture in 1924, titled *The Heart of Cleveland*, to promote the area and the benefits of electric living. By 1929, the company had built several new generating plants and covered a service area of nearly 1,700 square miles, including heat and electric power for the Van Sweringen brothers' Terminal Tower in downtown Cleveland.

During the Great Depression and the war years of the 1940s, CEI was there to provide power, and by 1955, the company achieved a key milestone, installing its 500,000th electric meter, as it continued to meet the demands of the era of suburban living and all of the new electrical conveniences customers desired in their homes. In 1957, Cleveland's first steel and glass skyscraper, the Illuminating Building, rose at 55 Public Square.

In the 1960s, CEI added a number of service centers to accommodate vast residential growth and purchased its first computer system. By the 1970s, in response to the energy crisis, the company invested in new energy sources, such as nuclear power plants, to ensure a stronger future.

From the age of Edison to the nuclear age, Centerior Energy and its predecessors have furnished the key to growth for Cleveland and northeast Ohio through clean, effective electric power. Today, the company continues to address sensitive environmental concerns by developing a number of important, innovative, earth-safe projects, including quiet, efficient electric cars. More than 50 years ago, it was the first Cleveland company to refer to this region as the Best Location in the Nation. Today, along with its new partners in FirstEnergy Corp., Centerior Energy is helping to keep it that way.

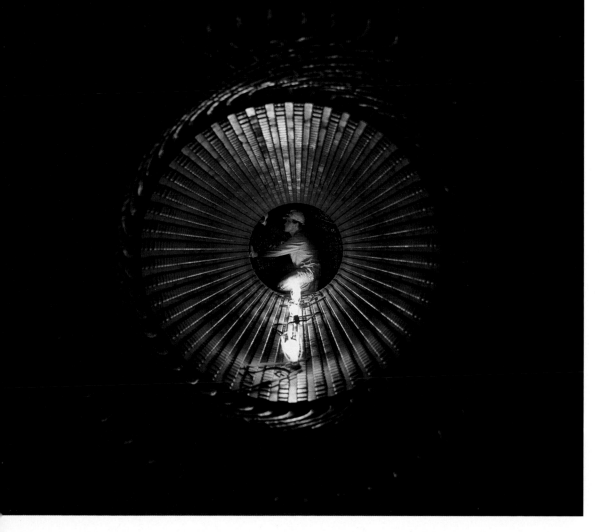

CENTERIOR ENERGY IS PROUD TO PROVIDE ENERGY FOR THE "BEST LOCATION IN THE NATION."

IN THE 18 YEARS SINCE CURRENT MANAGEMENT HAS BEEN IN PLACE, Invacare Corporation has grown from a small U.S. standard wheelchair manufacturing company with 350 employees and $19 million in annual sales to the world's leading manufacturer and distributor of

home medical products, currently offering more than two-dozen product lines in more than 80 countries, employing 4,200 people, and generating $619 million in sales in 1996.

Invacare Corporation's mission is to provide the highest value in mobility products and home medical equipment for people with disabilities and those requiring home health care worldwide. To accomplish this, the company focuses on two basic fundamentals—innovation and distribution. Invacare continuously strives to achieve excellence through improved products, processes, and services. The breadth and depth of the company's distribution system, together with the continuous search for new channels and expansion opportunities, have

allowed Invacare to literally explode new products into the marketplace.

INNOVATIVE PRODUCTS MEET CONSUMER NEEDS

The company's products are marketed primarily through independent home medical equipment (HME) providers that in turn sell or rent products directly to consumers. The company's consolidated brand strategy makes Invacare® the primary brand for home care products and Action the primary brand for high-tech, customized mobility and sports equipment. Both of these brands are available only through HME providers. Consumers interested in locating a provider of these products can contact Invacare's account ser-

vices department for referrals to the location nearest them.

The Aurora™ brand was developed and launched in 1996 to serve the newly emerging mass retail channels of distribution for home medical equipment considered to be "off the shelf." The Aurora products are available at mass merchants, drugstore chains, hardware stores, and home centers nationwide.

MARKETING PROGRAMS REACH CONSUMERS

Ever the innovator, Invacare continues to make improvements to its existing sales and marketing programs to generate greater consumer awareness of the company and its products. Through its consumer marketing program, Invacare sponsors a vari-

A. MALACHI MIXON III (LEFT) SERVES AS CHAIRMAN AND CHIEF EXECUTIVE OFFICER OF INVACARE CORPORATION.

THE COMPANY MANUFACTURES A WIDE VARIETY OF PRODUCTS DESIGNED TO IMPROVE THE LIVES OF PEOPLE WITH DISABILITIES (RIGHT).

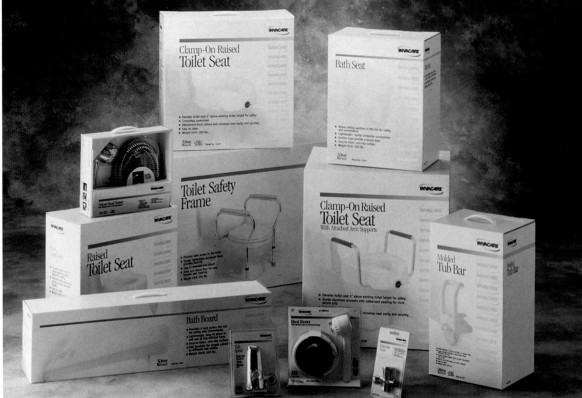

ety of wheelchair sports activities and supports causes that are important to people with disabilities. At the 1996 Atlanta Paralympic Games, athletes sponsored by Invacare's Action brand won 89 medals—more than double the amount of the nearest competitor—competing in the company's high-performance racing and sports chairs. These products make use of new materials, such as aerospace-grade aluminum, as well as high-tech design features also used in today's top racing bicycles and luxury automobiles. Consumers ultimately benefit because Invacare incorporates these same high-tech design features and materials into its everyday Action chairs.

Invacare also reaches out to millions of children and adults with disabilities through its national corporate sponsorship of the National Easter Seal Society. Each year, the company sponsors Action Days at Easter Seals Camps throughout the United States, where athletes teach wheelchair sports to young campers and act as positive role models.

Invacare also is an active sponsor of the Paralyzed Veterans of America (PVA) and its annual Veterans Wheelchair Games; the Cleveland Ballet Dancing Wheels; and more than 75 wheelchair athletes and teams, including wheelchair tennis, basketball (including the Cleveland Cavaliers and Dallas Mavericks wheelchair teams), quad-rugby, and track and racing.

RECOGNIZED BY THE FINANCIAL COMMUNITY

*I*nvacare Corporation, a publicly held company traded on the NASDAQ system under the symbol IVCR, has been recognized by the business and financial community with numerous awards. In 1995, the company's five-year performance ranked 37 out of all listed NASDAQ stocks.

Financial World magazine ranked the company number 78 on its list of the 100 Best Growth Companies for 1996. Additionally, the magazine included Invacare as one of the top 50 midcap companies in 1995 and in the list of the 200 best growth companies in 1994.

Invacare was included in *Business Week*'s 1993 list of 50 Little Giants in manufacturing, as well as the magazine's 1992 list of the 200 best small companies. *Inc.* recognized Invacare for its entrepreneurial leadership in 1992; *Forbes* included the company in its list of the 200 best small companies in 1992; *U.S. News & World Report* listed it as one of the 50 top small stocks with superior earnings in 1991; and *Crain's Cleveland Business* named Invacare the best performing public company in northeast Ohio for 1990-91, as well as number one in five-year stock price appreciation from 1989 to 1993.

INVACARE'S CUSTOMERS HAVE COME TO RELY ON SUCH INNOVATIVE PRODUCTS AS THE VENTURE™ DEMAND OXYGEN DELIVERY DEVICE.

A BRIGHT FUTURE

*I*n the extremely competitive and rapidly changing environment in which Invacare operates, the company has a proven track record. With the continuing demographic trend of the aging population, home health care has proved to be a cost-effective solution to the nation's health care delivery system problems. Invacare is strongly positioned for future growth to take advantage of this trend.

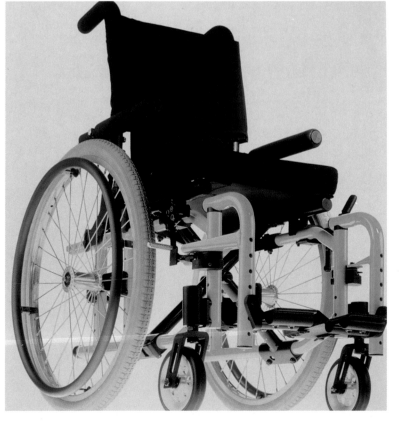

THE COMPANY INCORPORATES HIGH-TECH DESIGN FEATURES AND MATERIALS USED IN ITS COMPETITION CHAIRS INTO ITS EVERYDAY ACTION CHAIRS.

ENERGIZER

ENERGIZER IS THE WORLD'S LARGEST MANUFACTURER OF DRY-CELL batteries and flashlights, and a global leader in the dynamic portable power business. A member of the local business community for more than 100 years, Energizer has three key facilities located in the Cleveland area: the worldwide operations management and technology facility in Westlake, a satellite location in Cleveland, and a sales office in Independence.

Energizer offers full product lines in alkaline, carbon-zinc, miniature, and rechargeable batteries, and in lighting products. Each year, the company's global workforce of more than 15,000 produces billions of batteries that are marketed and sold in more than 160 countries.

A PROUD CLEVELAND HISTORY

Energizer was formed in Cleveland as the National Carbon Company in 1886. Founder W.H. Lawrence bought the company's first facility on East 55th Street to produce open-arc carbons for street lamps, carbon brushes for dynamos, and porous plates for wet batteries. In 1890, the facility produced the first dry-cell battery.

In 1896, National Carbon introduced the 1.5-volt Columbia,

the first dry battery produced and distributed to consumers on a large scale. Used to power telephones, the Columbia was so popular that the company built the first factory in the world devoted to dry-cell battery production.

In 1906, National Carbon purchased half interest in American Ever Ready, owned by flashlight inventor Conrad Hubert. The Cleveland company bought the remaining interest before becoming part of Union Carbide Corporation in 1917.

World War I and the radio craze of the 1920s caused dry battery sales to boom. As a result, Union Carbide opened a new plant on West 73rd Street in Cleveland. By 1930, the company's manufacturing operations were consolidated there.

As new battery types and battery-powered devices proliferated, the company expanded globally. In 1956, Union Carbide opened a battery research center in Parma, sparking a flurry of innovations. Among them were the first 9-volt battery, the first standard alkaline battery, the first batteries for transistor radios,

◄ BARNEY TAXEL

miniature silver oxide batteries, the first watch battery, rechargeable nickel-cadmium batteries, and lithium battery technology.

The 1980 introduction of Energizer-brand alkaline batteries heralded a new era in battery technology. Energizer Super Heavy Duty batteries, lithium batteries, and powerful halogen flashlights soon followed.

A GLOBAL RESEARCH LEADER

In 1982, one of the world's largest battery research and development centers opened on a 35-acre site in Westlake, uniting the R&D functions formerly located at the Parma and West 73rd Street sites. In 1986, Ralston Purina bought Union Carbide's Battery Products Division to create Eveready Battery Company, Inc., known by its flagship brand, Energizer.

In the well-equipped Westlake facility, projects range from fundamental electrochemistry to development of battery designs and unit manufacturing operations. R&D teams focus on specific electrochemical systems and battery sizes for the world market. Analytical, engineering, battery applications, information, and other technical service groups support these teams.

Battery testing and customer service centers are located at the West 73rd Street site. Up to 100,000 batteries are discharged simultaneously under computer-controlled schedules. Data collection, analysis, and reporting are fully automatic. Up to 750,000 batteries, including those tested under various environmental conditions, simultaneously undergo long-term surveillance testing.

ENERGIZER'S WEST 73RD STREET SITE DATES BACK TO THE 1920S. NOW A SATELLITE LOCATION FOR BATTERY TESTING, TRAINING, AND SPECIAL PROJECTS, THIS FACILITY BOASTS BEAUTIFUL INTERIOR ARCHITECTURE AND MAGNIFICENT VIEWS OF LAKE ERIE AND THE CITY SKYLINE.

R&D TEAMS AT ENERGIZER'S WORLDWIDE OPERATIONS MANAGEMENT AND TECHNOLOGY FACILITY IN WESTLAKE FOCUS ON PRESENT AND FUTURE BATTERY DESIGNS.

This facility also is a training center and satellite location for special projects.

Synergy between these Energizer facilities creates a dynamic environment for designing customer-focused products. Results include the introduction of the first AA-sized 1.5-volt lithium battery, the first one-hour rechargeable battery, and the first on-battery tester. The company's Independence sales office provides the link between research innovation and customers.

AN ENVIRONMENTAL LEADER

Energizer continues to lead the industry in providing environmentally responsible battery products. Programs include source reduction of heavy metals, reducing package waste, targeting zero emissions and discharges in manufacturing, conserving energy, and recycling. Energizer's achievements include introducing the first ultra-low mercury battery, reducing packaging waste material by 70 percent, introducing packaging composed of 90 percent recycled materials, introducing the first no-added mercury battery in the United States (Super Heavy Duty), and introducing the Energizer no-added mercury alkaline battery.

A COMMUNITY OF PEOPLE WHO CARE

Energizer's employees are dedicated to making an impact on the Greater Cleveland community, especially on the development of its young people.

The company is especially proud of the students and staff of Cleveland's Wilbur Wright Middle School, who are making a positive impact on the community through their achievements in the Character Building Program. This Energizer-supported incentive program, which highlights and reinforces behaviors that demonstrate courtesy and respect for other people, is being expanded to include more local schools.

The company sponsors many other initiatives such as DARE, fire safety programs, and the Special Olympics. The long-established Christmas Basket Fund provides holiday meals to Clevelanders in need through year-round employee-organized fund-raisers.

A VISION FOR THE FUTURE

For more than a century, Energizer has been an industry leader and a proud part of Cleveland's business community. The company is setting an agenda for the 21st century that addresses the environment, quality, innovation, and customer service: "Energize the World . . . through Superior People, Products, and Service."

THE INTERNATIONAL LAW FIRM OF SQUIRE, SANDERS & DEMPSEY L.L.P. has seven U.S. offices and seven more throughout Europe. The Cleveland office—the firm's first and largest—occupies eight floors in Key Tower on Public Square. Quartered there are 160 of the more

than 375 attorneys who keep the firm among the country's 50 largest. It delivers professional services in practice categories such as litigation, public law, environmental, corporate law, regulatory, taxation, labor/employment law, intellectual property, and computer and information systems technology.

The Cleveland office serves clients divided almost evenly between the public and private sectors. Itself a public/private partnership, the Cleveland office synergistically addresses the needs of both of those client base elements.

Squire, Sanders & Dempsey L.L.P. helped form the Ohio Turnpike Commission and helped devise the referenda for amending the Ohio Constitution to permit issuing tax-exempt bonds as incentives to retain companies tempted to relocate out of state. The firm also helped establish the now widely adopted techniques used to determine utility rate bases.

The heart of any major law firm is its business clients, and Squire, Sanders & Dempsey L.L.P. serves a wide array of such entities, from privately held businesses to Fortune 500 corporations. Particularly significant is the firm's extensive representation of privately held and family corporations. The firm's attorneys advise owner/managers and participate in business planning to equip client companies and their owners with the tools to thrive and prosper. Frequently, this participation means addressing such matters as succession, ownership transfer, executive compensation, and tax and estate planning issues.

The attorneys often assist private companies in deciding whether to go public or determine what other forms of corporate and tax-exempt financing will best provide the capital the companies need.

ACCOUNTABILITY AND GLOBAL EXPERTISE

The hallmark of Squire, Sanders & Dempsey L.L.P. attorneys is accountability. That quality includes remaining on the client account and assuming frontline responsibility; serving, if appropriate, on the client company board of trustees; networking the client into the business and financial community; and coordinating the firm's resources to benefit the client.

Each client is assigned an attorney who knows and understands that client's business and who cost-effectively delivers the firm's expertise and other resources—when, where, and how they are needed.

Squire, Sanders & Dempsey L.L.P. attorneys provide in-depth expertise in such diverse specialties as acquisitions, dispositions, reorganizations, joint ventures, tender offers, contracts, international investment and trade, and real estate. They also handle all facets of employer/employee relationships, among them pensions and profit sharing plans, labor negotiations, NLRB representation, unionization avoidance, EEO discrimination counseling and litigation, and employee benefit plans.

In 1996, the firm's attorneys represented the City of Cleveland in its highly visible legal battle over the Cleveland Browns NFL team. Although the old team's players and management left town, the team name and colors were saved for a replacement franchise expected by century's end. The NFL, in turn, made unprecedented pledges of economic support toward the city's efforts to build a new stadium.

Over the past 30 years, Squire, Sanders & Dempsey L.L.P. attorneys also have advised the NCAA, including defining in 1972 its right to regulate extracollegiate competition, which resolved the long NCAA/AAU feud.

THE FIRM'S FIRST AND LONGEST-ESTABLISHED PRACTICE OFFICE IS IN CLEVELAND, WHERE ANDREW SQUIRE, WILLIAM B. SANDERS, AND JAMES DEMPSEY FOUNDED THEIR LAW PRACTICE ON JANUARY 1, 1890.

With half of its offices located overseas, the firm plans to increase its presence in those regions as well as by fostering development of individual nations' economies. By no means, though, does this emphasis on expanding into foreign markets equate to plowing untilled territory. For more than two decades, the firm has staffed a large office in Brussels, and has represented numerous high-profile clients, including the U.S. Embassy. Since 1990, the firm has helped lead the economic transformation of central European countries that, freed from communistic regimes, have been eagerly striving to open their markets to international trade.

For example, when Hungary privatized its telephone system, when the Czech Republic decided to sell a major brewery, and when Nike needed legal representation in negotiating distribution in Russia, Squire, Sanders & Dempsey L.L.P. handled the arrangements. The firm also represents such diverse entities as the State Property Fund in Ukraine on privatization issues, a Czech cigarette company on a $400 million privatization agreement with Philip Morris, and Sara Lee Corporation on its investment in a Czech food-processing business.

"Our firm has always been world class," notes Chairman R. Thomas Stanton. "In fact, what we have done in recent years is built on strong, long-standing propositions that we already held, in both client base and expertise."

COMMUNITY FOCUS

The longtime commitment that the firm has demonstrated to the local community mirrors the magnitude of its worldwide operations.

Office Managing Partner John F. Lewis, a labor and employment law specialist who joined the firm in 1958, is a strong supporter of—and active participant in—the civic,

educational, and social arenas. As he emphasizes, "Squire, Sanders & Dempsey has always believed it is both a privilege and a necessity that its attorneys give of their time and resources to the community they call home. We are committed to the community and to giving back to it." He knows whereof he speaks, having helped launch the community's first major private/public venture—the Playhouse Square Foundation—during his 1980-1985 service as chair of the foundation's board of trustees. With pride for what the city is able to accomplish, Lewis points out, "The $41 million Playhouse Square renovation has been more than a neighborhood project. Today, as the largest theater restoration in the world, it's a way of life, with the entire community joining in its continued development."

Squire, Sanders & Dempsey L.L.P. has always generously funneled its energies back into the community—a legacy begun by its founders, who helped establish the Cleveland Metroparks System, the world-renowned Cleveland Museum of Art, and Cleveland's widely respected University

School. Today, as board chairman of Case Western Reserve University and of the Ohio Foundation of Independent Colleges, Lewis is building on the tradition of the firm's founders. He also has chaired the Education Committee of the Greater Cleveland Roundtable and has guided creation of the Scholarship-in-Escrow and School-to-Work programs, which together have raised some $16 million to motivate students to remain in school.

A VISITOR CHECKS IN AT THE SQUIRE, SANDERS & DEMPSEY L.L.P. RECEPTION AREA ON THE 49TH FLOOR OF KEY TOWER, LOCATED ON PUBLIC SQUARE AT THE CITY'S CENTER (TOP).

CONFERRING ARE MARY ANN JORGENSON, WHO HEADS THE FIRM'S CORPORATE GROUP; R. THOMAS STANTON, CHAIRMAN OF THE FIRM; AND JOHN F. LEWIS, MANAGING PARTNER OF THE CLEVELAND OFFICE (BOTTOM).

OR MORE THAN A CENTURY, THE OSBORN ENGINEERING COMPANY has been at the heart of Cleveland's growth, helping to shape an extraordinary skyline. The city's oldest engineering firm, Osborn provides the professional services required for the development and construction of Cleveland's built environment.

With a staff of more than 100 engineers, architects, technicians, and support personnel, Osborn stands as one of the region's finest multidisciplinary firms. The company integrates structural, civil, mechanical, electrical, and process engineering; industrial safety; machine design; and architecture to create the most effective and efficient design solutions for its clients. To meet the demands of its successful service policy, Osborn utilizes the most up-to-date developments in design, drafting, and project management technology.

Osborn stands ready to serve its clients with extensive capabilities for projects ranging from large industrial, commercial, and institutional developments and feasibility studies to architectural and structural designs and investigations, including historic restoration, renovation, and remodeling. The expertise of the company's team of

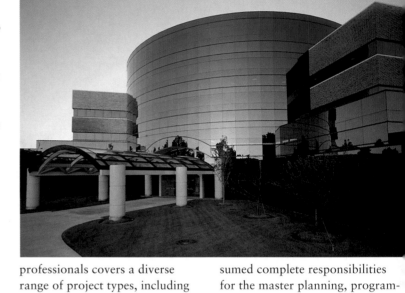

professionals covers a diverse range of project types, including industrial plants, laboratories, commercial offices, sports facilities, and bridges/roadways.

PART OF THE RENAISSANCE

Osborn's participation in Cleveland's recent renaissance includes involvement in a number of high-profile projects that will impact the vitality of the city far into the next century. As a significant contributor to the success of the nationally renowned and award-winning Jacobs Field, Osborn's role entailed the complete planning and design of structural engineering systems for the 42,000-seat baseball stadium.

To enable the facility to open on schedule, the company implemented a daunting fast-track schedule, completing in five months what would normally require a full year. For its inventive approach to this substantial landmark project, Osborn received national and state awards for its engineering innovations and technical excellence.

For Lubrizol Corporation, a Fortune 500 giant, Osborn as-

sumed complete responsibilities for the master planning, programming, and design of a gleaming, new, 200,000-square-foot corporate headquarters facility. Osborn tastefully integrated the office building into the existing campus-like setting by coordinating the style and materials of the new structure with the old. Special features included complete design of a 17,000-square-foot, state-of-the-art computer operations center and an interface with the corporation's broadband system, LAN network, and fiber optics. This example of a successful fast-track design and construction project allowed Lubrizol to meet its tight schedules.

A CENTURY OF ENGINEERING EXCELLENCE

The Osborn Engineering Company began contributing its renowned approach to world-class quality engineering and architecture in 1892, when Frank C. Osborn left his position as chief engineer for the King Bridge Company and founded the firm that still proudly bears his name.

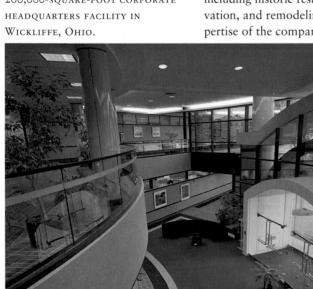

FOR LUBRIZOL CORPORATION, OSBORN ASSUMED COMPLETE RESPONSIBILITIES FOR THE MASTER PLANNING, PROGRAMMING, AND DESIGN OF A GLEAMING, NEW, 200,000-SQUARE-FOOT CORPORATE HEADQUARTERS FACILITY IN WICKLIFFE, OHIO.

Osborn had received acclaim for developing new methods for concrete testing, and in 1902, he published the forerunner of today's *American Institute of Steel Construction Manual*.

Throughout the years, Osborn's new enterprise went on to perform engineering work for such notable Cleveland landmarks as League Park, the Rose Building, Public Auditorium, the Union Club, Grays Armory, Municipal Stadium, the old Cleveland Trust Building on East Ninth Street, and many others.

The firm also attained early acclaim for its design of legendary sports facilities nationwide—from Yankee Stadium and the Polo Grounds in New York City to Comiskey Park in Chicago, Tiger Stadium in Detroit, Notre Dame Stadium in South Bend, the University of Michigan Stadium in Ann Arbor, and Fenway Park in Boston. More recently, Osborn furnished design and engineering services for Three Rivers Stadium in Pittsburgh; Miami University's Yager Stadium in Oxford, Ohio; and Youngstown State University's Stambaugh Stadium. And two of the most renowned jewels in American sports, Wrigley Field in Chicago and Ohio Stadium in Columbus, have been entrusted to Osborn for the tasteful and sensitive renovations that will maintain their heritage and traditions for decades to come.

After more than 11,000 projects, the personalized attention Osborn's original staff extended to their first client has been refined and developed into a highly successful service concept, resulting in more than 80 percent of each year's design volume recorded with previous clients.

The size and diverse skills of the firm also empower Osborn to react quickly to problem situations. When a client's Arkansas subsidiary was damaged by a tornado, for example, an Osborn

As a significant contributor to the success of the nationally renowned and award-winning Jacobs Field in Cleveland, Osborn's role entailed the complete planning and design of structural engineering systems for the 42,000-seat baseball stadium (top).

The firm put its signature on Plus Mark's 1 million-square-foot corporate headquarters and manufacturing facility in Greeneville, Tennessee (bottom).

team was on its way within hours, prepared to assess damage and plan repairs.

Clients also benefit from the firm's involvement in professional organizations. Since Frank Osborn started the Civil Engineers Club, the forerunner of the Cleveland Engineering Society, company principals have actively sought to update technological knowledge. Their service on committees and

as officers of state and national professional organizations has brought international recognition to Cleveland talent.

Coupling its past accomplishments with a firm commitment to the latest in design and engineering innovations today, Osborn Engineering continues to fulfill its mission and practice its motto: Designing Tomorrow since 1892.

IN 1995, THE LINCOLN ELECTRIC COMPANY CELEBRATED ITS centennial and began its next 100 years with the slogan "A Century of Excellence—A Future of Innovation." The first century saw the company grow from a small, local enterprise that produced electric

motors to a worldwide corporation with manufacturing facilities in 14 countries. And the second promises even greater growth.

Founded in 1895 by brothers John C. and James F. Lincoln to build and sell electric motors, the business soon expanded to include arc-welding and metal-cutting products. Throughout its history, one of the distinguishing characteristics of Lincoln Electric has been its product and operational innovations. Such progressive thinking has propelled the company to achieve sales of $1.05 billion and a net income of $61.5 million in 1995.

100 YEARS AND COUNTING

From early on in its existence, Lincoln Electric has introduced new products and processes to the world. In 1911, for example, the company invented the variable-voltage, single-operator portable welding machine. Three years later, Lincoln Electric established its piecework system of manufacturing, which continues to this day. The company also created the Employee Advisory Board, which includes elected representatives from every department of the company who meet with top management; the board has convened every two weeks

since its genesis in 1914. In addition, the Lincoln Electric Welding School, founded in 1917, has trained more than 100,000 people.

The company continued to grow through the years, even during the Great Depression. In fact, Lincoln Electric paid its first year-end employee bonus in 1934. Annual sales grew from $4 million that year to $24 million in 1942, and in 1951, the company made giant strides into the modern era by opening a new plant on St. Clair Avenue in Euclid, Ohio.

It was during the 1980s that Lincoln Electric truly expanded into an international company, growing from five plants in four countries to operations in 16 countries. Today, Lincoln Electric has manufacturing facilities in Australia, the Netherlands, Canada, Norway, France, Spain, Ireland, the United Kingdom, Italy, Mexico and the United States.

In recognition of its commitment to quality and providing outstanding service to its customers, Lincoln Electric was awarded ISO 9002 certification in 1993. And on June 8, 1995—designated John C. Lincoln Appreciation Day in honor of the company's centennial—Lincoln Electric opened a state-of-the-art motor plant in Cleveland. Today, the company is led by Chairman Donald Hastings, who has been with Lincoln Electric since 1953. Hastings was appointed president in 1986 and was named to his current position in 1992.

MOTORS, AND WELDING AND CUTTING PRODUCTS

Lincoln Electric's product line is divided into two areas: motors, and welding and

utting products. Motors manufactured by Lincoln Electric include TEFC, ODP, and specialty motors. Unique features include such world-class components as the ventilation system, winding methodology, insulation system, rotor, and bearing system. The company's motors range from one-third to 1,250 horsepower and come with a five-year warranty.

In the area of welding and cutting products, Lincoln Electric produces stick, TIG, CV, CC/CV, and engine-driven welders, as well as wire feeder/welders, semiautomatic and automatic wire feeders, robotic/automatic systems, plasma, magnum guns, torches and accessories, and environmental systems. Lincoln Electric also assembles carbon and low-alloy steel, stainless steel, hard facing, and cast-iron/nonferrous consumables.

In addition to these products, Lincoln Electric provides specialized services to its customers and employees, including technical

representatives, welding seminars, the Weld Tech Center, and the Lincoln Electric Welding School. The company has also produced several technical books, manuals, and training aids. And its comprehensive *Procedure Handbook*, considered the bible of the welding industry, has reached a printing of more than 2 million copies.

A GREAT PLACE TO WORK

*A*fter its products and services, Lincoln Electric is perhaps best known for its innovative incentive performance system, a corporate philosophy centered around several precepts: people, Christian ethics, principles, simplicity, competition, and the customer. In accordance with this philosophy, Lincoln Electric promises that each employee who has been on board for more than three years will be paid for a minimum of 30 hours of work each week, that jobs will be put on a straight piecework system whenever possible, and that no limits will be

placed on the amount of piecework pay an employee can earn.

In addition, all employees are responsible for their own quality of work. Twice a year, the company evaluates the performance of its workers on the basis of four categories: ideas and cooperation, output, dependability, and quality. Lincoln Electric then gives year-end bonuses to employees—on the basis of their merit ratings—in recognition of their efficient operation and their contributions to the company's success for the year. Although Lincoln Electric does not guarantee the bonus, it has rewarded its employees in this way every year since 1934.

Now that the company has passed its centennial mark, the "future of innovation" takes on even greater significance and prominence. Based on its history of success, Lincoln Electric is well prepared to build on its past as it begins a second century of innovative manufacturing and management.

KPMG PEAT MARWICK LLP

FOR THE PAST CENTURY, BUSINESSES HAVE BEEN TURNING TO KPMG Peat Marwick for guidance. And the top-notch accounting firm wants to ensure that these and other companies will continue to do so. As it prepares to enter the 21st century, KPMG has realigned its operations into a market-oriented structure that is tailored to meet the unique needs of customers for accounting, auditing, corporate finance, tax and management consulting, and other professional services.

KPMG is committed to offering the highest-quality professional services and becoming the world's undisputed leader in accounting and consulting services. While providing added value to clients, the firm also pledges to meet or exceed their expectations.

A LONG TRADITION OF INDUSTRY LEADERSHIP

In 1897, little more than a decade after the formation of the first American accounting firm, James Marwick and Roger Mitchell established Marwick, Mitchell & Co., the predecessor of today's KPMG Peat Marwick. The firm established its international focus in 1911 through a merger with the British practice of Sir William B. Peat. In 1975,

KPMG again went out ahead of the pack, establishing what has become an industry standard for quality control by engaging another firm to audit its work.

In 1978, Peat Marwick International, an umbrella partnership of member firms, was formed to foster a singular, prestigious image worldwide. And in 1981, it became one of the first firms to automate its audit process. In joining with Klynveld Main Goerdeler in 1987, the firm created the first truly global accounting and consulting organization, and two years later it was the first major professional services firm to establish a formal quality service measurement process. All these steps contributed to KPMG's passing the $8 billion mark in annual revenues in the 1990s.

A WORLDWIDE PRESENCE

One of the world's leading professional services firms, KPMG Peat Marwick has clients across the world—from Nairobi to Beijing, Chicago to Singapore, Adelaide to Amsterdam. The firm operates more than 1,000 offices in 829 cities in 145 countries. Its global workforce includes 75,000 partners and staff.

The Cleveland office, located downtown at 1500 National City Center, provides clients ready access to an unparalleled network that stretches from Costa Rica to Ireland, Latin America to the Netherlands, South Africa to Sweden. No matter the location,

JAMES T. SORENSEN SERVES AS OFFICE MANAGING PARTNER FOR KPMG IN CLEVELAND (TOP).

THE FIRM DELIVERS VALUE THROUGH ITS FIVE LINES OF BUSINESS: HEALTH CARE AND LIFE SCIENCES; INFORMATION, COMMUNICATIONS, AND ENTERTAINMENT; FINANCIAL SERVICES; MANUFACTURING, RETAILING, AND DISTRIBUTION; AND PUBLIC SERVICES (BOTTOM).

KPMG can bring the world economy home or take a client's business worldwide—crossing oceans, time zones, and entire continents to maximize a company's effectiveness.

More of the world's top international corporations turn to KPMG for auditing than to any other firm. These companies and other international forces also rely on KPMG for management consulting advice, including reengineering, international tax restructuring, and other complex business strategies. Today, KPMG is a full-service consulting firm with a worldwide perspective.

STRUCTURED ACCORDING TO MARKETS

To succeed in markets made even more complex by high technology and the world economy, U.S. companies require assistance from experts uniquely concerned with the issues that will drive their enterprises to higher levels of success. To meet this need, KPMG has organized itself along several lines of business: financial services; health care and life sciences; information, communications, and entertainment; manufacturing, retailing, and distribution; and public services.

Each area is further divided to maximize the benefit to clients. For example, the financial services line of business includes concentrations in banking and finance, insurance, real estate, investment banking, investment management services, and financial services.

In addition to its unique industry focus, the firm offers a full range of products and services. Its assurance services practice assists companies by improving the reliability and relevance of information used by decision makers. Through a greater emphasis on

business ethics, KPMG clients are prompted toward responsible solutions to the most daunting dilemmas facing businesses today. The firm's business process solutions reshape the way business is done in an increasingly competitive environment. KPMG also provides expert assistance in areas such as compensation and benefits, information risk management, international services, litigation and forensic services, personal financial planning, and strategic services.

Business leaders travel from all over the world to conferences sponsored by KMPG. For example, in late 1996 educators attended the 10th annual 21st Century Higher Education Confer-

ence for a variety of perspectives on trends affecting regulatory, transformation, and technology issues.

A CENTURY OLD

In late 1996, KPMG Peat Marwick named a new pair of national leaders to take the firm into the 21st century, Chairman and CEO Stephen Butler and Deputy Chairman Roger S. Siboni. In 1997, the first of their six years at the helm, KPMG celebrated its 100-year anniversary in Cleveland.

"My vision for KPMG is simple," Butler says. "The only place for us to be is unequivocally number one in the markets we choose to serve."

KPMG's Cleveland offices are located on the 15th and 16th floors of National City Center.

F OR MORE THAN 100 YEARS, PENTON PUBLISHING HAS PROVIDED communications to specialized markets. From the time its founder, John Augustus Penton, launched his first magazine in 1892, to the company's development of CD-ROM products in the 1990s, Penton

Publishing has long enjoyed a reputation as one of the best business publishing companies in the United States.

As it approaches the end of the 20th century, Penton Publishing produces more than 90 titles and employs more than 1,250 professionals worldwide. The company also operates a state-of-the-art printing facility and is rapidly expanding its operations into other areas of business communications, such as conferences, trade shows, and electronic publishing. By following the philosophy "If we serve our readers first, we serve our advertisers best," Penton Publishing has become a leader and innovator in the publishing industry.

A CENTURY OF GROWTH

P enton immigrated to Detroit from Canada in 1862 when he was 21 years old. He soon began working as a machinery molder, later becoming president of the Brotherhood of Machinery Molders and editor of the *Machinery Molders Journal*. By 1890, Penton was determined

to begin publishing a magazine for his fellow foundry workers. The first issue of *Foundry* appeared in September 1892.

In 1901, Penton moved to Cleveland to run the Iron and Steel Press Co., which took over the publishing of *Foundry* and the *Iron Trade Review*. In 1912, newly founded Penton Publishing purchased the Whitworth Brothers Co., which had been printing the Penton magazines, and took over the Whitworth headquarters at the southwest corner of East 12th Street and Chester Avenue.

During the 1920s and 1930s, Penton's role as a premier printer and publisher of business magazines flourished. Such titles as *Machine Design*; *New Equipment Digest*; *Steel*, which later became *IndustryWeek*; and *Daily Metal Trade* were added to the company's roster. It was during this time that Penton introduced the publishing industry to pioneering marketing techniques such as controlled circulation, and conducted the first Business Publications Audit, a survey of readers' functions. From 1938 to 1945, the company

assisted the U.S. Bureau of the Census in developing the Standard Industrial Classification (SIC) system and created the first Census of Manufacturing.

During World War II, Penton publications contributed to the war effort by distributing important information to the metalworking industries that were engaged in war contracts. In the postwar years, Penton continued its growth. In the 1950s the company came up with more innovative ways to serve its advertising customers, such as psychographic research, multiunit tabloid advertising, and a reader management service. Penton also remained a leader in discerning manufacturing industry trends; in 1962, the company received an E award from President John F. Kennedy for its contributions to the expansion of the nation's international trade.

In 1976, Penton Publishing was purchased by Pittway Corporation of Chicago and merged with another industrial magazine publishing giant, Industrial Publishing Co. (IPC), which owned 15 magazines and six catalogs

and directories. In the 1980s and 1990s, Penton Publishing expanded its business-to-business marketing services to its product lines. Known in the publishing industry as the company that is "not business-to-business as usual," Penton Publishing offers its customers services such as direct mail, printing, research, list rentals, conferences, custom publishing, and trade shows, as well as a variety of products, including more than 20 annual directories and buyers' guides, CD-ROMs, newsletters, postcard packs, reprints, advertorials, and educational materials. A Penton subsidiary, Curtin & Pease/Peneco in Dunedin, Florida, is a direct mail marketing and custom printing company that serves clients in the pharmaceutical, health care, and business services markets.

MEETING CUSTOMERS' NEEDS

*I*n recent years, Penton's commitment to total quality management and ongoing employee training and education has been critical to its success. These programs not only give employees a larger role in the success of the organization, but also produce more efficient, cost-effective products and services for customers.

Penton's commitment to excellence is nowhere more evident than in its expertly written magazines. The company's editors and designers win countless awards annually. In fact, more editors at Penton have won the coveted G.D. Crain Award for outstanding career contributions to the business press than any other business-to-business publishing company. And Penton is the only publishing company to have four of its executives serve as chairman of the American Business Press.

Thomas Kemp, Penton's current chairman and CEO, believes the company's ongoing mission is

to provide useful, unique, need-to-know information to business professionals, and to provide advertisers with access to the markets that Penton serves. These markets include management, electronics, design and engineering, hospitality and food service, transportation and logistics, government and compliance, and aviation and airlines.

Penton magazine titles include *Air Transport World*, *Computer-Aided Engineering*, *Restaurant Hospitality*, *Welding Design & Fabrication*, *Machine Design*, *Forging*, *Government Product News*, *Lodging Hospitality*, and *IndustryWeek*, a 233,000-circulation publication for executives and other key decision makers in manufacturing.

Innovative people and new approaches to trade publishing have transformed Penton into a full-service business communications company that offers marketing and advertising services, as well as timely business information. In the coming years, Penton Publishing will continue to use electronic media, trade shows, conferences,

AWARD-WINNING EDITORS AND DESIGNERS ARE AMONG PENTON PUBLISHING'S 1,250 EMPLOYEES WORLDWIDE (TOP).

A STATE-OF-THE-ART PRINTING FACILITY HANDLES ALL OF PENTON'S PRINTING NEEDS (BOTTOM).

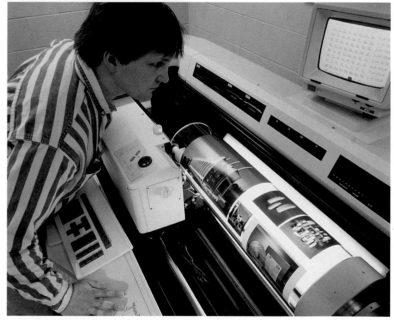

seminars, and further expansion into international markets to serve customers' changing needs.

Penton Publishing has a proud history in Cleveland. By seizing—and initiating—trends in its own industry and by staying in touch with what is happening in others, the company has remained a strong presence on the local, national, and international business scenes.

ROYAL APPLIANCE MFG. CO. HAS BEEN CLEANING UP AMERICA SINCE the company was established in 1905 by Clevelander P.A. Geier. From its inauspicious beginning in Geier's backyard garage, the P.A. Geier Company—as the business was originally named—was to become the world's oldest vacuum cleaner company.

Soon after its formation, Geier's company produced a new cleaning device that gained immediate popularity and soon demanded larger manufacturing facilities. From its new plant on Cleveland's east side, the company quickly grew and began producing mixers, hair dryers, and washing machine units in addition to vacuum cleaners, which prevailed as the company's dominant product. In 1937, the P.A. Geier Company introduced the industry's first handheld vacuum, the Royal Prince. Since that time, the vacuum cleaning industry has never been the same.

After World War II, during which time the company used its operations to manufacture military goods, P.A. Geier resumed producing vacuum cleaners. Its shipments remained strong until 1953, when the company was sold to an investment group headed by Walter E. Schott, who renamed the business Royal Appliance Manufacturing Company. Shortly after, in 1954, a group of employees headed by Stan Erbor purchased the company. Royal Appliance thrived under Erbor's leadership, moving to its present address in 1969, where it expanded and refined all phases of operation.

The 1980s brought a number of changes for Royal Appliance. In 1981, after Erbor's death, a small group of investors purchased the company and quickly initiated a fresh, new approach to sales and marketing. They adopted an aggressive advertising strategy and upgraded the company's distribution efforts into mass retail outlets. Under the new leadership, Royal's sales grew dramatically, and the company increased its focus on product design and development, as well as marketing and advertising innovation.

In 1984, Royal Appliance introduced a new, innovative product—the Dirt Devil® Hand Vac—revolutionizing the industry by making powerful hand vacs that were lightweight and easy to use. But the innovation did not stop with the product; it continued with advertising that "morphed" an upright vacuum into a hand vac. At the time, the cutting-edge concept of morphing clearly communicated the idea that consumers could "put the power of an upright in the palm of your hand." The Hand Vac has grown to become Royal's signature product and the largest-selling handheld vacuum cleaner in the world. Since its debut, more than 18 million Dirt Devil Hand Vacs have been sold, opening the door for many new product innovations under the Dirt Devil brand name.

The 1990s brought rapid changes to the increasingly competitive vacuum cleaner industry. Royal Appliance responded by renewing its commitment to innovation and the development of cleaning appliances that thrill customers. In doing so, the company also set new industry standards by

THE P.A. GEIER COMPANY—AS ROYAL APPLIANCE WAS ORIGINALLY NAMED—PRODUCED MIXERS, HAIR DRYERS, WASHING MACHINE UNITS, AND VACUUM CLEANERS IN ITS PLANT ON CLEVELAND'S EAST SIDE.

being the first to develop, mass market, and advertise upright vacuums with onboard tools, and by investing unprecedented dollars in print and broadcast advertising—initiatives that seem commonplace in the floor care industry today, but were revolutionary at the time. As awareness of the Dirt Devil brand name increased, the company also experienced rapidly growing customer acceptance of a variety of Dirt Devil products, including hand vacs, upright vacuums, stick vacuums, canister vacuums, wet/dry vacuums, and sweepers. In fact, Royal Appliance today enjoys more than 90 percent brand awareness in the Dirt Devil name.

While Dirt Devil products have already enjoyed tremendous success, Royal Appliance is committed to making its quality products even better. In 1996, the company upgraded two of its most popular products, the Hand Vac and the MVP upright, with the new and improved Ultra series.

The Ultra MVP® upright vacuum and Ultra Hand Vac put even greater power and convenience into consumers' hands, with innovative, patented onboard tools and overall enhanced product features. Consumers were offered more than 20 feet of cleaning reach with the Ultra MVP's exclusive Hide-a-Hose™ system that made it possible to clean an entire flight of stairs without ever moving the vacuum. And the unit's triangular, patented EDGE WEDGE™ tool made it much easier to clean corners and stairs. New product features for the Ultra Hand Vac included a unique built-in stretch hose and crevice tool, and an extra-long cord for greater cleaning versatility.

In 1996, Royal Appliance also launched an entirely new product category with the Dirt Devil Broom Vac®—a cordless, rechargeable broom that sweeps

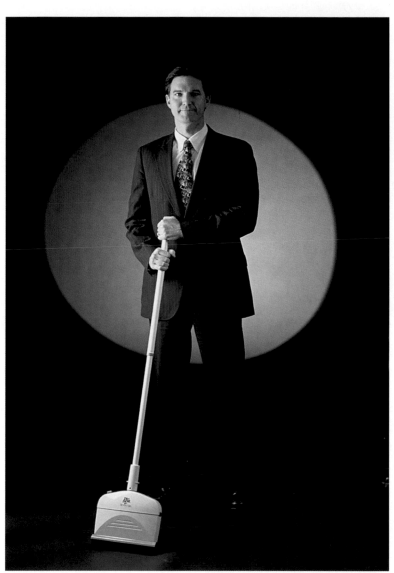

and vacuums in one simple step, making the dustpan virtually obsolete. According to Michael Merriman, who was appointed president and CEO in 1995, the new Broom Vac product launch was only the beginning. In keeping with the times and the prospects new technology offers, Dirt Devil will continue to introduce new, innovative products that provide easier, more enjoyable cleaning experiences for consumers.

In 1997, the company maintained its spirit of innovation, introducing three new products: the Dirt Devil Swivel Glide™, the Dirt Devil RoomMate™, and the Dirt Devil Mop Vac™. The Dirt Devil Swivel Glide is a full-size, upright vacuum cleaner with

enhanced maneuverability, while the Dirt Devil RoomMate is a lightweight, portable, upright vacuum cleaner. These two products were unveiled at the 1997 International Housewares Show and received enthusiastic responses from the company's major retail customers. The third product— a cordless, rechargeable mop called the Dirt Devil Mop Vac— represents another new category for the company and its retailers.

Royal Appliance will continue into the next millennium with new product innovations and enhancements, thanks to its renewed vision and dedicated personnel, all of which make Dirt Devil a true leader in the vacuum cleaning industry.

CLOCKWISE FROM LEFT: IN 1996, UNDER THE LEADERSHIP OF PRESIDENT AND CEO MICHAEL MERRIMAN, ROYAL APPLIANCE LAUNCHED AN ENTIRELY NEW PRODUCT CATEGORY WITH THE DIRT DEVIL BROOM VAC®—A CORDLESS, RECHARGEABLE BROOM THAT SWEEPS AND VACUUMS IN ONE SIMPLE STEP.

ENHANCED PRODUCT FEATURES FOR THE ULTRA HAND VAC INCLUDE A UNIQUE BUILT-IN STRETCH HOSE AND CREVICE TOOL, AND AN EXTRA-LONG CORD FOR GREATER CLEANING VERSATILITY.

THE ULTRA MVP® OFFERS THE EXCLUSIVE HIDE-A-HOSE™ SYSTEM WITH MORE THAN 20 FEET OF CLEANING REACH, WHILE THE UNIT'S TRIANGULAR, PATENTED EDGE WEDGE™ TOOL FACILITATES CLEANING OF CORNERS AND STAIRS.

ABCOCK & WILCOX (B&W), AN OPERATING UNIT OF MCDERMOTT International, Inc., has been a name synonymous with excellence in the power generation industry since 1867, when the company was founded by George Babcock and Stephen Wilcox. Among their

favorite adages was the phrase "there must be a better way." In fact, that philosophy was the impetus behind the birth of the company, as the two childhood friends worked to invent and market a water tube boiler that was not only safer but also more efficient than existing models. That saying, as well as the founders' belief in continually looking for ways to improve the company's products, remains within B&W today.

What began as a simple boiler engineering and manufacturing operation has evolved into a company that supplies complete power plants, environmental equipment, and construction services for utilities and industries worldwide. The company also serves as a major contractor to the U.S. government, providing fuel, propulsion systems, and other products for the

navy's nuclear fleet, as well as environmental remediation services under government contract. Through B&W's Diamond Power Specialty Company, based in Lancaster, Ohio, the corporation provides a complete line of boiler cleaning systems and equipment for customers worldwide.

Babcock & Wilcox has earned a reputation as an industry leader for its commitment to excellence and for its quality, integrity, teamwork, and outstanding customer service. It is a company truly dedicated to powering the world by providing innovative energy solutions and total-scope services to its customers. Yet today, even with offices and facilities in 17 states, international operations across the globe, and more than 10,000 employees worldwide, Babcock & Wilcox is proud to call Barberton, Ohio, its home.

B&W AND OHIO

B&W has been in Barberton since 1906, when the company purchased the local Stirling Consolidated Boiler Company plant. From its earliest days in northeast Ohio through the Great Depression and the war years, and from the turbulent 1960s and the energy crisis of the 1970s through today's era of extremely competitive business conditions, Babcock & Wilcox has demonstrated a steadfast commitment to Ohio and its residents.

B&W is known and recognized around the world for its superior products, technological leadership, and innovative employees who receive scores of patents each year for products or processes they create for the power generation industry.

Yet even as B&W's challenges have been many, particularly in the past decade, the company has refused to be daunted by even the greatest adversity. B&W's Nuclear Equipment Division plant, for instance, faced a dramatically reduced demand for its products

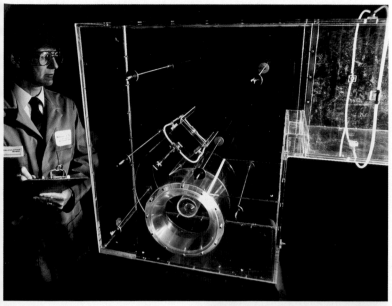

as the country, and the world, entered a new era of peace. To address this challenge, the B&W management team and its employees have strived to improve their work processes and reduce costs to better the division's chance of winning the limited work available to the country's defense contractors.

For B&W's Power Generation Group, the challenges have been just as great. Deregulation and privatization in the electric utility industry, which has traditionally provided the group's base business, have caused a dramatic decline in the domestic market for B&W's products. But the company shifted its focus to the growing international market, and has learned to successfully rival the most aggressive overseas competitors, even while maintaining its strong ties to its domestic customer base. B&W's success is reflected in more than $1 billion in new contracts over the past two years. Although most of that work is for international power generation projects, much of it will be engineered and project managed at B&W's Barberton headquarters.

World-class technology is also a cornerstone of B&W, and the company has dedicated exten-

sive resources to staying at the forefront of new and emerging developments. The company boasts a research facility in Alliance, Ohio, where a highly qualified professional staff uses state-of-the-art measurement, diagnostic, and analysis equipment; advanced numerical modeling and testing techniques; and critical test facilities to study combustion processes, coals and other fuels, nuclear steam generating systems, materials development and evaluation, and manufacturing technology. B&W's dedication to research and development ensures it will continue to design and engineer

some of the best steam generating equipment in the world—equipment that will meet or exceed the performance standards and environmental regulations of customers across the globe.

A HERITAGE OF COMMUNITY SPIRIT

Even as it excels on the world stage against the most fierce competition, B&W believes in maintaining strong community ties. The company is one of the largest employers in the Akron area, and has formed strong affiliations with a wide range of community organizations. B&W is proud of its rich history of community service in the area.

Whether providing aid to area charities, supporting the local school systems, or contributing to city beautification projects, B&W remains dedicated to helping the community and its residents, and to making Barberton and all of northeast Ohio an even better place to live and work.

Babcock & Wilcox is also committed to maintaining the high standards set by its founders and to finding "a better way" to continually meet the needs and exceed the expectations of an ever changing industrial world.

CLOCKWISE FROM TOP LEFT: B&W STRIVES TO MEET THE ENERGY CHALLENGES OF THE FUTURE THROUGH CONTINUOUS AND DEDICATED RESEARCH AND DEVELOPMENT EFFORTS.

COMPANY EMPLOYEES HAVE A STRONG SENSE OF COMMUNITY SPIRIT AND FREQUENTLY VOLUNTEER FOR A NUMBER OF CHARITABLE ORGANIZATIONS.

B&W WAS NAMED THE STATE OF OHIO'S EXPORTER OF THE YEAR IN 1996, IN RECOGNITION OF THE COMPANY'S SUCCESS IN THE GLOBAL MARKET.

QUITE LITERALLY, CLEVELAND PUBLIC POWER (CPP) HAS HELPED propel the revival of the city's fortunes. While other organizations might make similar declarations, none has played such an important part in Cleveland's civic rebirth. As the city's municipal electrical

power company, CPP provides the electricity that energizes local government buildings, businesses, and homes, as well as such landmark structures as the Rock and Roll Hall of Fame and Museum, the world-renowned centerpiece of the city's revitalized lakefront.

Having moved ahead of its competition by purchasing electricity on the open market for a better price, Cleveland Public Power is poised to capitalize on opportunities presented in a deregulated era, where more customers will be able to pick their provider. In coming years, the company will complete a $450 million expansion, allowing more individuals, businesses, and institutions in northeastern Ohio to make Cleveland Public Power their choice for electric power.

"There's a powerful story behind Cleveland's renaissance. It's the growth and expansion of our city's municipal electric system—Cleveland Public Power," says Mayor Michael R. White.

EXPANDING FOR THE FUTURE

Since the mid-1990s, the City of Cleveland has been expanding its power distribution system. While enlarging its existing network, CPP had already increased its customer base by nearly 50 percent—from 50,000 in 1993 to 74,000 in 1996.

"Our intention by the year 2002 is to serve at least 100,000 customers. We are significantly more than halfway to our goal," says Public Utilities Director Michael G. Konicek. Meeting this target would double Cleveland Public Power's base of satisfied customers in just 10 years.

Customers have saved more than $220 million during the past decade, and Cleveland Public Power's operating revenues nearly doubled from $60 million in 1993 to $100 million in 1996.

"The nearly one-half-billion-dollar expansion of Cleveland Public Power is a vital building block to the city's rebirth," White says. "In just three years, we are well on our way to fulfilling the vision of former Mayor Tom L. Johnson, who created municipal electric power to benefit the citizens of Cleveland in their

homes and businesses throughout the city."

A HISTORY OF COMMITMENT TO THE COMMUNITY

In 1906, Cleveland began producing its own electrical power through the annexation of the village of South Brooklyn and its power station. Four years later, another power station was added in Collinwood. In 1911, Cleveland residents approved a bond issue to build what would become the country's largest steam-generated power plant,

CLEVELAND PUBLIC POWER'S MULTI-COLORED LIGHTING OF BRIDGES SPANNING THE CUYAHOGA RIVER SYMBOLIZES THE UNIFIED EFFORT OF THE CITY'S 60 ETHNIC GROUPS IN MAKING CLEVELAND THE NEW AMERICAN CITY. THE BRIDGE LIGHTING PROJECT ALSO HELPED CELEBRATE THE CITY'S BICENTENNIAL IN 1996.

which represented the state of the art at the time. After growing significantly, the power system stagnated for almost 40 years, as community leaders turned their vision elsewhere.

In the late 1970s, the focus returned to the electric power system, which was renamed Cleveland Public Power in the early 1980s. Today, CPP redistributes electric power purchased on a national electricity grid, bypassing the regional monopoly for cheaper sources available through this wholesale market. In 1996, as regional monopolies struggled to maintain financial stability, Cleveland's municipal electric power company—streamlined for the future through a reorganization—received the highest bond rating in its history.

"As deregulation becomes a reality, the way we do business

and the benefits we can offer Cleveland Public Power customers will set us apart," says Konicek.

CPP supplies energy to City Hall, plants operated by the Division of Water, and other municipal buildings, thereby saving Cleveland—and its taxpayers—the expense of contracting for any electrical power. In addition to the Rock and Roll Hall of Fame and Museum, the municipal electric power company provides the power that energizes the Great Lakes Science Center and major University Circle institutions, including University Hospitals of Cleveland, Case Western Reserve University, and Severance Hall.

Along with the Divisions of Water and Water Pollution Control, CPP makes up the Department of Public Utilities, winner of Cleveland's Department of the Year award in 1993 and

1995. Working with Cleveland's city council and the city administration, CPP seeks to employ top professionals in the electrical power industry and encourages employee growth and continued education, which translate to high-quality customer service in everything from installation to repair to billing.

Cleveland Public Power's 363 employees participate in a wide variety of civic programs benefiting the community. They are recognized for going beyond the call of duty through the annual Looking Out for You Award. However, few go as far as Ken Bauer, a Cleveland Public Power employee who, in February 1996, rescued a man who had fallen from a raft into five-foot waves on Lake Erie. In attempting to rescue the man's friend, Bauer nearly drowned. He was awarded the Gold Medal Lifesaver Medal—the highest honor for heroism issued to citizens by the federal government—and the Looking Out for You Award by the City of Cleveland.

"I am deeply honored, but I'm no hero," Bauer told reporters. "Someone was in trouble, and I knew something had to be done." Heading into the 21st century, Cleveland Public Power aspires to bring this same level of commitment to providing Greater Cleveland with affordable, reliable electrical power.

DONN R. NOTTAGE

CLEVELAND PUBLIC POWER ILLUMINATES HISTORIC LIGHTING SURROUNDING THE WEST SIDE MARKET, A NEAR WEST SIDE LANDMARK (LEFT).

ELECTRIC POWER AND WATER FOR CLEVELAND'S NEW GREAT LAKES SCIENCE CENTER ON THE SHORES OF LAKE ERIE ARE SUPPLIED BY CLEVELAND PUBLIC POWER AND THE DIVISION OF WATER (RIGHT).

N 1908, BROTHERS-IN-LAW YANK ULMER AND JOE BERNE graduated from Case Western Reserve University Law School in Cleveland and founded the firm that still bears their names. With their strong commitment to the ethical practice of law at the highest skill

level, to active civic involvement, and to courtesy in all dealings with others, the firm steadily grew in prominence within the community. Today, some 90 years later, Ulmer and Berne's time-tested principles are passed along to the firm's new arrivals by partners who learned from Yank and Joe themselves.

A COMMITMENT TO EXCELLENT LAWYERING

Jordan Band, the retired chair of the firm's Business Department, recalls working with Berne: "Joe was a little guy—a soft-spoken man; modest; a courtly, polite, and consummate gentleman in the truest sense of the word. He had a great sense of social justice, and he was a great lawyer. He literally created the standard of excellence and

dedication to his clients under which we in this firm have operated from the beginning.

"He was productive to the very end. On the day before he died in surgery at the age of 81, he called me from his hospital

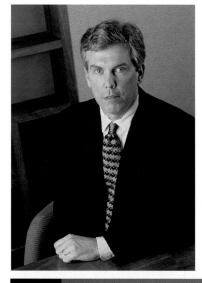

bed and carefully went over every matter on his pending list. He was quite a guy."

The firm continues to carry Berne's standard of excellent lawyering. Perhaps the truest measure of a lawyer's proficiency is recognition by his or her peers as an expert in a field of law. For example, five members of Ulmer & Berne are included in the current edition of *The Best Lawyers in America*. In addition, Marvin Karp, chair of the firm's Litigation Department and a perennial "best lawyer" selection, was identified in a recent *Cleveland Magazine* article as one of the six best trial lawyers in Cleveland. As a note of interest to local football fans, in the 1980s, Karp represented the minority owner of the Cleveland Browns football club in a series of lawsuits against majority owner

Art Modell. Karp, working almost single-handedly, defeated the team of lawyers representing Modell, and ultimately won the cases in the Ohio Supreme Court. Under Karp's stewardship, the firm has developed one of the premier business litigation practices in Ohio.

In recognition of clients' increasing demands for special expertise in their lawyers, Ulmer & Berne has created 20 practice groups covering nearly every aspect of the law, including health care, liability defense, tax, employment law, real estate, and employee benefits. As an example of the firm's versatility, in 1992, the Bankruptcy and Creditors' Rights Group represented a company in its successful Chapter 11 bankruptcy reorganization; just three years later, the Corporate Finance and Securities Group represented that company's successor in its initial offering of shares to the public.

A COMMITMENT TO THE COMMUNITY

Throughout its history, Ulmer & Berne's lawyers have contributed their time and energies generously to many civic causes. The standards for this commitment were set by founders Berne and Ulmer. Berne led the early development of what is now Playhouse Square and served for nine years as the head of Cleveland's Jewish Welfare Federation. Ulmer's most significant efforts arose from his own two-year blindness caused by cataracts. Upon regaining his sight in the late 1940s, after surgery to remove the cataracts, Ulmer campaigned for many years throughout the world to raise money for research on the causes of blindness.

This tradition of civic leadership has been carried on recently by firm member Ron Kahn, who devoted innumerable hours to supervising the construction of the new Ronald McDonald House on Euclid Avenue, and by Ulmer & Berne lawyers Ruth Anna Carlson, Inajo Davis Chappell, and Bill Gagliano, each of whom is active in the leadership of the American Red Cross. Partner Craig Miller has a keen appreciation for this commitment. When he joined the firm in 1996, Miller was serving in a pro bono capacity as the chairman of Gateway Economic Development Corporation. Ulmer & Berne continued to support Miller's efforts on behalf of Gateway, enabling him to successfully resolve lingering disputes with the project's contractors and the major tenants—the Indians and the Cavaliers.

Says Miller, "The lawyers of Ulmer & Berne embrace commitment to civic activities for the enrichment of the community that in turn supports the firm. The firm has a great culture, one that supports its tradition of providing leadership to many of the communities that make up the city of Cleveland."

PROMISE FOR THE FUTURE

Ulmer & Berne has witnessed Cleveland's growth as an industrial force earlier in the 20th century, its gradual decline, and now its rebirth as a host for emerging technologies and as a destination city with expanding cultural and entertainment attractions. Through it all, Ulmer & Berne has remained true to its roots because, as retired Managing Partner Bob Lewis says, "This is a firm with great optimism and vitality, a great promoter, supporter, and believer in the renaissance of Cleveland."

As a consequence of its faith in Cleveland and in Clevelanders, Ulmer & Berne has enjoyed steady growth and now numbers approximately 100 lawyers. The firm attracts top-ranking students from law schools and has added established practitioners with particular specialties to meet the evolving

needs of its clients. The result is a fine blend of savvy experience and emerging talent.

Managing Partner Kip Reader expects this pattern to continue: "I foresee sustained growth of the firm, enabling us to continue our vigorous representation of an expanding client base. We will continue to add lawyers of top academic and professional credentials who are dedicated to our clients' success and who meet our founders' standards of professional excellence." Ulmer & Berne confidently looks forward to a future full of promise for continued success of the firm, its clients, and the community it serves.

TOP: ULMER & BERNE LAWYERS BILL J. GAGLIANO (STANDING, LEFT), INAJO DAVIS CHAPPELL (STANDING, RIGHT), AND RUTH ANNA CARLSON (SEATED, LEFT) HAVE ACTIVE LEADERSHIP ROLES IN THE AMERICAN RED CROSS AND OFTEN WORK WITH CLEVELAND CHAPTER CHIEF EXECUTIVE OFFICER STEVE D. BULLOCK (SEATED, RIGHT).

BOTTOM: MANY OF THE FIRM'S YOUNG LAWYERS ARE CONTINUING THE WORK YANK ULMER AND JOE BERNE BEGAN NEARLY 100 YEARS AGO, INCLUDING (STANDING, FROM LEFT) JENNIFER HAYS GORMAN, BRIAN N. RAMM, MICHAEL N. UNGAR, (SEATED) STEPHANIE E. DUTCHESS TRUDEAU, PETER A. ROME, AND JOHNINE P. BARNES-PANNELL.

ITH ROOTS REACHING BACK TO 1906, THE HISTORY OF Cleveland Energy Resources' district energy system is a reflection of the renaissance of the city itself. Miles of pipe deliver steam and chilled water for heating and cooling through two independently distributed and centrally located production plants.

During the first three quarters of the 20th century, the steam system flourished with urban growth. At its peak, the district steam system served more than 300 customers who utilized the centrally produced steam to heat their buildings. As in many other metropolitan areas across the country, businesses began to migrate out of downtown. In addition, the original investors' commitment to the steam system was reduced in order to pursue other energy investments. As a result of these two events, the steam system experienced an erosion of customers and concern arose that this key infrastructure for early downtown development might not survive into the 21st century.

That is when Mid-America Energy Resources of Indianapolis, the parent to Cleveland Energy Resources, stepped in to reestablish the commitment to district energy in Cleveland. With experience in other district energy

THE BENEFITS OF CLEVELAND ENERGY RESOURCES' DISTRICT ENERGY SYSTEMS ELIMINATE THE NEED FOR CAPITAL EXPENDITURE AND FURTHER REDUCE LABOR, ENERGY, AND OTHER OPERATING COSTS FOR BUILDING OWNERS (TOP).

CURRENTLY, DISTRICT CHILLED WATER SERVICE IS PROVIDED TO SUCH LOCAL LANDMARKS AS CITY HALL, CLEVELAND CONVENTION CENTER, CLEVELAND PUBLIC LIBRARY, JUSTICE CENTER COMPLEX, AND WYNDHAM CLEVELAND HOTEL AT PLAYHOUSE SQUARE (BOTTOM).

systems, Mid-America Energy Resources purchased the system in 1991. Investments were made in new technology and refurbishment of the steam system, which resulted in immediate improvements in efficiency, performance, and cost of service.

Not only was the commitment toward investing capital in the steam system, but also in developing a new district chilled water system for air-conditioning. In 1993, an investment of $28 million was made to install 10,000 tons of cooling capacity, as well as a distribution system consisting of 17,000 feet of underground pipe in the Cleveland downtown business district.

Timing could not have been better. With the impending phase-out of CFCs used for air-conditioning, many building owners were faced with the need to invest significant capital into their air-conditioning systems. The benefits of Cleveland Energy Resources' district energy systems eliminate the need for capital expenditure and further reduce labor, energy,

and other operating costs for building owners. Currently, district chilled water service is provided to such local landmarks as City Hall, Cleveland Convention Center, Cleveland Public Library, Justice Center Complex, and Wyndham Cleveland Hotel at Playhouse Square. Cleveland Energy Resources plans to more than double its service capabilities over the next few years.

In addition, district energy systems benefit downtown in ways beyond offering energy alternatives for business development. Cleveland Energy Resources' fuel efficiency and emission control provide important environmental impacts on the improvement to air quality for downtown, which is important to any city's skyline.

Clevelanders, businesspeople, and visitors alike enjoy the benefits of district energy. Whether relaxing at the Renaissance Hotel, enjoying a show at Playhouse Square, or shopping in Terminal Tower, they can rely on district energy service provided by Cleveland Energy Resources.

TONY FESTA PHOTOGRAPHY

1909

1910
KENT STATE UNIVERSITY

1911
STATE INDUSTRIAL PRODUCTS

1916
ELSAG BAILEY PROCESS AUTOMATION

1919
FERRO CORPORATION

1921
THE CLEVELAND CLINIC FOUNDATION
CCF HEALTH CARE VENTURES, INC. (1986)
CLEVELAND HEALTH NETWORK (1994)

1921
FOREST CITY ENTERPRISES, INC.

1921
PLAYHOUSE SQUARE CENTER

1922
HKM DIRECT MARKET COMMUNICATIONS, INC.

◆ BILL GANCE

1923
RIDGE TOOL COMPANY

1925
CLEVELAND DEPARTMENT OF PORT CONTROL

1926
WDOK 102.1 FM AND WRMR AM 850

1928
FINAST FRIENDLY MARKETS

1928
TELEDYNE FLUID SYSTEMS

1929
NORTH AMERICAN REFRACTORIES COMPANY

1930
CHASE FINANCIAL CORPORATION

1930
LTV STEEL COMPANY, INC.

1930
MELDRUM & FEWSMITH COMMUNICATIONS

1930

KENT STATE UNIVERSITY

FROM ITS EARLIEST DAYS AS A SCHOOL DEDICATED TO THE TRAINING of teachers, Kent State University has been committed to academic excellence and student success. At the turn of the century, the university's pioneering programs trained educators to teach reading,

writing, and arithmetic, as well as agriculture and harness making. Today, as the state of Ohio's third-largest public university, with 135,000 alumni worldwide, Kent has matured into a world-class research and teaching institution with nationally and internationally recognized programs in areas from liquid crystal research to fashion design.

"Kent State University has a strong sense of pride and tradition," says Kent's president, Dr. Carol A. Cartwright. "As we embrace the new technologies and innovations that will carry us into the 21st century, we remain steadfast to our mission. Student success is our foremost priority."

ABOUT THE UNIVERSITY

Kent State University was founded in 1910 on 85 acres of prized farmland donated by William S. Kent. Originally known as Kent State Normal School, the early campus featured seven classical-style buildings on a hillside overlooking the city of Kent. The school prospered as a resource for Ohio and Ohioans, and in 1935 university status was conferred.

Today, the Kent campus embraces 825 gently rolling acres. With 29 residence halls housing more than 5,000 students, it is the largest residential campus in northeast Ohio. Great care has been taken to preserve the wooded hills, meadows, and gardens that distinguish the campus as one of the most beautiful in the nation.

Kent is at the heart of an eight-campus system encompassing 2,305 acres. The university's seven regional campuses, located in communities throughout northeast Ohio, constitute the oldest and largest regional

educational system in the state, and one of the largest in the nation.

COMMITTED TO STUDENT SUCCESS

Nearly 30,000 students from across the nation and from 67 countries choose from 170 undergraduate programs, a full range of graduate degrees, and a six-year medical school program through the Northeastern Ohio Universities College of Medicine. Students pursue careers from architecture to zoology in Kent's four colleges—Arts and Sciences, Business Administration, Education, and Fine and Professional Arts—as well as in the university's independent schools of nursing and technology.

Opportunities for international study abound, including faculty and student exchanges with institutions in such countries as England, Germany, Greece, Italy, Japan, Poland, Russia, Spain, and Switzerland.

Across the university, students benefit from a distinguished and caring faculty, many of whom are

THE KENT STATE UNIVERSITY CAMPUS IS DISTINGUISHED BY ITS TRADITIONAL SETTING AND MAGNIFICENT GARDENS.

KENT'S HONORS COLLEGE IS RECOGNIZED AS A NATIONAL LEADER IN NURTURING THE TALENTS OF ITS GIFTED STUDENTS. WITH AN ENROLLMENT OF MORE THAN 900, THE HONORS COLLEGE IS ONE OF THE OLDEST AND LARGEST OF ITS KIND IN THE COUNTRY.

internationally recognized in their fields. The faculty counts 24 Fulbright scholars among its ranks.

A spirited student life provides more than 230 clubs and organizations for student activities and interests. Kent's Honors College, striving to meet the challenges of nearly 900 of the university's gifted students, is one of the oldest and largest of its kind in the nation.

The university is among just 37 institutions nationwide to earn the Carnegie Foundation's prestigious Research University II designation, which recognizes comprehensive undergraduate programs and focused research and graduate programs in carefully selected areas.

Kent is an institution clearly on the move. "The university has taken a tradition of excellence and used it as a launchpad to leadership in areas from teaching to technology," Cartwright says.

Faculty and students are on the leading edge of learning—from designing fashions at the nationally respected Shannon Rodgers and Jerry Silverman School of Fashion Design and Merchandising to developing new liquid crystal applications at the world's liquid-crystal capital, the Glenn H. Brown Liquid Crystal Institute. Research under way at the institute's new, $13.3 million head-

quarters has the potential to revolutionize the multibillion-dollar display industry and attract new commerce and jobs to northeast Ohio.

A public university that is genuinely interested in serving the public, Kent's emphasis on scholarship that addresses real-world problems and issues is attracting national attention.

Faculty and students at the Center for Applied Conflict Management are creating violence-prevention programs for public schools; students and faculty in the School of Architecture and Environmental Design are planning user-friendly neighborhoods to help spark an inner-city renais-

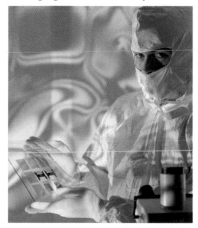

sance in Cleveland; faculty of the Water Resources Research Institute are developing new methods to ensure safe drinking water for communities; and researchers at the Applied Psychology Center are formulating effective nonmedical AIDS-prevention strategies.

LEADING IN EDUCATIONAL INNOVATIONS

*K*ent is also attracting a great deal of national attention for its most ambitious initiative of the 1990s: the $24 million Moulton Hall Technologies and Learning Center, which will serve as home to the university's technological innovations in teaching and learning as well as research and corporate training and development.

Kent has forged ahead in pioneering distributed education and other academic resources via a wide variety of state-of-the-art technologies. The transformation of traditional chalkboard and textbook lesson plans into highly interactive multimedia courses distributed through sophisticated computer networks began with the fiber-optic networking of Kent's eight campuses.

In keeping with Kent's commitment to public service and economic development, the Technologies and Learning Center will enable the university to share its educational innovations with businesses, institutions, and communities worldwide, acting as consultant and contractor for their information delivery and training needs.

Kent has stepped to the forefront in responding to the tidal wave of changes that have swept higher education in the 1990s. Cartwright says, "We are standing at the threshold of a new era in education. Beyond this threshold are dramatic changes in the way education is delivered, students learn, and teachers teach."

As Kent State University looks to the challenges of the 21st century, it reaffirms its proud tradition of teaching excellence and public service, and continues its unwavering commitment to student success.

TATE INDUSTRIAL PRODUCTS STANDS POISED AS IT ENTERS THE 21st century with an ideal combination: business experience drawn from nearly 100 years of service to customers and dynamic leadership with a clear vision of the future. ❖ Since the company opened its

doors for the first time, a single principle has been the foundation of State Industrial Products' growth and success year after year—solving customers' maintenance problems with high-quality products and personal service.

In today's world, constant change is the norm, but all too often organizations react slowly, if at all, to new challenges. State Industrial Products' approach is aggressive and proactive. New ideas are valued, cultivated, and implemented with a great sense of urgency. This commitment to continual improvement has been a core belief throughout the five generations of ownership by the Zucker and Uhrman families, allowing the organization to set industry standards in product development, service, and innovation.

State Industrial Products' world headquarters is in Cleveland, just east of downtown on Hamilton Avenue. Corporate employment is rapidly approaching 2,000. However, with the company's current strategic growth and expansion plans, worldwide employment will grow by leaps and bounds.

In addition to the Cleveland facility, State Industrial Products operates state-of-the-art manufacturing and distribution facilities

around the world. A perfect example is the plant in Tulsa. Strategically located, outfitted with cutting-edge manufacturing technology, and designed for expansion, this facility exemplifies the company's commitment to excellence and its focus on the future.

State Industrial Products operates three divisions within the maintenance, repair, and operation (MRO) industry: State Chemical Manufacturing Company, UZ Engineered Products, and Neutron Industries.

State Chemical is a worldwide leader in the manufacturing and distribution of specialty maintenance products. Its product line—designed to promote a cleaner environment through technology—is virtually limitless, given the constant introduction of new products. All around the world, State Chemical products are at work in manufacturing plants, water treatment facilities, schools, hotels, and hospitals. Whether it's supplying lubricants for multimillion-dollar machinery or floor finish for a gym floor, State Chemical provides solutions to maintenance problems.

In both industrial and institutional organizations, maintaining production equipment, fleets, and physical plants is demanding and vital. Having the right part at the right time is essential. UZ Engineered Products provides its customers with the products and services to keep equipment running and downtime minimal. UZ offers a comprehensive line of fasteners, anchors, electrical supplies, drill bits, abrasives, cutting tools, battery terminals, and many other specialty items.

STATE CHEMICAL'S COMMITMENT TO ITS IN-HOUSE TRAINING PROGRAMS ENSURES THAT THE DIVISION'S LEVEL OF CUSTOMER SERVICE IS CONSISTENTLY PROFESSIONAL AND SUPPORTIVE (TOP).

THE ASSOCIATES OF STATE INDUSTRIAL PRODUCTS STRIVE TO SUCCEED BASED ON THE COMPANY'S THREE FOUNDING PRINCIPLES: GET IT RIGHT THE FIRST TIME, BE EASY TO DO BUSINESS WITH, AND LOWER THE CUSTOMER'S TOTAL COST OF DOING BUSINESS (BOTTOM).

Twice ranked among the nation's fastest-growing companies by *Inc.* magazine, Neutron Industries is a premier telemarketer of maintenance supplies to schools, hospitals, offices, and retail stores. Utilizing sophisticated customer-based computer software, Neutron is able to meet the needs of its expanding customer base. Operated from its main office in Phoenix, Neutron markets its products throughout North America and Europe.

LOOKING TO THE FUTURE

State Industrial Products continues to chart a growth strategy that will position the organization for even greater success in years to come. With strategic plans in place to exceed $200 million in sales, President Hal Uhrman is focused on the next plateau, $500 million in sales.

"Our intent is to be the largest privately held organization in our industry," says Uhrman. "We are confident that our quality products, service, and commitment

to growth will enable us to achieve these goals."

To hit this target, State Industrial Products continues to invest in education, training, and recognition programs for its worldwide team of sales professionals. Millions of dollars are allocated annually to attract and train sales representatives.

The same diligence is applied to product development. "The challenge is to continually improve our products in conjunction with increasing regulatory and service demands," Uhrman says. "We are meeting the challenges head-on and creatively using new technologies to provide solutions that work and provide an overall positive impact on our customers' operations."

State Industrial Products is committed to the latest advances in technology. Take, for example, the installation of a new computer system that is three times as fast as the previous one. The increased speed and capacity translate into better customer service.

STILL ACTIVE IN CLEVELAND

While its business strategy now spans the globe, State Industrial Products remains an active participant in local community affairs. More than 400 employees work at the Cleveland headquarters, and the company and its employees traditionally participate in the United Way, the Cleveland Corporate Challenge, the Harvest for Hunger program, and other charitable organizations.

The multinational company remains focused on the three basic principles that built its long-standing tradition: Get it right the first time, be easy to do business with, and lower the customer's total cost of doing business.

Keeping those goals in mind, State Industrial Products has seen its influence reach far and wide. Says Uhrman, "Today and every day, the sun never sets on the company's products."

BACKED BY A WELL-TRAINED, DEDICATED STAFF, COMBINED WITH STATE-OF-THE-ART COMPUTER TECHNOLOGY, STATE INDUSTRIAL PRODUCTS IS ABLE TO EFFICIENTLY AND EFFECTIVELY PROCESS ORDERS (LEFT).

STATE CHEMICAL IS PROUD OF ITS REPUTATION FOR QUALITY PRODUCTS THAT PROVIDE SOLUTIONS FOR A VARIETY OF CUSTOMER NEEDS (RIGHT).

INNOVATION FLOURISHED DURING THE INDUSTRIAL AGE, BUT IF ONE invention could be credited with putting the finishing touch on the industrial revolution it would be the Bailey Boiler Meter. The popularity of this device—which measured boiler air flow, fuel bed conditions, and steam output—led to the formation in 1916 of Bailey Meter Company. Today known as Elsag Bailey Process Automation, the Cleveland company is the world's second-leading supplier of process automation systems, with 40 operations in 25 countries and more than 12,000 employees worldwide. Operating as an umbrella for such individual companies as Bailey Controls, Hartmann & Braun, Applied Automation, and Bailey-Fischer & Porter, Elsag Bailey helps customers monitor and control high-tech processes in global industries. The company provides state-of-the-art control and business support systems with true one-stop shopping for all of a customer's process automation needs.

FROM BAILEY METER TO ELSAG BAILEY

On January 1, 1916, Ervin G. Bailey founded the Bailey Meter Company, providing a manufacturing outlet for the revolutionary Bailey Boiler Meter. In its first year of operation, the company produced a total of 46 boiler meters. Within two years, Bailey had sold 700 of his popular units. By the time the company was purchased by Babcock & Wilcox in 1925, thousands of Bailey Boiler Meters had been sold worldwide. As a testament to its contributions to the industrial revolution—and to the genius of its inventor—the Bailey Boiler Meter today is on permanent display in the Smithsonian Institution in Washington, D.C.

Over the years, Bailey Meter Company became a leading force in the control and instrumentation industry, supplying automation devices to electric power, marine, and other industries around the world. During World War II, its boiler control systems were so prevalent in engine rooms on

BAILEY CONTROLS, A UNIT OF ELSAG BAILEY PROCESS AUTOMATION, WAS FOUNDED IN 1916 AS BAILEY METER COMPANY. TODAY, IT MANUFACTURES ADVANCED PROCESS CONTROL SYSTEMS AT ITS 42-ACRE SITE IN WICKLIFFE.

merchant vessels and warships that sailors referred to the panels as "Bailey boards."

The company remained a subsidiary of Babcock & Wilcox until 1978, when both firms were purchased by New Orleans-based McDermott, Inc. In 1989, Bailey was purchased by the Elsag Group of Italy and, as a result, was renamed Elsag Bailey Process Automation in 1991.

The leap from coal-fired steam boilers that powered warships to digital systems that control entire manufacturing processes is a long one, but one that Elsag Bailey has made with ease. While technology has changed over the decades, the company remains committed to engineering excellence, quality, and, above all, meeting the needs of its customers.

"You have to be close to customers wherever they are and give them the local service and support they need," says Vincenzo Cannatelli, Elsag Bailey's managing director and chief executive officer. "The development of the technology has to be done in a centralized way and from a global point of view. Our customers in Brazil, Bahrain, Norway, and New Delhi want support services from someone who speaks their language, understands their culture, and visits their plant on a regular basis."

MAKING EXISTING SYSTEMS BETTER

While the work and the company itself have changed dramatically over the past 80 years, Elsag Bailey has maintained its reputation for being a technological leader, producing control systems for process industries such as power generation plants, oil refineries, steel and paper mills, and breweries. The company's control systems ensure that a business runs safely and efficiently.

Introduced in 1980, NETWORK 90 was Bailey's first

microprocessor-based distributed control system. It was faster and more powerful than the standard digital-based technology and allowed the company to diversify within the process control market. Bailey's utility customers used the system for monitoring and controlling boiler operations. However, the system's technology was equally useful for processing industries such as chemicals, refining, and pulp and paper.

Distributed control systems are distinctive in that they consist of a series of solid-state control and monitoring modules in cabinets that are installed near the customers' machines. If a plant expands, new cabinets and cables can be added similar to the way memory is added to a computer. Elsag Bailey's design is unique in that it offers forward and backward compatibility, meaning that as engineers develop a next-generation component or system, it is designed to be compatible with the installed system.

NETWORK 90's successor, INFI 90, was introduced in 1988 and ushered in the concept of strategic process management. With this new technology, the control system communicates with a company's other computerized systems, permitting simultaneous real-time access to process data. INFI 90 was followed by INFI 90 OPEN in

1994, featuring advancements in system architecture and information management tools.

The next-generation system, SYMPHONY, was introduced in 1996. SYMPHONY is designated as an enterprise management and control system. Its unique architecture supports sophisticated business software, integrates with business information systems, and provides Internet access for multiplant site communications. SYMPHONY allows true global coordination capabilities.

As Elsag Bailey looks to the future, the company remains committed to being a world leader in process control innovations. With the introduction of SYMPHONY, Elsag Bailey Process Automation continues to put the customer first, offering the latest in cutting-edge technology.

FERRO CORPORATION

HETHER IT'S YOUR REFRIGERATOR, THE TILE IN YOUR BATHROOM and kitchen, your lawn mower, or the dashboard of your car, most likely a Ferro specialty material had a key role in its creation. As a leading global producer of specialty materials, Ferro Corporation

helps enhance the performance and appearance of products in many markets, including building/renovation, major appliances, household furnishings, transportation, and industrial products.

AN EARLY GLOBAL PRESENCE

Ferro's beginnings date back to 1919, when Harry D. Cushman established the Ferro Enameling Company to manufacture porcelain enamel frit, a specialty glass material used to coat metal. Since that beginning on East 56th Street in Cleveland (where Ferro still maintains a facility), the company has grown and its product line has diversified into many other value-added materials for industry.

Ferro attributes much of its growth to Cleveland's centralized location for manufacturing in North America and its accessibility to overseas markets. In fact, the company has had an international presence since 1927, when it established operations in Canada, followed two years later by facilities in England and Holland. Still based in Cleveland, Ferro currently maintains manufacturing operations in 21 countries, operates sales offices in another dozen countries on five continents, and sells its products in more than 100 countries. At a time when many companies are struggling to establish an international presence, Ferro's truly global network gives it a strong competitive edge. The company is not only the world's largest producer of glass coatings, but also a world leader in the production of a variety of specialty materials.

PRODUCTS THAT ADD VALUE

Ferro has always prided itself on the quality of its products and service in supplying materials to some of the world's largest companies. In fact, the Ferro logo—a check-in-a-circle insignia established in 1921—remains an ongoing reminder of that commitment to quality. All of the company's products are rigorously checked at every stage of production to ensure quality, a testament to the founder's belief that "things are only worth what we make them worth."

Today, Ferro's products are organized into three major segments. The largest segment is specialty coatings, colors, and ceramics, which includes porcelain enamel, ceramic glaze, and powder coatings. Specialty plastics encompasses plastic colorants and compounds. And the principal business of specialty chemicals is focused on polymer additives.

Ferro's performance materials have earned leading shares of diverse markets worldwide. In building and renovation markets, the company's porcelain enamel coats building panels, and its colors and ceramic glaze materials finish and decorate tiles and sanitary ware. Many major appliances, including refrigerators and washing machines, are finished with Ferro powder coatings. Cookware and other household furnishings are frequently coated with Ferro porcelain enamel, while tableware incorporates the company's

FERRO WAS FOUNDED AT THIS LOCATION ON EAST 56TH STREET IN 1919 (TOP). THE PLANT, MUCH EXPANDED TODAY, REMAINS THE COMPANY'S MAIN MANUFACTURING FACILITY IN CLEVELAND.

HEADQUARTERED ON LAKESIDE AVENUE IN THE HEART OF CLEVELAND'S DOWNTOWN (BOTTOM), FERRO CORPORATION HAS OPERATIONS IN 21 COUNTRIES AROUND THE WORLD AND SELLS ITS PRODUCTS IN MORE THAN 100 COUNTRIES.

ceramic glaze. The transportation market, mainly automotive, uses Ferro powder coatings for primers and for coating aluminum wheels and various exterior parts; its plastic colorants and compounds for parts and trim; and its petroleum additives for fuel efficiency. Finally, the company's products go into a variety of other markets, from leisure products, such as scuba equipment and toys, to electronics, such as personal computers and televisions.

RENOWNED RESEARCH

*O*ne of Ferro's main competitive strengths is its customer-driven research and development capabilities. The company has continually been a leader in its industries through the development and application of product solutions for its customers. Ferro's research and development is product-line centered at various facilities, with the Corporate Research and Development Center located in Independence, Ohio, just south of Cleveland.

Ferro holds more than 500 patents worldwide. Recent product innovations include specialized polypropylene compounds, lead-free glazes for dinnerware, and polymer alloy powder coatings for appliance "blanks." Ferro's most revolutionary new product under development is a low-temperature-cure powder coating that can be applied to substrates, such as plastics and wood, in addition to the traditional application to metals. New products of this kind could open new markets for Ferro and solidify its position as a market leader.

Beyond its own research and development projects, Ferro helps support specialized research programs conducted by leading colleges and universities to advance the state of the art in materials science and process technology. The company also seeks to collaborate with federal laboratories

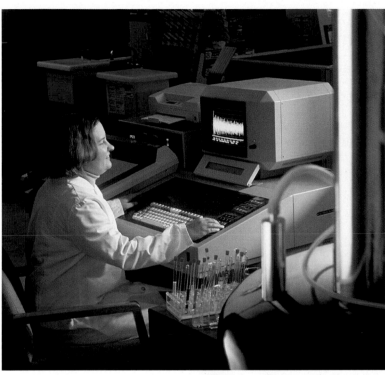

where combined strengths can be leveraged.

COMMUNITY PARTNER

*F*erro is committed not only to continually improving its products and technology, but also to enhancing the communities in which it operates. The company has had a long history of community involvement in the Cleveland area and contributes to a great variety of arts, education, and community development organizations through the Ferro Foundation.

An example of the company's commitment to shaping the talent of tomorrow is its partnership with Charles W. Elliott Middle School in Cleveland's inner city. The partnership began in 1986 as a once-a-week science lab, but has blossomed into a full-time plan to further the development of the school's students. Ferro employees volunteer their time to develop weekly science labs and offer tutoring in math and science. In addition, company employees help students in areas ranging from the school newspaper to spelling bees, assist teachers in

improving computer skills, participate in career days, and host an awards program and facility tours at Ferro.

With a solid foundation, a dedication to innovation, and a commitment to helping both its customers and communities find solutions to their challenges, Ferro is poised for continued growth in Cleveland and around the world into the next century and beyond.

SCIENTISTS AT FERRO'S CORPORATE RESEARCH AND DEVELOPMENT CENTER IN INDEPENDENCE, OHIO, PROVIDE PRIMARY RESEARCH AND TECHNICAL SUPPORT FOR CORE TECHNOLOGIES THROUGHOUT THE WORLD. FERRO'S RESEARCH CAPABILITIES REPRESENT ONE OF THE COMPANY'S MAIN COMPETITIVE ADVANTAGES.

STUDENTS FROM THE CHARLES W. ELLIOTT MIDDLE SCHOOL IN CLEVELAND PARTICIPATE IN A WEEKLY SCIENCE LAB CONDUCTED BY FERRO EMPLOYEES. SINCE 1986, WHEN THE SCIENCE LABS BEGAN, FERRO'S INVOLVEMENT WITH THE SCHOOL HAS GROWN TO ENCOMPASS A COMPLETE PROGRAM TO FURTHER ALL ASPECTS OF THE STUDENTS' EDUCATION.

HE YEAR WAS 1921. THE MEMORY OF THE GREAT WAR WAS beginning to fade. A heat wave gripped the nation in the summer. An experimental two-way radio was installed in a Detroit police car. And Cleveland was on the threshold of medical history.

An idea born during long evenings at a military base hospital in France during World War I, the Cleveland Clinic came to fruition in 1921 when four local physicians opened an outpatient clinic on the southwest corner of East 93rd Street and Euclid Avenue. Doctors Frank E. Bunts, George Crile Sr., William E. Lower, and John Phillips built their group practice on the same foundation that would soon become their mission: "to think and act as a unit." Their premise was that collaboration stimulates innovation, thereby improving patient care and expanding medical knowledge.

The four-story clinic had doctors' offices, examining rooms, treatment rooms, an X-ray department, laboratories, and a pharmacy. The top floor housed executive offices, a library, and Crile's biophysics laboratory, where he studied the effects of shock, transfusion, and anesthesia. In this early facility, the Cleveland Clinic began to take shape—a cooperative medical practice and a place for education and research. And from that time on, the organization has secured its position as a major presence in this progressive city.

GETTING ESTABLISHED

Clevelanders accepted the new clinic enthusiastically as soon as it opened its doors. The staff continued to have hospital privileges at Lakeside, Charity, and Mt. Sinai hospitals, but the four physicians knew they would soon need their own hospital beds. To that end, they purchased two old houses on East 93rd Street, just north of Carnegie Avenue, and converted them to one 53-bed hospital. Another house was used for radiation therapy. Known as the Oxley Homes, this facility was named for the very capable English nurse in charge of the hospital. This early incarnation of the Cleveland Clinic Hospital was little more than a nursing home.

In a fourth house, Dr. Henry John treated diabetes with the newly discovered drug called insulin. The founders soon installed an operating room. Convenience was a bit lacking, however: Since the houses did not have elevators, orderlies, nurses, and doctors had to carry their patients up and down the stairs of the Oxley Homes.

In 1924, the Cleveland Clinic opened a modern, 184-bed hospital on East 90th Street. This building had elevators, as well as

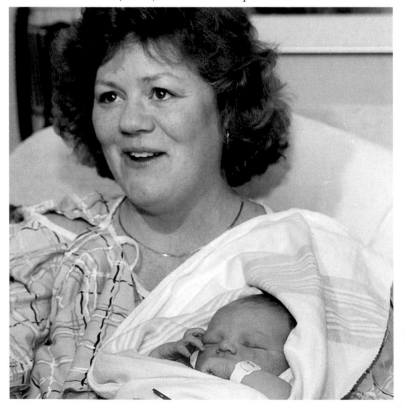

operating rooms, living quarters for residents in training, and anatomic and clinical pathology laboratories.

Even with a total of 237 beds, however, the clinic was unable to meet the growing community's demand for hospital care. Therefore, in 1926, two floors of the Bolton Square Hotel on Carnegie Avenue were equipped for the care of 40 more patients, and two years later the clinic added an eastern extension to the modern hospital facility. The clinic building boasted a penthouse machine shop, and the campus also had its own laundry, power plant, and ice plant.

With the growing popularity of motorcars, the clinic bought more property in order to build a parking lot. And when Crile's biophysics laboratory became inadequate, a narrow, eight-story research facility sprang up between the clinic building and the hospital.

Along with the rest of the country, the Cleveland Clinic rode a wave of prosperity in the 1920s, growing by giant leaps. The rising demand for both outpatient and inpatient services provided the impetus for expanding the clinic's professional staff and existing departments. Because it had money left in the building fund, even after the expansion, the clinic purchased a gram of radium and installed a radium emanation plant that made radon seeds for

the treatment of cancer. This plant was the first of its kind in the region.

In 1922, the Cleveland Clinic added a state-of-the-art X-ray therapy unit and placed Dr. U.V. Portmann, a highly trained specialist in radiation therapy, in charge. Working with Valentine Seitz, the clinic's chief engineer, and biophysicist Dr. Otto Glasser, Portmann developed the first dosimeter to accurately measure the amount of radiation administered to a patient.

In 1924, pioneer neurosurgeon Dr. Charles Locke began performing delicate brain surgery at the Cleveland Clinic, making it one of a small group of elite centers that offered the expertise of a neurosurgery department. As medicine became increasingly more specialized, the clinic added other depart-

ments, such as orthopedic surgery and endocrinology, a newly created specialty.

Tragedy nearly brought the clinic to its knees in May 1929, when toxic fumes from X-ray film caused two explosions and killed more than 100 people. The accident also seriously damaged the main building of the bustling medical center and resulted in another discovery that would change the face of medicine. Investigation of the explosions resulted in the worldwide adoption of revised safety codes for storing X-ray film and the widespread use of safety film that would not ignite.

Today, the Cleveland Clinic is still an independent, not-for-profit, multispecialty academic medical center recognized as an international health resource that

A LEADER IN THE EFFORT TO UNRAVEL THE CAUSE OF HYPERTENSION AND THEREBY ESTABLISH ITS TREATMENT, DR. IRVINE H. PAGE HELPED THE CLINIC DEVELOP A MULTIDISCIPLINARY APPROACH AIMED AT SOLVING PROBLEMS IN CARDIOVASCULAR DISEASE (TOP).

CARDIOLOGIST F. MASON SONES JR., M.D. (BOTTOM), DEVELOPED CORONARY ANGIOGRAPHY, A METHOD FOR VIEWING THE HEART AND ITS VESSELS THROUGH MOVING X RAYS. THIS LANDMARK DISCOVERY INITIATED THE MODERN ERA OF CARDIOLOGY AND MADE POSSIBLE THE DEVELOPMENT OF BYPASS SURGERY.

cares for patients from around the world. Known more broadly as The Cleveland Clinic Foundation, it still includes an outpatient clinic and a hospital with more than 900 beds, in addition to an education division and a research institute.

MAKING HISTORY

*I*n the more than 75 years since its opening, some of the most notable advances in medical history have occurred at the Cleveland Clinic. In the 1940s and 1950s, for example, researcher Dr. Irvine H. Page made important discoveries about high blood pressure and its link to heart disease. Page recruited a team of clinicians and scientists to help in the study of hypertension and its quiet destruction of the heart and other organs. The resulting research led to many important innovations in the years to come.

In 1958, the discovery of cine-coronary angiography at the Cleveland Clinic paved the way

for corrective cardiac surgery, and in 1963, it became one of the first hospitals to install beds for fathers to stay with mothers and newborns. Also in 1963, Dr. William Kolff, inventor of the kidney dialysis machine, teamed up with two surgeons, Dr. Ralph Straffon and Dr. Eugene Poutasse, to pioneer a kidney transplant procedure. The team performed one of the first successful transplants of an organ taken from a cadaver. Later that year, Straffon and Dr. Bruce Stewart performed one of the first live-donor kidney transplants.

In 1967, heart surgeon Dr.

René Favaloro pioneered coronary bypass surgery at the Cleveland Clinic, grafting a healthy vein taken from a patient's leg onto a diseased coronary artery to increase blood flow to the heart. This breakthrough procedure took advantage of an earlier clinic advancement—the development of a method of observing the heart and its vessels by moving X rays—and paved the way for further advancements in the specialty.

In the early 1970s, the Cleveland Clinic was one of the first medical centers in the United States to buy a CAT scanner to X-ray "slices" of the head with unprecedented detail. A short time later, the clinic assisted a Cleveland firm with the design of an improved CAT scanner that allowed full-body scanning, a technique that is especially helpful in diagnosing cancer and other diseases.

The expert care that can currently be found at the Cleveland Clinic is the result of these early advancements. Today, brain tumors are being treated with such revolutionary methods as immunotherapy, which actually turns the cancer against itself. The Department of Nephrology and Hypertension reinforces the clinic's leadership in hypertension research by taking part in several medical trials that evaluate treatments for high blood pressure. Likewise, cardiac surgery for a bypass or valve repair/replacement can now be done through a small incision that heals much more quickly than with previous methods.

After a 29-year hiatus, the Cleveland Clinic is again delivering babies with a variety of birthing options, including midwives. In the 1990s, heart, lung, kidney, liver, pancreas, bone, bone marrow, and corneal transplants have become established procedures at the clinic. However, these radical procedures are only an alternative to such innovative options as grafting back muscles to the heart to boost its pumping power, removing only the diseased portion of the kidney in kidney-sparing surgery, and improving the efficiency of the lungs through volume-reduction surgery.

LOOKING TO THE FUTURE

*T*he Cleveland Clinic and the National Aeronautics and Space Administration's Lewis Research Center in Cleveland have joined forces to conduct research that will expand current knowledge of disease and treatment. Among the projects now under way is a study of the effect of weightlessness on bone density and muscle loss, the results of which could improve weight-bearing exercises for both space travelers and earthbound patients with bone diseases.

The Cleveland Clinic's excellent medical treatment has not gone unnoticed or unrewarded. Since 1990, *U.S. News & World Report* has ranked it among the 10 best hospitals in the nation, making the Cleveland Clinic the only Ohio hospital with that distinction. In 1996, of the 16 specialties evaluated, the clinic was named among the top-rated institutions in cardiology, gastroenterology, gynecology, neurology, orthopedics, rheumatology and urology.

As the Cleveland Clinic enters the last quarter of its first century, it is working toward the opening of the Research and Education Institutes, a 410,000-square-foot complex that will consolidate the clinic's education, research, and biomedical engineering activities. For the first time in its history, all of these activities will be housed in a single location that will include classrooms, laboratories, conference rooms, and an expanded medical library. The Research and Education Institutes will also link the new facilities with the John Sherwin Research Building, which houses the Betsy de Windt Cancer Research Laboratory.

Designed for maximum interaction between scientists and physicians and between staff and students, the center will encourage collaboration—thinking and acting as a unit—the key factor responsible for many breakthroughs in the past and a necessary component for the next generation of advances at the Cleveland Clinic.

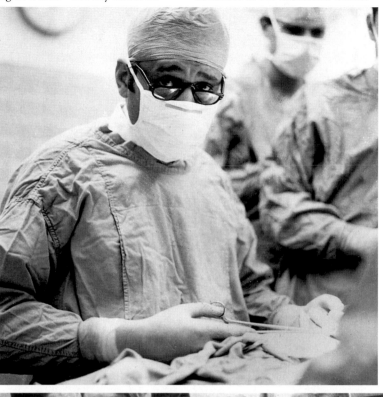

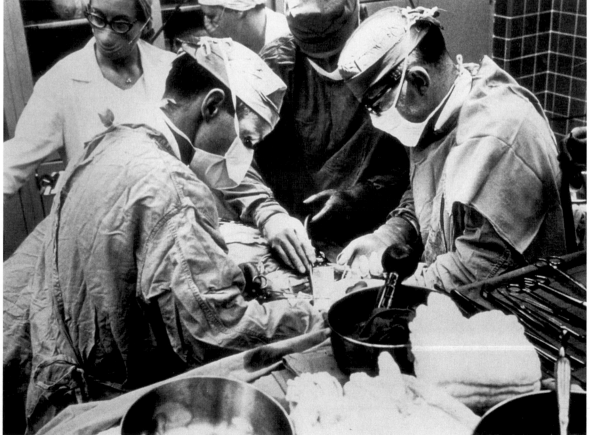

IN 1967, CLEVELAND CLINIC HEART SURGEON RENÉ FAVALORO, M.D., PERFORMED THE FIRST DOCUMENTED AORTOCORONARY BYPASS OPERATION (TOP).

A PIONEER IN THE FIELD OF KIDNEY TRANSPLANTS AND REVASCULARIZATION, DR. RALPH STRAFFON, ASSISTED BY DR. BRUCE STEWART, PERFORMED A SUCCESSFUL KIDNEY TRANSPLANT ON A CLEVELAND CLINIC PATIENT IN 1964 USING AN ORGAN TAKEN FROM A CADAVER (BOTTOM).

ETTING THE STANDARD IN HEALTH CARE IS A FAMILIAR ROLE FOR The Cleveland Clinic Foundation (CCF). It is not surprising that CCF Health Care Ventures (CCFHCV) was among the first to provide home health care in the Cleveland area or that it is among the largest home health care providers in the nation.

In a little more than 10 years, CCFHCV has grown into a nationally recognized leader in alternate-site care and a valuable administrative resource to the health care industry.

MAKING HOME HEALTH CARE A REALITY

CF Health Care Ventures began in 1986 when Carol L. Schaffer, J.D., R.N., M.S.N., M.B.A., became the general manager of Clinicare Health Resources (CHR). A joint venture between Clinitec, a wholly owned subsidiary of The Cleveland Clinic Foundation, and Caremark's Home Health Care of America, CHR had been established in June 1985 to care for patients at home who needed intravenous nutrition therapy.

CCF physician Dr. Ezra Steiger pioneered home total parenteral nutrition (TPN) therapy. The program was advanced by other CCF physicians, such as Dr. Susan Rehm and Dr. Robert Wyllie, who developed programs for the care of intravenous and TPN therapy patients at home.

In the mid-1980s, because insurance companies were not convinced that home care programs were much more than an experiment, reimbursement of costs was a problem. Additionally, Ohio state laws prohibited nurses, who are the cornerstones of home health care, from performing the procedures needed for TPN therapy.

Despite the heavy regulatory restrictions, Cleveland Clinic Home Care Services (CCHCS), as the venture had come to be known, continued to grow, with increasing numbers of referrals from CCF physicians. The organization created a professional advisory board in July 1986, and, under the leadership of Rehm, the group developed home care standards, policies, and procedures for ensuring the highest-quality care in a home setting. The board's expertise and vision enabled CCHCS to identify areas for expansion of care as well as new areas of patient need within the services that were being provided. The board's guidelines, published by Aspen, are widely recognized as an industry standard.

In the spring of 1990 Cleveland Clinic Home Care Services received accreditation from the Joint Commission on Accreditation of Healthcare Organizations. During preparation for the accreditation process, CCHCS opened a satellite office in Florida, offering patients of the Cleveland Clinic Florida the full spectrum of home care services that are available in Cleveland. By that time, the operation—through a variety of local and national health care providers—was serving patients in a seven-state area.

CCF HEALTH CARE VENTURES MAKES IT POSSIBLE FOR THOUSANDS OF PEOPLE TO RETURN HOME QUICKLY AFTER HOSPITALIZATION OR TO AVOID HOSPITALIZATION ALTOGETHER. HOME CARE MAY INCLUDE INTRAVENOUS THERAPY, RESPIRATORY THERAPY, AND USE OF DURABLE MEDICAL EQUIPMENT.

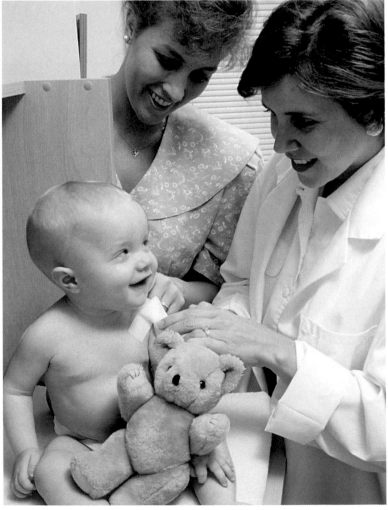

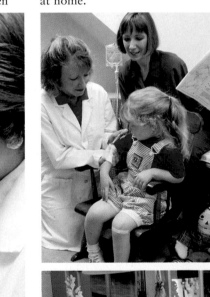

VENTURING FORTH

*I*n 1991, CCHCS severed its ties with Caremark and re-entered the market as an independent home infusion company with pharmacy and administrative headquarters in Valley View, a suburb of Cleveland.

In 1993, The Cleveland Clinic Foundation approved the creation of CCF Health Care Ventures, Inc., the umbrella organization that manages an increasing number of alternate-site care programs. In addition to providing home health care, CCF Health Care Ventures provides varying degrees of services to patients in numerous subacute facilities throughout Ohio. The facilities serve patients who no longer need the acute care of a hospital, but are not yet ready for home care.

In 1994, CCF Health Care Ventures teamed up with 10 area hospitals and affiliated network providers to offer its home health care services. This program, by 1996, took legal form as Venture-Net for the Cleveland Health Network. VentureNet will rapidly result in the administration of more than 1 million annual visits.

Today, clinical coordinators identify potential home care patients within 48 hours of their admission to the hospital, thereby reducing the cost of long hospital stays. In addition to home care, which includes intravenous therapy, respiratory therapy, and durable medical equipment, the organization opened a 59-bed, hospital-based skilled nursing facility in December 1995 on The Cleveland Clinic Foundation campus. At the facility, patients receive restorative, rehabilitative therapy and skilled nursing care before returning to their homes.

In addition, more and more community hospitals are looking to CCF Health Care Ventures to manage their home care depart-

ments. According to Schaffer, the organization's medical and business services are ideal for smaller facilities that need the state-of-the-art systems required to manage an efficient home health program.

"Home care has traditionally been a fragmented business. The patient received equipment from one dealer, nursing from another company, and infusion therapy from yet another vendor. But all that is changing," says Schaffer. "Coordination of home health care, such as we offer, is enabling smaller hospitals to expand their services and stay true to their mission."

The Cleveland Clinic Foundation's Hospice Program also became part of CCF Health Care Ventures. This move, which occurred in late 1995, allows the Hospice Program

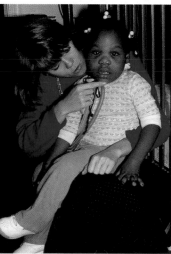

to benefit from CCF Health Care Ventures' management expertise and to expand both programs, providing CCF Health Care Ventures with the final component in the total continuum of care.

The physical and occupational therapy programs also came under the direction of CCF Health Care Ventures in 1995. The move enhances continuity as more and more patients are seen in alternate sites. In 1996, CCF Health Care Ventures launched its Comprehensive Outpatient Rehabilitation Facilities (CORF) to care for patients in need of therapy in ambulatory sites, as well as nursing care and pain management. A comprehensive approach, CORF has been expanded from the main campus into the satellite locations, a process that will continue in 1997.

ROACTIVE IS THE BYWORD FOR CLEVELAND HEALTH NETWORK (CHN), a dynamic regional health care delivery system created through the collaboration of local physicians and hospitals. Committed to improving the health of the communities it serves, the

network constantly strives toward its mission of providing high-quality, cost-effective, comprehensive health care services throughout the region.

Formed in 1994, Cleveland Health Network has quickly become northeast Ohio's largest and most comprehensive integrated delivery system. Its goal is to "link physicians and hospitals in a unique relationship that is responsive to the needs of both patients and payors," explains Cleveland Health Network President Martin P. Hauser.

With The Cleveland Clinic Foundation as its cornerstone, the network is composed of more than 3,000 physicians and other health care professionals, as well as more than 20 hospitals in northern Ohio. These skillful professionals practice expertly within a complete range of facilities, from acute care

community hospitals to tertiary care facilities and centers of excellence. Physicians from a full spectrum of medical specialties provide what the network describes as a seamless system of coordinated health care.

"This is a locally developed system, created by the physicians

and the hospitals," explains CHN Medical Director Alan E. London, M.D. "We are building relationships that give people broad access to a full spectrum of coordinated health care services." The Cleveland Health Network can be defined as an integrated delivery system, which means that previously independent doctors and hospitals have organized so that they are able to provide top-quality care with the patient's best interest in mind.

The effects and influence of the Cleveland Health Network are far reaching. For example, its formation has made the expertise of world-class doctors available to patients in smaller community hospitals.

CREATING A NETWORK

The roots of the organization can be found in activities such as the 1994 linking of the cardiovascular surgery programs at the Cleveland Clinic and EMH Regional Medical Center in Elyria, a union that made highly specialized heart care easily accessible to patients in Lorain County.

THE CLEVELAND HEALTH NETWORK LINKS PHYSICIANS AND HOSPITALS TO FORM NORTHEAST OHIO'S LARGEST AND MOST COMPREHENSIVE INTEGRATED HEALTH CARE DELIVERY SYSTEM (TOP).

AT CHN, THE PRIMARY CARE PHYSICIAN REMAINS KEY TO AN INDIVIDUAL'S HEALTH CARE (BOTTOM).

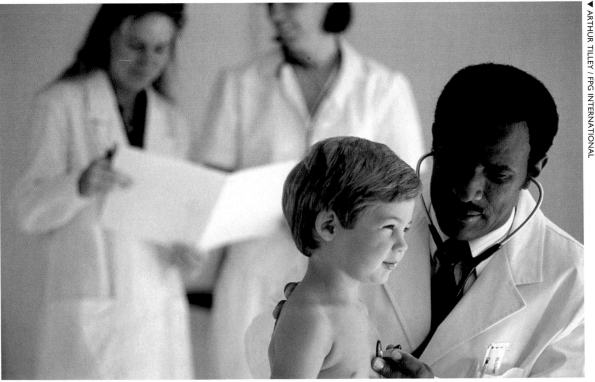

◀ ARTHUR TILLEY / FPG INTERNATIONAL

Later that year, Fairview General Hospital on Cleveland's west side and the Cleveland Clinic agreed to relocate 15 obstetric and 17 nursery beds from Fairview Hospital to the Cleveland Clinic campus. This arrangement marked the clinic's reentry into obstetrics after a 29-year absence.

"This type of collaboration led to broader-based discussions and the formation of the Cleveland Health Network," says Hauser. Initially, two institutions and their affiliated physicians found they could collaborate to improve the overall health of the communities they serve.

As time passed, other institutions and physicians with the same commitment, vision, and values became participants in CHN. By linking themselves with the Cleveland Health Network, health care providers have become able to share services and administrative costs, design the best kinds of

treatment for patients based on shared information, and offer the best care to the largest number of people at the most reasonable price. "Through case-managed referrals, physicians are assured of getting the patient to the appropriate physician and hospital for the appropriate treatment in a timely way," London adds.

That doctor-patient relationship remains the focus of health care in the Cleveland Health Network. "Health care is still a local relationship, and we want to keep it that way," says London. To that end, the primary care physician remains the key to an individual's care and, along with the medical management team at Cleveland Health Network, determines which care options are the most appropriate for the patient.

Physicians are also key participants in the governance of the Cleveland Health Network, given that 50 percent of its board is

composed of physicians. In addition to their contribution to the governance of CHN, participating physicians from throughout the region are actively involved in developing and defining the standards of care for the network members.

Hauser calls Cleveland Health Network an "innovative approach" to community health care, noting that it takes into account many of the concerns of consumers, as well as employers and insurance companies. "We are addressing how to control costs while focusing on preventive and quality care," says Hauser. "Instead of rationing health care, we are looking at it rationally."

What's the rational way to approach health care in northeastern Ohio? Looking to the future, the Cleveland Health Network is poised to answer that question for people and communities throughout the region it serves.

IT WAS 1971. THE PERMITS HAD BEEN ISSUED. THE WRECKING balls had been readied. But in place of a death knell, a handful of theater lovers successfully orchestrated a last-minute reprieve that saved the area known as Cleveland's Theater District from becoming another

parking lot. Today, that area, which stretches along Euclid Avenue from East 12th to East 18th streets and from Chester to Prospect avenues, is the fourth-largest performing arts center in America.

Come 1998, it will rank as the second largest.

"It was the beginning of Cleveland's rebirth," Art Falco, president of the Playhouse Square Foundation, says with great satisfaction. "We thought that if we could get people to come downtown to the theater once, they would come back again. It worked."

ON THE SCENE

The rebirth of the Cleveland Theater District is the result of a $40 million public/private partnership that not only has revived the area and four of its historic theaters, but also has served as the impetus for the revival of the city's entire downtown area. The project is estimated to bring more than $50 million in new capital to the city each year.

Back in the 1920s, local newspapers had coined the moniker "Playhouse Square" to describe the budding entertainment district in downtown Cleveland. Those were boom times in this first-tier

industrial city, and people craved entertainment. In 1916 the Stillman, an elaborate motion picture house with 1,800 seats, opened at East 12th Street and Euclid Avenue. It was the beginning of a dream that would see the nearby State and Ohio theaters open within a week of each other in 1921. The State Theatre boasted one of the longest lobbies in the world and, in those days of silent movies, featured an orchestra in the pit. The 1,200-seat Ohio Theatre next door featured touring dramas and musicals. Nine more theaters followed, including the Allen Theatre, the $2 million Palace Theatre, and the Hanna Theatre, which replaced the Euclid Avenue Opera House.

Thanks to Playhouse Square, locals could now enjoy legitimate theater, movies, and vaudeville acts featuring headliners like Fanny Brice, Burns and Allen, Jack Benny, Harry Houdini, and Sophie Tucker.

CHANGING WITH THE TIMES

During the decades that followed their establishment, the theaters at Playhouse Square reflected the moods of Cleveland and the nation. As vaudeville faded, new forms of entertainment took its place. But as the theaters began to age, lifestyle changes that were emerging would herald the demise of these grand venues. The popularity of television, coupled with the growth of suburban shopping centers, resulted in a waning interest in keeping downtown Cleveland and Playhouse Square alive. By the late 1960s, the once-lively city streets were virtually deserted after dark. The four stars in the Playhouse Square constellation—the Allen, State, Palace, and Ohio

TODAY, CLEVELAND'S THEATER DISTRICT, WHICH STRETCHES ALONG EUCLID AVENUE FROM EAST 12TH TO EAST 18TH STREETS AND FROM CHESTER TO PROSPECT AVENUES, IS THE FOURTH-LARGEST PERFORMING ARTS CENTER IN AMERICA. COME 1998, IT WILL RANK AS THE SECOND LARGEST.

theaters—were abandoned and crumbling.

On the 49th anniversary of the opening of the State Theatre, a local school employee who was looking for a place to hold meetings happened into one of the aged theaters. He was awestruck by the remnants of its glory days. His rediscovery led to the formation of the Playhouse Square Foundation, an organization that promised to breathe new life into the area. During the ensuing 10 years, restoration of the theaters and limited-scale theatrical productions took place on a shoestring. In 1982, however, the foundation began to assemble a professional management team that would raise the $40 million needed to make the theater district's true renaissance a reality.

The process, which began as an urban redevelopment laboratory, continues as a contemporary model for other cities across the United States, as well as Australia and Japan. Cleveland has reaped the rewards with a revived downtown that includes the magnificent Tower City, a restored railway station boasting 130 stores, bistros, and theaters; the Rock and Roll Hall of Fame and Museum; the Great Lakes Science Center; the Gateway Complex, housing the Indians' Jacobs Field and the Cavaliers' Gund Arena; the restored Warehouse District; the lively riverfront district known as the Flats; and several new high-rise office buildings.

The Theater District's master plan calls for major physical changes to the area: narrowing Euclid Avenue to discourage vehicular traffic; widening the sidewalks to accommodate outdoor cafés and kiosks; lining the avenue with mature shade trees; and placing colorful theatrical signage on billboards and building tops throughout the district. Falco also anticipates more housing and restaurants, plus a party center in the

mix. "We are creating a vibrant, exciting neighborhood," he says.

"Our prevailing hope," Falco adds, "was that the theaters would serve as people magnets, drawing both suburbanites and investment capital back downtown. We have been wildly successful, having welcomed our 10 millionth patron to Playhouse Square Center early in 1997. Not only are the four the-

aters historic and architectural attractions in their own right, which invite tours, but the entertainment variety they host, including theater, dance, comedy, and all genres of music, continues to attract diverse audiences. Now our focus widens. Playhouse Square Center becomes a major player in Cleveland's future as a premier destination city."

THE PALACE THEATRE, WHICH INITIALLY COST $2 MILLION TO BUILD, IS ONE OF THE NEWLY RESTORED BUILDINGS IN CLEVELAND'S REVITALIZED THEATER DISTRICT.

BACK IN THE 1920S, LOCAL NEWSPAPERS COINED THE MONIKER "PLAYHOUSE SQUARE" TO DESCRIBE THE BUDDING ENTERTAINMENT DISTRICT IN DOWNTOWN CLEVELAND. BY 1928, THERE WERE A DOZEN THEATERS FEATURING LEGITIMATE THEATER, MOVIES, AND VAUDEVILLE.

OREST CITY ENTERPRISES, INC. HAS CHANGED DRAMATICALLY since its founding in 1921 as a lumberyard on East 93rd Street and Harvard Avenue in Cleveland, but its values have stayed constant. ❖ "Our company was named after Cleveland, known as

the Forest City, which suggests our community commitment," says Charles Ratner, president and chief executive officer. "Although we now operate in dozens of cities, we try in every one of them to be good neighbors, good business partners, good landlords, and good citizens. I think that's why we've been successful."

From that east side lumberyard, founded by Polish immigrant brothers Charles, Leonard, and Max Ratner, Forest City today is one of the largest publicly traded real estate investment companies in the United States, with assets of more than $2.5 billion. Forest City plans, finances, constructs, leases, markets, and manages new and renovated retail, residential, commercial, and mixed-used developments in 20 states and the District of Columbia.

The lumber business is still an important component of Forest City Enterprises, although it bears

scant resemblance to the original lumberyard. The Trading Group, one of Forest City's four strategic business units (SBU), is the nation's second-largest lumber wholesaler, moving some $3 billion in wood products a year. The Trading Group buys lumber from 1,000 mills and sells it in all 50 states and in all Canadian provinces.

The other SBUs are commercial, residential, and land.

The Commercial Group owns, acquires, develops, and manages retail, office, and entertainment projects nationwide. In Cleveland, Forest City Enterprises was an early and important player in the city's renaissance, investing $600 million to transform the largely abandoned downtown railroad terminal into a glittering mall called The Avenue at Tower City Center. The center includes new and renovated office buildings and a hotel—all at the heart of Cleveland on Public Square.

Forest City has pioneered the concept of bringing major retail development to inner-city neighborhoods ignored by major retailers. In Brooklyn, for example, the company developed Atlantic Center, the first new retail complex to open in the borough in 30 years. The project brought 1,200 taxpaying jobs to the inner city. Forest City has completed similar developments in The Bronx and Queens, as well as in Philadelphia, Chicago, and downtown Pasadena.

For outstanding contributions to the revitalization of the American downtown marketplace, Forest City received the AGORA Award from the U.S. Department of Housing and Urban Development

In a pioneering effort of a different sort, Forest City is adding entertainment projects to new and existing retail facilities to enhance their appeal to shoppers. A 333,000-square-foot entertainment and retail complex on 42nd Street in

THE SHOWCASE ENTERTAINMENT AND RETAIL COMPLEX IS LOCATED ADJACENT TO THE MGM GRAND CASINO IN LAS VEGAS.

New York City is a key component in the revitalization of Times Square. And on the Strip in Las Vegas, the Showcase, a 190,000-square-foot entertainment and retail complex, includes theaters, an interactive game park, and restaurants. In the Las Vegas suburb of Henderson, Forest City is involved in the first gaming and entertainment complex in the United States attached to a regional shopping center, adding a hotel/casino and Olympic-sized ice rink to The Galleria at Sunset.

A notable office project is the MetroTech complex in Brooklyn. Forest City owns six buildings there totaling 3.2 million square feet, including one housing New York City's fire department headquarters. Nationwide, the Commercial Group has 7 million square feet of office space, 15 million square feet of retail space, and five hotels boasting more than 1,500 rooms.

Forest City's Residential Group is meeting the increased national demand for rental apartments with a portfolio that includes more than 32,000 units in 20 states and the District of Columbia. Projects are tailored to local market conditions, and monthly rentals range from less than $300 to more than $1,500 for a one-bedroom apartment. In Greater Cleveland, the company manages 21 properties.

The Land Group has unmatched expertise in developing raw land into master-planned

communities and other residential developments. It provides all infrastructure improvements and then sells lots to home builders who are creating unique urban and suburban projects that fill special local needs, including the Aberdeen golf course community in Greater Cleveland. The Land Group has more than 50,000 acres of holdings in 10 states.

"Forest City creates each project to respond to the needs of its community," says Ratner. "What makes us unique is our total involvement in every aspect of ownership and development—from concept through completion and operation."

Although it is now a company with operations from coast to coast, Forest City still has its headquarters in Cleveland. Its local commitment not only includes continued development but, through its For-

est City Charitable Foundation, involves donations of some $1 million a year to more than 300 Cleveland-area organizations serving education, health, and human services needs. In addition, Forest City employees have volunteered to partner with Thomas Jefferson Middle School on West 44th Street and Clark Avenue in Cleveland, and have painted the interior, carpeted the library, and bought books for the children.

"Our actions demonstrate our belief that to be successful, we must develop meaningful relationships with our customers and our communities," says Ratner. It's a philosophy that has driven the growth of Forest City Enterprises from that single lumberyard to preeminence in real estate development.

FOREST CITY PLANS, FINANCES, CONSTRUCTS, LEASES, MARKETS, AND MANAGES NEW AND RENOVATED RETAIL, RESIDENTIAL, COMMERCIAL, AND MIXED-USED DEVELOPMENTS IN 20 STATES AND THE DISTRICT OF COLUMBIA, INCLUDING THE AVENUE AT TOWER CITY CENTER IN CLEVELAND (RIGHT).

A LOT HAS CHANGED SINCE 1922, WHEN THE FOUNDERS OF HKM Direct Market Communications, Inc. opened a small printing and mailing operation. Today, the company is a full-service communications source that offers a complete line of printing and mailing

services, as well as creative support, graphic design, art production, desktop publishing and electronic prepress services. In addition, HKM provides bindery, information management, on-demand personalized laser printing, and fulfillment programs.

Despite the firm's evolution, one thing has remained constant: HKM maintains the highest level of customer service in the industry. "Every project we do for our customers is the continuation of a partnership," says Scott L. Durham, chief operating officer. "This partnership is based on common goals. That's why all of our customers feel like they're special—because they are our partners."

From its headquarters on Cass Avenue in Cleveland—and from its Elyria Graphics facility located approximately 20 miles to the west—HKM provides an environment for innovation, an

ability to encourage change, and a commitment to quality and service.

"Our ability to anticipate and encourage change has fueled HKM's growth," says George Q. Durham, chairman of the board. "One constant through the years, however, has been the dedication of our people to quality and service. Their commitment has always been at the core of our growth, and touches everything we do."

A TEAM APPROACH

The foundation of HKM's approach to meeting customers' needs is the sales and account service team, who stay with a project from concept to completion. By tracking progress, these representatives can ensure efficient and effective management of each individual project, as well as the overall account. From the moment the project reaches the Cleveland or Elyria office, an HKM team

begins planning, scheduling, and tracking progress—meeting daily with production managers and supervisors to assess company-wide production needs and to ensure that projects are completed on time and within budget.

Knowledgeable about each aspect of graphics, prepress, and printing processes and facilities, sales and account service representatives are able to troubleshoot potential problems and make optimal choices, ranging from using the proper press and paper to determining the most effective mailing services. Also available are database management, target marketing list selection, addressing, and fulfillment programs.

Should a client require creative services, HKM can meet a full range of marketing needs—from print and video to CD-ROM and Internet communications. The creative staff provides planning, scripting, and production skills.

FROM ITS HEADQUARTERS ON CASS AVENUE IN CLEVELAND, HKM PROVIDES AN ENVIRONMENT FOR INNOVATION, AN ABILITY TO ENCOURAGE CHANGE, AND A COMMITMENT TO QUALITY AND SERVICE (LEFT).

THE FIRM IS EQUIPPED TO MEET A DIVERSITY OF PRINTING AND BINDERY NEEDS (RIGHT).

In addition to producing original artwork, typesetting, illustration, and working with images, HKM specialists are skilled at copy writing, graphic design, layout, and desktop publishing. Whether creating a visual image, designing an attractive brochure, or conceiving an innovative direct mail campaign, HKM can deliver the specialists, technology, and materials to complement and enhance a company's communications program.

MAKING A DIFFERENCE

*H*KM's on-site electronic prepress department scans original color images, artwork, and photographs with the latest in hardware and software, ensuring the highest resolution and finest detail. The system is capable of correcting flaws in coloration and enhancing images to accentuate the visual effect. Customers can review color proofs quickly and inexpensively because HKM is able to evaluate images electronically before anything is finalized on film. While equipped for electronic images, the firm also responds with the latest technologies for reproducing conventional artwork.

Once a job is ready to print, HKM can support customer needs whether they call for large-run, high-quality-color, sheet-fed work or for short-run, one- and two-color work. HKM's full-service bindery can trim, fold, stitch, and drill, as well as perfect bind, pad, shrink-wrap, and carton-print

products. All equipment is operated by highly qualified craftsmen.

HKM's computer technologies are universally compatible: Whether a customer uses a mainframe system, a network of personal computers, desktop publishing equipment, or an electronic prepress system, programmers can customize software for specific jobs. Database management services range from inputting data to reproducing information on labels, magnetic tape, and disks, or via computer modem. HKM's laser printers produce high-quality letters, mailers, and forms, as well as on-demand electronic documents.

The company follows through on its projects to the very end. HKM's team of experts determine the ideal mix of mailing techniques at the lowest postal rate, while ensuring the project complies

with postal regulations. Mail rooms in Elyria and Cleveland then function as small post offices. A fleet of trucks guarantees delivery within hours of completion, and manual and machine inserting services are available to meet the full range of customer needs.

HKM has refined warehousing and fulfillment to a science. All transactions are logged into a computer system and prepared for shipping to destinations worldwide. In addition, HKM can provide its customers with detailed reports that carefully analyze the effectiveness of its direct mailings.

"One of the things people notice most about HKM is our impressive facilities," says Robert A. Durham, president. "We maintain a thoroughly modern and efficient working environment. I believe this illustrates our commitment to the future, and we're very proud of that."

A QUINTESSENTIAL NORTHEASTERN OHIO FIRM, RIDGE TOOL CO. has been selling quality products to the pipe working and construction industries since 1923, while changing with the times and adjusting to its customers' needs. At the same time, the company has maintained

its high quality standards, as well as its state-of-the-art plants, and has grown to become one of the world's largest manufacturers of tools for the professional craftsman, selling its products under the RIDGID brand name in 130 countries. From humble beginnings as a small-town supplier to local plumbers, pipe workers, and builders, Ridge Tool has become a major presence both in the United States and worldwide.

The company was founded in North Ridgeville, Ohio, by Carl Ingwer Sr., William Thewes, and Arthur Smith. Starting with fewer than 80 employees working in a tiny building at the intersection of two country roads, the men designed and produced a new style of heavy-duty pipe wrench. Gradually, the company began to broaden its market base, expanding its product line to include other hand tools for the pipe working industry.

By 1943, the company's significant growth had necessitated a move to a larger headquarters facility in Elyria, where it is still located. In 1966, Ridge Tool expanded further with the acquisition of the Kollmann Co., a manufacturer of drain cleaning equipment.

Ridge Tool's sparkling headquarters today employs around 1,000 people on a 26-acre campus. A key part of the company's marketing approach is its strategic positioning of manufacturing, warehousing, and sales operations throughout the world. For example, Ridge Tool has manufacturing facilities in Pennsylvania, Virginia, Ireland, Brazil, and Germany. Its distribution and sales offices are strategically located throughout

RIDGE TOOL'S SPARKLING HEADQUARTERS TODAY EMPLOYS AROUND 1,000 PEOPLE ON A 26-ACRE CAMPUS IN ELYRIA (TOP).

THE COMPANY BEGAN WITH THE CREATION OF A NEW STYLE OF HEAVY-DUTY PIPE WRENCH. TODAY, ONE OF ITS MOST POPULAR PRODUCT LINES IS STILL ITS VAST ARRAY OF WRENCHES (BOTTOM).

the United States, Canada, Europe, Latin America, the Pacific Rim, Australia, the Middle East, and Africa.

TODAY AND TOMORROW

Ridge Tool now makes more than 300 different types of tools in more than 4,000 models and sizes. Wrenches; pipe cutters and other power tools; threading equipment; tubing tools; pipe and drain cleaning equipment; and such general purpose tools as hammers, vises, and chisels are among the company's many well-known products. Its tools are sold primarily to professional craftsmen, but are also available in general retail stores.

In recent years, Ridge Tool, which became part of St. Louis-based Emersen Electric Co. in 1967, has implemented an aggressive marketing strategy. Along with the company's reputation for quality products, that strategy has boosted the percentage of new product sales tenfold in a five-year period. As a result, Ridge Tool has become a leading trade magazine advertiser, and has invested heavily in training programs to teach end users throughout the world the proper use of its tools. The company now participates in more than 100 shows and exhibits annually.

Ridge Tool is proud of its accomplishments in expanding into new markets, either by introducing new products or entering new geographic areas, and the company expects such expansion to continue into the foreseeable future. To that end, the company's philosophy of becoming a best-cost producer includes six elements: dedication to quality, knowledge of competitors' costs, a focused manufacturing strategy, formal cost-reduction programs, effective communications, and commitment to capital expenditures to improve productivity. As an example of how Ridge Tool has implemented that strategy, the company has made an extensive commitment in the last decade to computer-aided-design and computer-aided-manufacturing technology, which helps assure product quality and reliability. Operating under that progressive philosophy, Ridge Tool is sure to become an even tougher powerhouse in its industry.

A COLORFUL HISTORY

One can't talk about Ridge Tool without mentioning another part of its history. Over the years, the company has developed a reputation for its colorful product calendar. Ridge Tool established the tradition in 1935 and expanded it to feature pinup drawings and, later, photographs of live models alongside its wrenches and other products.

Today, internationally recognized photographers contribute to the calendar, for which the company receives more than 500,000 requests every two years. The calendar, like the company's products, has become an institution, and it is displayed in plants and shops around the globe.

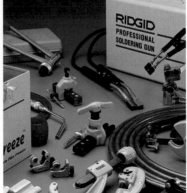

Despite exponential growth in the last 70-plus years, Ridge Tool hasn't forgotten its roots. The company has maintained a strong presence in Greater Cleveland by contributing to local charities, hospitals, and business programs for young people. Proud of its longtime reputation for a talented workforce, quality products, and service worthy of the best professional craftsmen, Ridge Tool, like northeast Ohio, has survived and thrived.

THREADING MACHINES AND OTHER POWER TOOLS ARE AMONG RIDGE TOOL'S EXTENSIVE PRODUCT LINE (TOP).

RIDGE TOOL MANUFACTURES TUBING TOOLS (BOTTOM RIGHT) AND PIPE AND DRAIN CLEANING EQUIPMENT (BOTTOM LEFT) FOR PROFESSIONAL CRAFTSMEN, AS WELL AS FOR GENERAL RETAIL SALE.

*I*T'S A NEW CLEVELAND, AND MORE AND MORE PEOPLE ARE HOPPING a plane to come visit. Cleveland is fortunate to have two strong airports as gateways to the community—Burke Lakefront and Cleveland Hopkins International. ❖ Cleveland's city-owned airports

serve as primary contributors to the economic prosperity of northeast Ohio as they facilitate business growth, tourism, and pleasure travel. They are prime locations for employment, with more than 5,000 people employed directly at the airports and 10,000 more employed due to airport activity. The total economic impact on the community currently exceeds $1.5 billion per year.

Upon completion of expansions now under way, Burke and Hopkins will play an even greater role in Cleveland's future. The economic impact of the airports is expected to grow to more than $2 billion per year by 2010.

CLEVELAND HOPKINS INTERNATIONAL AIRPORT

*H*opkins is continuing a trend of five straight years of record numbers of passengers. One of the driving forces in the increase in passenger activity has been the rapid growth of Continental Airlines. Northeast Ohio is better served than it ever has been, as the Continental hub means more air service for travelers, more destinations served, and more frequent flights.

The dramatic growth in passenger demand has necessitated the upgrading and expansion of the airfield and terminal facilities. This expansion is possible due to a recent agreement that brings within Cleveland's borders all airport-owned land needed for the expansion.

A new parking garage is under construction, with completion of more than 2,000 spaces and the connecting pedestrian bridges scheduled for early spring of 1998. The remainder of the 3,800 spaces will be finished a year later. Begin-

ning construction is a new, $80 million, state-of-the-art commuter aircraft terminal that will be connected by an underground tunnel to Continental's C concourse. When the project is completed, Continental will have 56 gates to dock its jet and commuter aircraft.

A 6,450-foot parallel runway is scheduled to be completed in late 1999 in order to increase the peak period capacity of the airport. A runway extension will then allow for the addition of direct flights to all major Asian and European airports. Also under way at Hopkins are an upgrading and expansion of the airport's merchandise and food and beverage facilities, and the development of a centralized car rental complex just north of the airport.

Founded as Cleveland Municipal Airport in 1925, Hopkins—the oldest municipally owned airport in the country—has served as a model for the subsequent development of other airports around the world. Hopkins saw the first scheduled passenger service in the United States (1926), construction of the country's first passenger

CLEVELAND'S AIRPORT FACILITIES HAVE LONG BEEN ON THE CUTTING EDGE, INCLUDING THE INSTALLATION IN 1930 OF THE NATION'S FIRST AIRFIELD LIGHTING SYSTEM (TOP).

THANKS TO ADDITIONAL FLIGHTS BY CONTINENTAL AIRLINES, CLEVELAND HOPKINS INTERNATIONAL IS ONE OF THE FASTEST-GROWING MAJOR AIRPORTS IN THE UNITED STATES (BOTTOM).

terminal building (1927), development of the country's first system to aid night landing (1930), and installation of the first airport control tower in the world.

BURKE LAKEFRONT AIRPORT

*B*urke is every executive's dream: a full-service airport located in the center of downtown Cleveland within sight of the business community's best addresses. The importance of Burke has grown with the development of the Rock and Roll Hall of Fame and Museum and the Great Lakes Science Center on sites just a few minutes' walk from the airport. Long popular with business executives, Burke is now getting a lot of use by people flying in to visit these North Coast Harbor attractions. The airport is also the home of the Cleveland Grand Prix (an IndyCar race held on the airfield

each summer) and the Cleveland Air Show (traditionally held on Labor Day weekend).

CITY OWNED AND OPERATED

*O*wned and operated by the City of Cleveland, both airports are professionally managed by the Department of Port Control. Because they are self-supporting, neither of the airports' operations or expansions require tax support from the City of Cleveland's general fund.

The airports have been good neighbors. At Hopkins, the department has an active noise mitigation program that has resulted in the purchase of more than 500 homes and the insulation of 150 homes and three schools.

"Cleveland is fortunate to have two strong airports—a large, rapidly growing international airport and a perfectly located

business jetport right in the center of Cleveland's downtown excitement," concludes Cleveland Mayor Michael R. White. "I'm proud of the accomplishments of our staff to provide safe, efficient, and customer-friendly service to all the traveling public."

BURKE LAKEFRONT AIRPORT IS A FULL-SERVICE AIRPORT LOCATED NEXT TO THE ROCK AND ROLL HALL OF FAME AND MUSEUM IN DOWNTOWN CLEVELAND.

TOM EMBRESCIA, TOM WILSON, AND LARRY POLLOCK—THE OWNERS of Cleveland radio stations WDOK 102.1 FM and WRMR AM 850—are local people who take great pride in serving the local community. They achieve this goal in a variety of ways—

including attracting and hiring a staff of talented on-air personalities and dedicated behind-the-scenes employees, carefully considering listener and advertiser feedback, and involving both WDOK and WRMR in a myriad of community activities. Embrescia and Wilson are native Clevelanders, and Pollock is a 30-year Cleveland resident.

This hands-on ownership group, who purchased the stations in 1987, have a combined 75 years of broadcasting experience. Likewise, members of the company's management team—led by General Manager Chris Maduri, Operations Manager Sue Wilson, Community Relations Director Rena Blumberg, Business Manager Kim Brown, and Chief Engineer Ted Alexander—are dedicated to serving the station's listeners and advertisers.

THE STATIONS

Both WDOK and WRMR feature music-based formats and friendly on-air personalities who complement each station's unique style. WDOK's format consists of soft rock favor-ites targeted at the 25- to 54-year-old age bracket, with a playlist that includes such artists as Billy Joel, Elton John, and Whitney Houston. Its distinctive sound makes it easy for people to listen for hours at a time. In fact, WDOK is Cleveland's number one in-office station—heard in more offices and businesses and on more telephone "hold" buttons than any other station in Cleveland. WDOK provides its listeners with nonstop entertainment throughout the day. Morning host "Trapper Jack" Elliot, along with sidekick Robin Benzlé and newsman Jim McIntyre, offers listeners a show that's topical, spontaneous, and just plain fun, while Cleveland's "Lady in Red," Nancy Alden, makes WDOK a favorite at-work radio station during midday. In the afternoon, Matt "the Cat," a Cleveland air personality for more than 20 years, helps ease the stress of the drive home. And in the evening, Rob Schuler and his easygoing style make *102 After Dark* a welcome alternative to primetime television.

On the AM side of the dial, WRMR offers its listeners "The Music of Your Life," featuring a playlist of adult pop standards by artists like Frank Sinatra, Barbra Streisand, Tony Bennett, and Nat King Cole, plus a lineup of veteran Cleveland broadcasters. Every weekday morning, "Tall Ted" Hallaman's laid-back style, observations on the human condition, wit, and dry humor fill the airwaves, while each midday, "Captain" Carl Reese, drawing from 40-plus years of experience, entertains the huge WRMR audience. In addition to the music, among Reese's more popular features is *The Good Neighbor Show* with Fred Embrescia, a daily rundown of special events, birthdays, anniversaries, and more. During the afternoon drive time, the legendary Bill Randle plays the music of the superstars whose careers he helped shape. In the evenings, Rick Majors hosts the *Music of Your Life All-Request Show*, taking requests and dedications from listeners. And then, Ronnie Barrett, another longtime Cleve-

THE WDOK/WRMR OWNERSHIP TEAM INCLUDES (FROM LEFT) LARRY POLLOCK, TOM EMBRESCIA, AND TOM WILSON.

MEMBERS OF THE WDOK/WRMR MANAGEMENT TEAM INCLUDE (STANDING, FROM LEFT) SUE WILSON, JOE RESTIFO, (SEATED) RENA BLUMBERG, CHRIS MADURI, AND KIM BROWN.

◀ BARNEY TAXEL

land favorite, takes listeners through the night and early morning hours with his relaxed signature style, delivered over a background of piano music that he performs live.

GOOD NEWS FOR ADVERTISERS

*F*or advertisers and clients interested in reaching the Cleveland market, WDOK and WRMR are among Cleveland's best media buys, thanks to consistently high ratings and sales results. And because the stations understand the difficult marketing challenges facing retailers, their creative staff can put together commercials that will sell products. Says Maduri, "Our account executives are actually trained sales consultants and problem solvers. Our entire sales and support team takes pride in its ability to work with clients to keep cash registers ringing. We know and understand the market and how to get results." In addition to Maduri, the sales management team includes WDOK Local Sales Manager Kevin Watts, WRMR Local Sales Manager Paul Guy, WDOK/WRMR National Sales Manager Janet Pierce, and WDOK/WRMR Regional Sales Director John Guzik.

WDOK's policy of "highlighting" commercial messages also works to advertisers' advantage. Commercial breaks are limited to three times each hour and a maximum of four spots per break. For listeners, this means more music and fewer interruptions. For advertisers, it means a listener is more likely to stay tuned during commercial breaks and hear their messages.

Similar results can be found on WRMR, with the added advantage that its listeners tend to be highly affluent and have significant discretionary income. Some 15.3 percent of the WRMR audience have liquid assets in excess of $100,000. The station's listeners

also have high annual household incomes, are opinion leaders, and are frequent travelers—an excellent target audience for advertisers.

SERVING THE PUBLIC

*I*n addition to their entertainment programming, WDOK and WRMR are leaders in the areas of public service and community involvement. The stations play an active and ongoing role in several community service projects, including the WDOK/WRMR Feed-a-Family Campaign, which helps feed Cleveland's hungry by raising donations to benefit the Salvation Army and the Hunger Task Force. The stations also work closely with the Make-a-Wish

Foundation, the Northeast Ohio Race for the Cure (Susan G. Komen Breast Cancer Foundation), and Providence House (a children's crisis nursery).

Owners Embrescia, Wilson, and Pollock, along with their dedicated staff members, have worked hard to make WDOK and WRMR the stations of choice for the Cleveland audience. At WDOK 102.1 FM, music is the focus of everything, thereby bringing about steady growth in listeners and advertisers. At WRMR AM 850, the popularity of its adult pop standards format has created tremendous listener loyalty. Both stations look forward to a long and successful future of serving the Cleveland community.

WDOK MORNING HOST "TRAPPER JACK" ELLIOT (FRONT), ALONG WITH SIDEKICK ROBIN BENZLÉ AND NEWSMAN JIM MCINTYRE, OFFERS LISTENERS A SHOW THAT'S TOPICAL, SPONTANEOUS, AND JUST PLAIN FUN.

CLEVELAND'S "LADY IN RED," NANCY ALDEN (LEFT), MAKES WDOK A FAVORITE AT-WORK RADIO STATION DURING MIDDAY.

EACH MIDDAY, "CAPTAIN" CARL REESE (RIGHT), DRAWING FROM 40-PLUS YEARS OF EXPERIENCE, ENTERTAINS THE HUGE WRMR AUDIENCE.

WHEN EDWARD SILVERBERG OPENED HIS FIRST RETAIL OUTLET, the Osborne Dairy Store, in 1928, he had no way of knowing what the future would bring. But his strong commitment to satisfying customers and providing the highest-quality products at the lowest

CLOCKWISE FROM TOP: FINAST'S OLDE WORLD BAKERY PRODUCES A VARIETY OF BAKED GOODS, FROM FRESH BREADS TO PASTRIES AND WEDDING CAKES.

THE NEW NAME FOR FINAST—FINAST FRIENDLY MARKETS—REFLECTS THE MERIT OF LISTENING TO CUSTOMERS AND SERVICE TO THE COMMUNITY, THE VALUES THAT HAVE REMAINED A STEADY INFLUENCE WITH FINAST MANAGEMENT THROUGHOUT ITS 69-YEAR HISTORY.

IN 1939, KNOWING THAT CUSTOMERS WANTED LARGER, MORE COMPLETE GROCERY STORES, CLEVELANDER EDWARD SILVERBERG OPENED HIS FIRST SUPERMARKET, THEN KNOWN AS PICK-N-PAY. STORE NUMBER EIGHT WAS LOCATED AT EAST 131ST STREET AND MILES AVENUE.

prices helped create one of Cleveland's largest supermarket chains, operating 43 stores and employing more than 7,500 people today.

Silverberg's company experienced success right from the start. In the 1930s, he established a retail chain called Farmview Creamery Stores. And in 1939, knowing that customers wanted larger, more complete grocery stores, Silverberg opened his first supermarket, then known as Pick-N-Pay.

Pick-N-Pay was an immediate success, and, one by one, every Farmview store was incorporated into the popular supermarkets. In 1951, with 10 stores in Greater Cleveland, the chain was acquired by the Cook Coffee Company, now Cook United, Inc., which operated retail truck routes, selling grocery and household items. Under Cook's management, Pick-N-Pay continued to grow and was soon serving more than 100,000 Cleveland families.

In 1959, the Cook Coffee Company added substantially to the chain when it purchased 24

Foodtown locations from ACF-Wrigley Stores of Detroit. After the acquisition, Pick-N-Pay increased to 38 stores and moved into the Foodtown headquarters located in the Cleveland suburb of Maple Heights. In addition, the company acquired the right to distribute Edwards-brand products and soon captured the largest share of the Cleveland market. In the early 1960s, the company also began to build its own food-manufacturing plants.

A NEW DIRECTION

By the mid-1960s, Cleveland was flooded with grocery store chains and competition was fierce. Financial and operating difficulties plagued the Pick-N-Pay chain, and its stores began to look run-down and old-fashioned. The Cook Coffee Company—unable to reverse the downward trend and concerned with the development of its discount store operations—sold the chain's 57 stores to a group of

investors headed by Julius Kravitz and Richard Bogomolny.

The new management team quickly set out to revamp the operation by upgrading the existing facilities and opening larger stores. "Pick-N-Pay enjoyed an almost immediate turnaround," according to retired Chairman and CEO Bogomolny. "Pick-N-Pay's newfound dedication to complete customer satisfaction soon enabled us to regain our status as Greater Cleveland's number one supermarket chain." By 1975, sales had reached $300 million and the company had more than 5,000 employees.

Not satisfied to rest on its established reputation, Pick-N-Pay created the ultimate in customer convenience when it opened one of the industry's first true superstores in 1975. Called Pick-N-Pay Food Palace, the store offered one-stop shopping and featured specialty departments, including fresh fish and gourmet meat counters, bakeries, and flower shops.

In 1976, Pick-N-Pay again showed that it was at the forefront of the supermarket industry by opening Edwards Food Warehouse stores in the nearby cities of Toledo and Canton, Ohio. At Edwards, shoppers received dramatic savings by buying products in larger quantities than were available at conventional stores, bagging their own groceries, and providing their own carryout. Dramatic savings were made possible by such innovations as palletized stocking on warehouse racks, drastically reduced overhead, and less product duplication.

Meanwhile, Pick-N-Pay continued its reign as the leading supermarket chain in Cleveland, but management sought to further diversify its holdings. In 1978, the company acquired First National Stores (Finast), a large, New England-based food chain, resulting in the formation of publicly owned First National Supermarkets, Inc.

Management restructured the organization and sold some of the declining New England stores. By introducing new product techniques, First National Supermarkets was soon ranked as one of the nation's top supermarket chains.

In 1986, a price war led management to realize that the smaller stores would not be able to absorb the costs of offering customers lower prices. As a result, 16 of the

largest Pick-N-Pay stores were closed for a two-day period to reduce prices on more than 7,200 products and to convert the facilities to Finast superstores. The unique blend of service, quality, variety, and everyday low prices gave Cleveland-area consumers first-class shopping at a lower cost.

The remaining 29 Pick-N-Pay stores were customized to better serve the individual neighborhoods in which they operated, offering convenience, value, and promotional pricing. On January 6, 1988, First National Supermarkets was acquired by Royal Ahold, a Dutch-based company.

FINAST TODAY

*U*nder Royal Ahold's ownership, Finast continued to replace the existing Pick-N-Pay Supermarkets with Finast Food and Drug Superstores. The last Pick-N-Pay neighborhood store was closed in 1995. Finast continued its expansion throughout northeastern Ohio and, by 1995, had 40 supermarkets, including

six large superstores and two conventional supermarkets in the city of Cleveland, one of the largest urban investments in the country.

In the fall of 1996, Finast merged with Tops Markets, Inc., headquartered in Buffalo, New York, with 74 food stores in western and central New York, as well as in Pennsylvania. The merger with Tops Markets, also owned by Ahold, produced economies of scale and efficiencies of operation that will continue to serve customers throughout Cleveland and northeastern Ohio with quality, value, variety, and innovation. The new name for Finast—Finast Friendly Markets—reflects the merit of listening to customers and service to the community, the values that have remained a steady influence with Finast management throughout its 69-year history.

CLOCKWISE FROM TOP:
THE FINAST DELI CAN HELP CATER ANY FUNCTION, FROM A SMALL LUNCHEON TO A LARGE EVENT.

FINAST FRIENDLY MARKETS HAS RAISED HUNDREDS OF THOUSANDS OF DOLLARS FOR CHARITABLE ORGANIZATIONS, INCLUDING THE MARCH OF DIMES, THROUGHOUT NORTHEASTERN OHIO.

FINAST IS KNOWN FOR ITS SUPERIOR-QUALITY PRODUCE AND HELPFUL ASSOCIATES.

TELEDYNE FLUID SYSTEMS HAS A LONG AND RICH HISTORY. ITS business units developed as individual companies in places as far away as California and as close as its own backyard in Cleveland. The original companies each date back half a century: Hyson in Brecksville, Ohio; Republic in Brookpark, Ohio; Sprague in Gardena, California; and Farris in Palisades Park, New Jersey. All were acquired by Teledyne, Inc. in the 1960s and 1970s and prospered as part of this high-technology, multiproduct corporation. In the 1990s, in order to align companies with shared technologies, all were united to form Teledyne Fluid Systems.

Today, Teledyne Fluid Systems encompasses three distinct business units that share core capabilities in pressure technology, hydraulic/pneumatic circuitry, material forming, and surface finishing. The company provides innovative solutions to a diversified customer base through the development, manufacture, and marketing of specialized products, including nitrogen gas springs and systems, pneumatic valves, hydraulic pumps, and pressure relief valves.

With Greater Cleveland providing a ready workforce and a superior transportation network, Teledyne Fluid Systems has consolidated its U.S. manufacturing facilities in Brecksville with international operations in Canada, Sweden, and Thailand.

A HISTORY OF OUTSTANDING SERVICE

Although the products available from Teledyne Fluid Systems are diverse, when it comes to customers, the company is of a single mind. The focus is providing state-of-the-art products and services, outstanding quality, and the highest degree of customer service. Each business unit approaches this in a unique way.

Hyson developed and manufactured the first pneumatic die cylinder in 1939. From that auspicious start, the Nitrogen Products business unit has become a world leader in nitrogen gas systems. Its position has been strengthened with the recent acquisition of Swedish-based Stromsholmens and its Kaller line of self-contained nitrogen gas springs. Nitrogen gas springs and manifold pressure systems, integral to metal-forming operations, are used to control the flow of material during part formation and to complement the action of the press or die. Teledyne Fluid Systems' Nitrogen Products business unit has expanded the technology of resistant force to develop roller cams, hydraulic cams, and high-frequency gas springs that extend the nitrogen line of products.

Customers in the automotive, appliance, and can-making industries choose Teledyne Fluid Systems' nitrogen products because they can count on high quality that

SINCE THE EARLY 1940S, THE FARRIS ENGINEERING UNIT OF TELEDYNE FLUID SYSTEMS HAS DESIGNED AND PRODUCED A WIDE RANGE OF SPRING-LOADED AND PILOT-OPERATED PRESSURE RELIEF VALVES (LEFT).

THE COMPANY'S NITROGEN PRODUCTS BUSINESS UNIT HAS BECOME A WORLD LEADER IN NITROGEN GAS SYSTEMS (RIGHT).

enhances long-running, problem-free operations.

Teledyne Fluid Systems' Vehicle Control Products, formerly Republic Valve, manufactures high-quality, lightweight directional control valves for automobile transport trucks and specialty pneumatic directional control valves for Class 8 truck transmissions. Long recognized as a quality leader in the valve industry, Vehicle Control Products was not content to rest on its laurels. Teaming with their OEM customers, Teledyne Fluid Systems engineers perfected the aluminum stack valve. This lightweight alternative to the traditional cast-iron unit not only saves money in terms of reduced fuel use, but makes a significant contribution in terms of weight limitations on domestic highways.

Innovations from Teledyne Fluid Systems' Sprague Products are applied in pressure testing, as well as hydraulic and pneumatic circuits in production machinery. Sprague air-driven pumps offer a cost-effective method of converting low air pressure to high hydraulic output pressure up to 30,000 psi. Sprague gas boosters compress shop air or gases up to 10,000 psi.

Customers had seen nothing new in the field of air-driven pumps since the 1940s, until Sprague introduced PowerStar™ 4 in 1996. This patented pump system can be used to pump a wide variety of liquids to high-output pressures. It is assembled from modules, resulting in a broader product offering with reduced inventory levels. Seemingly overnight, PowerStar™ has become an industry leader.

Since the early 1940s, the Farris Engineering unit of Teledyne Fluid Systems has designed and produced a wide range of spring-loaded and pilot-operated pressure relief valves. Used as safety devices, they prevent overpressurization of vessels, pipelines, and equipment. Farris

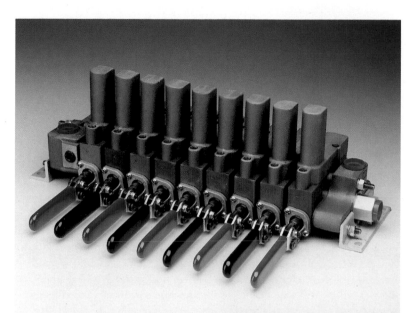

is a recognized leader in the hydrocarbon processing, refinery, petrochemical, natural gas production and transmission, pharmaceutical, and general processing industries worldwide.

A pioneer in the field, Farris Engineering created many products that remain industry standards. Integrating its core hardware technology with the information age, Farris originated computer software to assist customers in sizing and selection of valves. A recent reorganization of manufacturing plants and processes maximized production effectiveness to position the business unit at the forefront of the industry, with service and delivery second to none.

THE FUTURE: ACHIEVING EXCELLENCE IN CLEVELAND

Teledyne Fluid Systems is an operating company of Allegheny Teledyne Incorporated, a group of technology-based manufacturing businesses with significant concentration in advanced specialty metals, complemented by aerospace, electronics, industrial, and consumer products.

President Michael A. Gaudiani sums up the company's goals: "We are striving to be a company that achieves excellence in the eyes of our major stakeholders: customers, shareholders, and employees. We are serving customers with innovative, high-quality products delivered on time at a competitive price. We are helping provide Allegheny Teledyne shareholders with a solid and steadily growing return on investment. We are also developing a team-based work environment where employees' creativity and initiative are fostered, and where personal satisfaction and financial rewards from our company's success are significant enough to attract and retain the best talent available." And where better to do it than in Cleveland?

LONG RECOGNIZED AS A QUALITY LEADER, VEHICLE CONTROL PRODUCTS MANUFACTURES DIRECTIONAL CONTROL VALVES FOR AUTOMOBILE TRANSPORT TRUCKS AND CLASS 8 TRUCK TRANSMISSIONS (TOP).

IN 1996, SPRAGUE PRODUCTS INTRODUCED POWERSTAR™ 4, A PATENTED PUMP SYSTEM THAT CAN BE USED TO PUMP A WIDE VARIETY OF LIQUIDS TO HIGH-OUTPUT PRESSURES (BOTTOM).

ORTH AMERICAN REFRACTORIES COMPANY (NARCO) COMBINES THE basic elements of earth and fire to enable the creation of the most advanced industrial technologies. The company continues to pioneer the development of the essential products that help industries

NORTH AMERICAN REFRACTORIES COMPANY COMBINES THE BASIC ELEMENTS OF EARTH AND FIRE TO ENABLE THE CREATION OF THE MOST ADVANCED INDUSTRIAL TECHNOLOGIES (LEFT).

RESISTAL™ S60C PROVIDES EXCELLENT THERMAL SHOCK AND ABRASION RESISTANCE FOR SUCH STRUCTURES AS INCINERATORS (RIGHT).

worldwide do their job—refractory bricks, shapes, vessels, and other materials that can contain extremely high temperatures, withstand thermal shock and mechanical stress, and resist the physical and chemical attack of hot gases and molten metals.

As the foremost domestic provider of refractories and processing technology, NARCO supplies a wide range of consumer markets, including iron and steel, aluminum, cement, glass, foundries, waste incinerators, and other high-temperature process industries. From computer-assisted refractory design to the proven capability of planning, engineering, and constructing an entire plant, the com-

pany provides a broad range of services. NARCO also operates the largest research center of its kind in the United States.

Because of its technical capability, venerable reputation, and diverse product line, NARCO maintains strong supplier relationships with its customers, providing them with a full line of dependable, technically advanced products and services. Additionally, the company's extensive engineering and design capabilities allow it to work with customers to reduce refractory costs and enhance performance.

Moreover, with annual sales exceeding $300 million, NARCO distinguishes itself from the competition by achieving an intimate knowledge of its customers' operations, an understanding of what products might best suit a particular set of customer conditions, and an ability to supply its customers with the most cost-effective products. With a presence in 31 cities throughout the United States and Canada, the company's knowl-

edgeable sales force boasts comprehensive experience in related industries.

THE MERGER THAT STARTED IT ALL

NARCO was formed in 1929 in a merger of seven independent manufacturers of fireclay brick and specialty products that were located in Ohio, Pennsylvania, Kentucky, and Missouri. North American Refractories Ltd., a Canadian affiliate, was also acquired at that time. The company was headquartered in Cleveland because the Dover Fire Brick Company, the largest of the merging firebrick companies, was already located in the city.

The merger was quickly followed by diversification and growth throughout the 1930s and 1940s, including several acquisitions that added new manufacturing capacities and an expanded product line. In 1932, Fred Sweney—a student at the Cleveland School of Art whose wildlife

sketches later brought worldwide fame to the Brown and Bigelow calendars—designed the familiar NARCO Indian and arrowhead logo at the request of his father, the company's chief engineer. The colorful emblem symbolized NARCO's refractories made from flint fireclay.

Over the years, the company led the industry in procuring new raw materials from around the world. In 1960, NARCO began the manufacture of conventional, basic refractories. In 1965, the company became a subsidiary of Eltra Corporation, which was acquired by Allied Corporation in 1979. Subsequent acquisitions by Allied led to major reorganization, including the dissolution of Eltra Corporation, and NARCO became part of Allied's Chemical Division.

In the early 1980s, NARCO entered two new areas of the refractories business: the manufacture of slide gate systems for the steel industry and contract services, whereby the company not only manufactures the product, but also designs, installs, cures, and delivers it to the customer in a ready-to-use state.

CURRENT OWNERSHIP

*I*n 1986, NARCO engineered a leveraged buyout by a group of investors and top management to once again become a private, independent entity. After purchasing a 35 percent interest in the company in April 1988, Didier-Werke AG of Wiesbaden, Germany, obtained controlling interest in November 1989. In January 1991, NARCO merged with Didier Taylor Refractories Corporation, a 100 percent-owned Didier-Werke AG subsidiary located in Cincinnati, and the surviving company was named North American Refractories Company.

When the Veitsch-Radex Group of Vienna, Austria, acquired

controlling interest in Didier-Werke AG in 1995, the largest refractory company in the world was thus created. Currently, NARCO maintains its corporate offices in Cleveland's Halle Building and operates nine plants in the United States, which manufacture a variety of fireclay, high alumina, basic brick, and monolithic products. These facilities are located in Ohio, Kentucky, Pennsylvania, Michigan, Missouri, Indiana, and California. There are also seven warehouses throughout the country to facilitate distribution of products to customers in nearby territories. NARCO's Canadian affiliate, NARCO Canada Inc., oversees facilities in Burlington,

Ontario, and Bécancour, Québec. To date, eight of the facilities, including the two in Canada, are ISO 9002 certified.

Zircoa Inc., now a wholly owned subsidiary, was acquired in 1994 from Didier-Werke AG via a stock transfer. Located in Solon, Ohio, Zircoa manufactures zirconia-based ceramics.

As NARCO prepares for the challenges of the 21st century, the company's backbone remains its 1,400-plus people, who are responsive, results oriented, and ready for the future.

CLOCKWISE FROM TOP: NARCO'S PRODUCTS ARE USED TO LINE SUCH STRUCTURES AS PLANETARY COOLERS AND KILNS.

THE IRON AND STEEL INDUSTRIES DEPEND ON NARCO'S REFRACTORIES TO WITHSTAND THE EXTREMELY HIGH TEMPERATURES REQUIRED DURING WELDING AND FORGING.

AFTER CURING AND REMOVING THE MANDREL, THE PRECAST LADLE IS REMOVED FROM THE MOLD AND TRANSFERRED TO A DRYER FOR MOISTURE REMOVAL.

CHASE FINANCIAL CORPORATION HAS BEEN IN THE CONSUMER lending business in Cleveland since 1930. The company's products and services include home equity loans and lines of credit, as well as financing for manufactured homes. Chase Financial offers these

products and services to consumers through networks of dealers, brokers, and correspondents, as well as through retail and direct-to-consumer marketing channels.

Chase Financial is a subsidiary of The Chase Manhattan Corporation, the largest financial institution in the nation, with assets of $300 billion. Anchored by this solid financial base, Chase Financial has grown significantly since 1995.

Recent growth has been fueled by an increased demand for products and services, as well as new market penetration and geographic expansion. Between 1995 and 1997, Chase Financial doubled

its workforce, primarily in response to an expanding servicing portfolio. Today, the company employs approximately 1,100 people nationwide in the originations, servicing, and field sales areas. Roughly 700 of these employees work at Chase Financial's Cleveland headquarters.

Chase Financial employees are dedicated to developing innovative loan programs that meet the unique challenges of the company's niche markets. For all those who work hard to achieve or sustain a good life in a world of enormous opportunity and challenge, Chase strives to be the complete financial resource and ally that makes life easier.

CLEVELAND ROOTS

Chase Financial Corporation traces its Cleveland roots back to 1930, when Sun Finance and Loan Company was formed to provide community residents with small personal loans. Sun began to open offices throughout the country and was renamed SunAmerica. The company's national presence and profitability made it attractive to larger financial institutions, and, in 1975, Chemical Banking Corporation purchased SunAmerica and renamed the organization.

As Chemical Financial Services Corporation, the company's focus

IN 1992, THE COMPANY MOVED INTO ITS CURRENT HEADQUARTERS IN THE CHASE FINANCIAL TOWER IN DOWNTOWN CLEVELAND.

shifted from small loans to its current product mix. In the late 1980s, Chemical formulated a strategic plan to grow the businesses more rapidly and to integrate operations within the company. In 1992, Chemical Financial moved from its Euclid Avenue location into the company's present Tower City site.

In 1996, The Chase Manhattan Corporation merged into Chemical Banking Corporation, and the Cleveland entity was renamed Chase Financial Corporation.

PARTNERS IN THE COMMUNITY

*T*oday, Chase Financial is building a strong presence in the Cleveland community both as a major employer and as a corporate resource to the area's nonprofit organizations. Working with Cleveland's Business Volunteerism Council, Chase Financial has helped recruit volunteers and board members for the community's charitable and social service organizations. The company also supports the arts locally as a corporate benefactor to the Cleveland Museum of Art and the Cleveland Orchestra.

People who come to work for Chase Financial enjoy the convenience of the company's Tower City Center location downtown. This cosmopolitan business and retail complex houses an assortment of businesses, restaurants, and specialty and department stores. Employees from all points of the city have access to public transportation that can bring them within a short walk of Chase Financial Tower.

Firmly grounded in the Cleveland community, Chase Financial will continue to be a significant presence in the city well into the next century.

THE PLAZA IN THE TOWER CITY COMPLEX HOUSES CHASE FINANCIAL'S SERVICING OPERATION.

CHASE FINANCIAL CORPORATION TRACES ITS CLEVELAND ROOTS BACK TO 1930, WHEN SUN FINANCE AND LOAN COMPANY WAS FORMED TO PROVIDE COMMUNITY RESIDENTS WITH SMALL PERSONAL LOANS.

LTV STEEL COMPANY, INC.

UCH LIKE THE CITY IT CALLS HOME, LTV STEEL IS EXPERIENCING a renaissance. The company has a long and exciting history— punctuated by numerous mergers, a restructuring of the steelmaking industry, and the challenges of succeeding in a rapidly changing

industry. Nonetheless, LTV has focused on three objectives: to provide complete customer satisfaction, increase shareholder value, achieve profitable growth, and make a meaningful contribution to the communities in which it operates.

Today, LTV is a leading producer of high-quality, value-added, flat-rolled steel in the United States. And the company strives for continued growth—by using new technologies to maximize profit; entering new steel and steel-related businesses; and developing strategic business alliances to achieve growth and access to new technologies and markets. The $4 billion-plus company is preparing

to enter the 21st century with talents and technologies gleaned from many sources and high hopes for the future.

A LONG HISTORY IN GREATER CLEVELAND

LTV's lineage includes some of the oldest names in American industry—Jones & Laughlin Steel, Youngstown Sheet & Tube, and Republic Steel. The company's original investors were attracted to the venture for the same reason: the fundamental need for steel—in everything from cars to lawn mowers to appliances.

Local industrialist Cyrus Eaton created Republic Steel, one of LTV's predecessor firms, in 1930. To

fashion the new company, he merged Cleveland's Republic Iron and Steel Co.—which had been formed from 30 small iron companies in 1899—with Central Alloy Steel Corp. in Canton, Ohio, and Trumbull-Cliffs Furnace Co. in Warren, Ohio. Eaton was joined by Tom Girdler, then president of Jones & Laughlin Steel (J&L), who left J&L to become Republic's first president. Eaton added to Republic's operations by purchasing the Corrigan McKinney Co. in 1935, thereby providing the company with the east-side operations of its Cleveland Works.

Meanwhile, J&L was building substantial operations of its own, particularly in the Pittsburgh area and in Cleveland, with the acquisition of the Otis Steel Co. on the west bank of the Cuyahoga River. In 1968, J&L was acquired by The LTV Corp., a Dallas-based aerospace and electronics conglomerate. A decade later, LTV acquired Youngstown Sheet & Tube, giving LTV a flat-rolled steelmaking plant in northwest Indiana—strategically located in the heart of the industrial Midwest. Today, that integrated steel plant, the Indiana Harbor Works in East Chicago, Indiana, is a vital part of LTV's core flat-rolled steel operations.

In the early 1980s, global economic forces combined to create dramatic changes in the U.S. steel industry. The dollar rose astronomically, as compared to foreign currencies, and low-cost steel imports flooded the American market. In response, steel producers began a comprehensive restructuring. It was in this environment that Republic Steel and LTV merged, creating LTV Steel, a

LTV STEEL HAS INVESTED MORE THAN $1.5 BILLION IN ITS CLEVELAND OPERATIONS IN THE LAST 10 YEARS ALONE, STRENGTHENING ITS COMMITMENT TO A LONG-TERM FUTURE IN ITS HEADQUARTERS CITY.

BARNEY TAXEL

DESIGN PHOTOGRAPHY INC.

SCORE PHOTOGRAPHERS

wholly owned subsidiary of The LTV Corp. The merger gave the newly formed company two large flat-rolled operations in Cleveland and East Chicago, Indiana, each with the newest continuous slab casting facilities.

Since 1986, LTV has extensively modernized its core production facilities, enhancing the ability to produce flat-rolled steel for quality-critical markets, such as the automotive, appliance, and electrical equipment industries. Major capital projects have included state-of-the-art vacuum degassing and ladle metallurgy facilities; the Direct Hot Charge Complex and the Continuous Anneal Line at the Cleveland Works; and computerized gauge and tolerance controls at the company's hot strip mills and tandem cold mills. In addition, LTV formed two electrogalvanizing joint venture companies with Sumitomo Metal Industries, Ltd. The companies are located in Cleveland and Columbus, Ohio.

PROGRESS AND GROWTH FOR THE 21ST CENTURY

*T*oday, LTV Steel and its 14,000 employees are pursuing long-term profitable growth. Producing 8.8 million tons of continuously cast steel in 1996, LTV ranks as the third-largest integrated steel producer in the United States. In addition, the company is the second-largest maker of flat-rolled steel and the largest producer of ultralow carbon steels, carbon electrical steel sheets, and electrolytically galvanized (finished) steel sheets. LTV's sales climbed to more than $4.1 billion in 1996, a year in which its steel mills operated in excess of their industry-related capacity, reflecting improvements in productivity.

LTV places a high priority on its civic and community involvement, continuing its long-standing support and commitment to

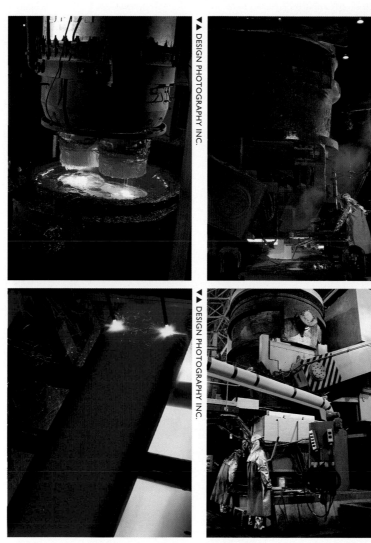

DESIGN PHOTOGRAPHY INC.

DESIGN PHOTOGRAPHY INC.

education by providing financial and other forms of support for the elementary and secondary schools in its plant communities. In Cleveland, the company sponsors the LTV Steel Science and Technology Institute summer study program for high school students. LTV participates in a number of college scholarship programs, including those designed to serve minority students. The company also continues to provide scholarships for children of LTV employees through the National Merit Scholarship Program. Both scholarship initiatives are funded by the LTV Foundation.

As part of Cleveland's Bicentennial Village project, the company provided financial support to Habitat for Humanity for the construction of 24 new steel-

framed houses—an inner-city community development project established in honor of the city's bicentennial in 1996. LTV employees play an important role in their communities as well, as they continue to give generously to the United Way, hunger prevention programs, and other local charities.

LTV Chairman David Hoag sums up the company's philosophy by saying, "LTV is committed to achieving lasting success, which is in the best long-term interest of our customers, shareholders, employees, and communities. Our future depends on our ability to satisfy our customers' needs, provide shareholder value, anticipate and benefit from rapid changes in technology, and grow profitably within the global steel industry."

CLOCKWISE FROM TOP LEFT: LADLE METALLURGY/VACUUM DEGASSING FACILITIES ENABLE LTV STEEL TO PRODUCE APPROXIMATELY ONE-THIRD OF THE PREMIUM ULTRALOW CARBON FLAT-ROLLED STEEL MADE IN THE UNITED STATES.

THE CLEVELAND WORKS NO. 1 CASTER HOLDS THE NORTH AMERICAN PRODUCTION RECORD FOR TWIN-STRAND SLAB CASTERS.

THE DIRECT HOT CHARGE COMPLEX IN CLEVELAND ENABLES LTV TO CHALLENGE THE PRODUCTIVITY OF MINIMILLS MAKING FLAT-ROLLED STEEL AND TO PROVIDE IMPROVED QUALITY STEELS FOR PIPE, TUBING, AND SERVICE CENTER CUSTOMERS.

GAS-FIRED CUTTING TORCHES CUT CONTINUOUSLY CAST SLABS TO SPECIFIED LENGTHS PRIOR TO ROLLING AT AN LTV HOT STRIP MILL.

WITH ITS LONGTIME ABILITY TO FIND THE EXCITEMENT— the electricity—in products where it is least expected, Meldrum & Fewsmith Communications has firmly established itself among the leading marketing communications agencies in the Midwest.

To communicate the electricity found in its clients' products, Meldrum & Fewsmith strives for truly great advertising. As a result, the agency has developed a reputation for providing an outstanding level of results-oriented strategic thinking, combined with an award-winning, highly memorable creative product.

In fact, no other Ohio-based agency can match Meldrum & Fewsmith's record of major national, regional, and local awards won over the past decade. "We have a strong heritage of creating great advertising," notes Chris Perry, chairman and chief execu-tive officer. "We recognize that, while many things have changed in the world of advertising, Meldrum & Fewsmith's commitment to that goal will never waver."

A TRADITION OF EXCITEMENT

Meldrum & Fewsmith's steadfast commitment to its mission of constantly provid-ing clients with new ideas that will drive their businesses has helped the agency grow from modest beginnings. From a four-person advertising shop founded 67 years ago with a handful of accounts, Meldrum & Fewsmith has been transformed into a $126 million, full-service agency with a staff of 115.

Meldrum & Fewsmith's quest for excellence has shaped the agency from the outset. Account man Joseph Fewsmith and copy chief Barclay Meldrum had al-ready established their ability to make advertising magic with their work for the Jordan motorcar in the Roaring Twenties. With more than 20 years' experience, Meldrum and Fewsmith struck out on their own, opening the doors of their own agency on the inauspicious date of April 1, 1930.

Yet, despite its beginning during the early months of the Great Depression, Meldrum & Fewsmith grew, with names like H.K. Ferguson, Carling Brewing, Ford Tractor, Bonne Bell, Durkee Foods, and Parker Hannifin join-ing the roster.

Over the years, Meldrum & Fewsmith created memorable, results-oriented work for these high-profile clients, along with scores of others. In fact, prior to her groundbreaking work for *Life* magazine, world-famous photo-journalist Margaret Bourke-White shot photographs used in Republic Steel ads created by the agency. Meldrum & Fewsmith helped Glidden launch Spred Satin, the world's first successful latex paint. And the agency introduced the now famous "A Company Called TRW" campaign.

NEW DIRECTIONS, POSITIVE RESULTS

As the agency moved into the early 1980s and beyond, the number of business-to-business and heavy industrial advertisers on Meldrum & Fewsmith's roster decreased

MELDRUM & FEWSMITH'S COR-PORATE OFFICES ARE LOCATED IN THE RENAISSANCE BUILDING IN DOWNTOWN CLEVELAND.

SCHUEMANN ARCHITECTURAL PHOTOGRAPHY

Every product has the **POWER** to excite. All you need is the **ELECTRICITY**.

▶ MICKEY JONES

THEY SAID IT WAS COARSE, OBSCENE, THE PATH TO MORAL DECAY. SOUNDS LIKE THE PERFECT GIFT.

ROCK AND ROLL ISN'T JUST SURVIVING. IT'S THRIVING. So GIVE YOURSELF OR SOMEONE ELSE WHO ROCKS A CHARTER MEMBERSHIP TO THE ROCK AND ROLL HALL OF FAME AND MUSEUM. YOU'LL GET A VERY COOL LIMITED-EDITION T-SHIRT. FREE ADMISSION FOR ONE YEAR. AND, WHILE THEY LAST, A SPECIAL HOLIDAY ORNAMENT. ALL FOR JUST $35. HEY, THEY SAID ROCK AND ROLL WOULD NEVER LAST. WELL, IT DID. BUT THIS SPECIAL CHARTER MEMBERSHIP OFFER MAY NOT. SO GET THE GIFT THAT ROCKS RIGHT NOW AT BORDERS BOOKS & MUSIC, RECORD REVOLUTION, VINTAGE RECORDS, THE AVENUE AT TOWER CITY CENTER, AND CAMELOT MUSIC LOCATIONS AT GOLDEN GATE AND THE GALLERIA. OR PICK UP THE PHONE AND CALL

1 - 8 0 0 - 3 1 7 - R - O - C - K

as more consumer brands and services joined the client ranks. Today, the agency has among its clientele such names as Libbey Glass, Mr. Coffee, University Hospitals of Cleveland, Continental General Tire, Health o meter, Grange Insurance, Rubbermaid, and Royal Appliance.

Meldrum & Fewsmith has also made important contributions to the community, with pro bono advertising work for clients such as the Rock and Roll Hall of Fame and Museum; Clean-Land, Ohio; Girl Scouts and Boy Scouts of America; United Way; and Health Hill Hospital for Children.

The agency has not grown solely with the addition of new clients. In 1992, Meldrum & Fewsmith nearly doubled in size overnight through its acquisition of Hesselbart & Mitten/Arocom, an advertising, direct marketing, and sales promotion agency located in Fairlawn, Ohio.

The combined agencies moved into new offices on three floors of the Renaissance Building, located on Euclid Avenue in downtown Cleveland. The move renewed Meldrum & Fewsmith's longtime commitment to the Playhouse Square neighborhood, while giving the expanded firm an up-

dated home with room for continued growth. Three years later, Meldrum & Fewsmith further differentiated itself from its competitors by eliminating the departmental hierarchy found at most agencies. Instead, it adopted a structure of client-centered teams in which all levels of client and

agency personnel are more directly involved with one another, and project responsibilities are intertwined at every step. These teams are physically located within specially designed office areas, creating an atmosphere of working in coordinated units to meet one goal: generating new ideas that will drive business for clients.

Today, Meldrum & Fewsmith can go beyond delivery of traditional advertising solutions to its clients and offer totally integrated marketing communications programs, including sales promotion, direct marketing, Yellow Pages, and even interactive options such as developing and maintaining client Web sites on the Internet.

No matter what the communications discipline, says Perry, Meldrum & Fewsmith continues to work from the position that "every product has the power to excite. All you need is the electricity. We believe there's human drama to be found in every brand relationship, no matter how pragmatic or mundane it may appear. The trick is finding it, then conveying it with excitement.

"Yet we haven't lost sight of the reason that message is created," adds Perry. "We strive to create an emotional bond with the target audience and make them take action in the marketplace. We have very definite standards all of our work must meet. It must be unexpected, insightful, well crafted. And, most important, it must have the power to excite."

CLOCKWISE FROM TOP LEFT: THE AGENCY'S SLOGAN EXEMPLIFIES ITS BELIEF THAT, ACCORDING TO CHAIRMAN AND CEO CHRIS N. PERRY, "THERE'S HUMAN DRAMA TO BE FOUND IN EVERY BRAND RELATIONSHIP, NO MATTER HOW PRAGMATIC OR MUNDANE IT MAY APPEAR. THE TRICK IS FINDING IT, THEN CONVEYING IT WITH EXCITEMENT."

PERRY TODAY OVERSEES A $126 MILLION FULL-SERVICE AGENCY WITH A STAFF OF 115.

MELDRUM & FEWSMITH HAS DEVELOPED A REPUTATION FOR PROVIDING AN AWARD-WINNING, HIGHLY MEMORABLE CREATIVE PRODUCT, AND HAS CREATED ADVERTISING CAMPAIGNS FOR SUCH CLEVELAND BUSINESSES AS THE ROCK AND ROLL HALL OF FAME AND MUSEUM.

1931

1946

OM GROUP, INC.

1947

RPM, INC.

1947

WEWS NEWSCHANNEL 5

1951

WYSE ADVERTISING

1953

REALTY ONE

1959

GARLAND FLOOR CO.

1962

MIDWESTERN NATIONAL LIFE INSURANCE
COMPANY OF OHIO

1963

CENTRAL RESERVE LIFE INSURANCE COMPANY

1963

CUYAHOGA COMMUNITY COLLEGE

1964

CLEVELAND STATE UNIVERSITY

1964

KAISER PERMANENTE

1965

DEVELOPERS DIVERSIFIED REALTY CORP.

1967

ASSOCIATED ESTATES REALTY CORPORATION

1967

PIERRE'S FRENCH ICE CREAM CO.

ONE TASTE IS ALL IT TAKES FOR CLEVELANDERS TO LOVE PIERRE's French Ice Cream Co. But once they learn about the company's proud history in and commitment to its hometown, they're likely to appreciate Pierre's even more. Pierre's was founded in 1932 as a small

ice cream shop at Euclid Avenue and East 82nd Street. Its gourmet French ice cream, prepared fresh daily, was sold by the cone or cup, or hand-packed for take-home orders. As the ice cream's popularity grew, Pierre's began selling its products to restaurants, country clubs, and grocery stores.

The company shared its first plant with the Royal Ice Cream Company at Hough Avenue and East 60th Street, and ultimately merged with Royal in 1960. Then, in 1967, Pierre's purchased the Harwill Ice Cream plant at East 65th and Carnegie, where the company's headquarters and manufacturing facilities remained until 1995. That year, Pierre's moved

into its newly constructed offices and distribution center on Euclid Avenue, just a mile from where the company originally set up shop.

Pierre's now makes more than 250 flavors of ice cream, sherbet, frozen yogurt, and novelty products. Through the years, the company has delighted local palates with such unique ice cream flavors as Pumpkin Pie, Cinnamon, Nutcracker Sweet, Chocolate Covered Pretzels 'n Cream, and Triple Play. In addition, Pierre's has added no-sugar and fat-free items to its product line, as well as sorbet and the new Frosted Smoothie™. It is also the exclusive distributor of Häagen-Dazs in northern Ohio. Customers include grocery stores, restaurants, hospitals, schools, amusement parks, and sporting arenas.

Pierre's currently sells its products in Ohio, Indiana, Michigan, Pennsylvania, Georgia, North and South Carolina, Aruba, Saudi Arabia, and Korea, but President Shelley Roth says the company

will further expand within the United States in the coming years.

COMMITTED TO CLEVELAND

Throughout its 60-plus years, Pierre's has maintained a strong commitment to the city of Cleveland, particularly its own neighborhood, the MidTown Corridor. A successful example of urban redevelopment just east of downtown, the corridor has evolved into a thriving commercial, industrial, and residential neighborhood over the past 15 years with the help of companies like Pierre's. "There wasn't a speck of green in MidTown before Pierre's persuaded some of its neighboring businesses to do some landscaping, fix the sidewalks, and make other aesthetic improvements to the area," says Roth. Since then, new businesses have moved into MidTown and others have expanded.

The company's other contributions to the community are numerous: Pierre's helps local organizations in their promotional efforts by providing the ice cream for their get-togethers. "Different organizations use our products to help them gain awareness. It seems like the community has adopted us as its local treat," says Roth. Pierre's has been especially active in Mothers Against Drunk Driving (MADD) and Students Against Driving Drunk (SADD)—passing out ice cream on Public Square to promote "don't drink and drive" themes.

Pierre's began its life making quality frozen desserts with creative flavors. Today, through its delicious desserts and ongoing contributions to the community, the company is still providing Clevelanders with tastes to savor.

CLOCKWISE FROM TOP:
THE COMPANY'S HEADQUARTERS AND DISTRIBUTION CENTER, BUILT IN 1995, IS JUST A MILE AWAY FROM ITS ORIGINAL LOCATION.

THE 40,000-SQUARE-FOOT PIERRE'S DISTRIBUTION CENTER IS KEPT AT 25 DEGREES BELOW ZERO AND HOUSES MORE THAN 36 MILLION SCOOPS OF ICE CREAM.

THE WIDE VARIETY OF PIERRE'S ICE CREAM AND FROZEN YOGURT OFFERS SOMETHING FOR EVERYONE.

MARCUS ADVERTISING, INC.

ADVERTISING HAS ALWAYS PLAYED AN IMPORTANT ROLE IN Cleveland's development as a major business center. And no other agency has played a bigger part in the development of the city's retail and consumer-based advertising than Marcus Advertising.

The agency was formed in 1946 as Marcus Advertising Art by brothers Marvin and Donald Marcus. Marvin, a graphic designer, and Don, a former movie publicist, recognized the need for an agency that could sell clothing and shoes in a town where others were selling metal ingots and machine tools.

MODEST BEGINNINGS

In the firm's initial years of operation, Don and Marvin had fewer than a handful of employees and counted General Television and Giant Tiger Stores as the agency's key retail clients. In 1979, Marvin retired and Don remained as president. In 1984, Don's nephew, Harvey Scholnick, returned to Marcus after 14 years as a senior vice president with J. Walter Thompson Advertising in Chicago. Today, Scholnick leads a team of more than 50 talented individuals and represents some of the most prominent companies in Ohio and throughout the nation, including Centerior Energy, Pizza Hut, Kelly-Springfield Tires, Manpower Temporary Services, Meridia Health System, Ohio Lottery, and TravelCenters of America.

The agency's growth has been steady—never the roller-coaster ride commonly associated with the dynamic business of advertising. Much of that steady rise is due to the family control of the agency and its strict adherence to five basic rules: "Manage clients' money like it was your own, produce great creative work, treat your employees fairly, think before being asked to think, and never be afraid to try new things."

INNOVATION AND EXPERTISE

In the late 1940s, Marcus was among the first agencies in the city to recognize the importance of television as an advertising medium. But the agency didn't settle on just producing television commercials. Marcus produced entire client-sponsored programs, including The Gene Carroll Show, the longest-running television show in Cleveland's history.

In the 1970s, the agency again demonstrated its expertise with broadcasting. Marcus developed a statewide television network for the Ohio Lottery and created the nation's first weekly lottery television show, now called *Cash Explosion Double Play*. The agency also produces an annual schedule of remote lottery broadcasts and regularly scheduled satellite videoconferences for the Ohio Lottery and other Marcus clients. Today, the agency is considered the nation's leading authority on lottery advertising.

Marcus also leads Ohio in its sports marketing expertise, having represented the Cleveland Indians, Browns, Cavaliers, and Lumberjacks with both image and ticket-sales campaigns.

The agency's entrepreneurial spirit is evident in its efforts to develop on-line marketing capabilities for clients. In the early 1990s, for example, Marcus created an on-line advertising system for one of the nation's largest banks, making it possible for bank staff members to access their ads and make changes on-line, 24 hours a day. Marcus was also among the first agencies to establish a digital marketing division. Today, DigiKnow, the advanced projects division of Marcus Advertising, is a national leader in on-line marketing. DigiKnow clients include the Cleveland Indians, Detroit Red Wings, Kelly-Springfield, Summa Health System, and other leading companies.

SINCE 1946, MARCUS ADVERTISING HAS HELPED SELL EVERYTHING FROM MRS. FIELD'S COOKIES TO PEPPERONI PIZZA, OHIO LOTTERY GAMES TO BROWNS AND INDIANS SEASON TICKETS, ELECTRIC POWER TO DIESEL FUEL AND TIRES, AND HEALTH CARE TO TEMPORARY HELP.

SEALY, INC.

EALY, INC. MAY BE PERCHED ATOP THE MATTRESS INDUSTRY, BUT the company doesn't take its challenges lying down. Serving more than 7,000 retail outlets from 26 facilities in 25 states, as well as Canada, Mexico, and Puerto Rico, Sealy remains the largest manu

facturer of bedding in North America. Through its subsidiaries, the company produces and sells a complete line of mattresses under the Sealy, Sealy Posturepedic, and Stearns & Foster brands.

Under the leadership of President and CEO Ron Jones, who joined the company in March 1996, Sealy has reaffirmed the position it has maintained since the early 1970s as the industry leader. Having weathered some difficult challenges from competition and ownership changes in the late 1980s and early 1990s, the company has introduced a significant number of new products and implemented a number of aggressive marketing and sales programs to enhance its approximately 20 percent market share in the $3.2 billion U.S. bedding market.

TAKING SEALY BEDDING WORLDWIDE

Recognizing the exciting potential for sales expansion around the globe, Sealy created a rapidly growing international division in 1994; the group features specialists in international marketing, bedding merchandising, manufacturing, and finance. In an effort to solidify its world leadership position, the company continues to initiate strategic expansion plans into a number of markets beyond North America.

"The rationale for our expansion is clear: There are 280 million people in the United States, where Sealy is the market leader, yet there are over 5 billion people outside of North America," says Jones. "Our goal is to strategically introduce our quality brands into new markets where they will be strongly supported with appropriate targeted marketing, sales education, and point-of-purchase efforts."

In 1995, the company began direct exporting of Sealy Posturepedic sleep sets, the world's largest-selling premium mattresses, to South Korea through a network of distributors in that country. In 1996, Sealy opened a 100,000-square-foot plant in Toluca, Mexico, where it has begun manufacturing Sealy-brand bedding for the Mexican market. Currently, the company is analyzing demographic, financial, legal, and market factors in a number of other foreign markets. The company also has licensees operating in Australia, Israel, Jamaica, Japan, New Zealand, South Africa, Thailand, and the United Kingdom.

FROM TEXAS ROOTS TO CLEVELAND HEADQUARTERS

The company has come a long way from its humble origins in Sealy, Texas, a small town near Houston, where an industrious cotton gin and gristmill builder began making cotton-filled mattresses for his neighbors in 1881. His inventive method for compressing long-staple cotton fiber into an "air

"voven" batt resulted in a resilient, tuftless mattress. By 1906, the innovative mattress maker had sold his patents and equipment to a Texas corporation, which kept the Sealy trade name for the popular mattresses.

The company continued to grow through a licensing program, and, by 1924, it had 28 licensed plants. The thriving business prevailed over the Great Depression of the 1930s by introducing a new product, the button-free innerspring, as springs began to outrank cotton in popularity. During the 1940s, the company developed a specially constructed mattress that incorporated the recommendations of orthopedic surgeons regarding the benefits of a firm sleeping surface. This new product served as the prototype of the now-famous Sealy Posturepedic line of mattresses, unveiled in the 1950s. In addition, Sealy claimed the introduction of king-size bedding in 1956.

During the 1960s, the company commissioned the first major research study to define the profile of the Posturepedic consumer, and to this day, Sealy carefully monitors consumer buying patterns and comfort preferences. Capitalizing on the growing power of television advertising, in 1967, Sealy instituted another first for the industry by running prime-time television commercials. Key product refinements occurred over the next decade, including programmed coils for increased support and the development of the torsion bar module for box spring foundations.

In December 1983, Sealy purchased the Stearns & Foster Company, which was founded in 1846 and had grown into one of the largest premium-brand manufacturers in the United States.

By 1989, Sealy had taken two major steps to achieve further growth. The first was the introduction of the industry's newest innerspring innovation, the Posturetech® Coil. The second, which had a more far-reaching impact on the company, was the resolution of decades of litigation with one of Sealy's largest licensees, the Ohio Mattress Company, owned and operated by Ernest Wuliger, a Cleveland native. Wuliger quickly completed acquiring all but one domestic licensee and consolidated them into a single enterprise. As a result, Sealy relocated its headquarters operations from Chicago to the Cleveland home of Ohio Mattress and moved into new offices in the Halle Building. In April 1989, a leveraged buyout (LBO) took the company private. Although the business remained healthy, the timing of the LBO eventually led to Sealy's

being resold to an investment fund, which has retained it as a private company.

Today, with retail sales exceeding $1.3 billion, Sealy employs more than 4,900 people throughout North America, including approximately 150 in the Cleveland offices and the world's premier bedding R&D center in Middleburg Heights. The company sells its products through furniture stores, leading department stores, sleep shops, and mass merchandisers, and is a key supplier to the hospitality industry. After more than 110 years of prominence in providing people with the ultimate in correct back support and sleeping comfort, Sealy remains committed to serving in its role as the industry leader.

CLOCKWISE FROM TOP LEFT:
THE COMPANY SELLS ITS PRODUCTS THROUGH FURNITURE STORES, LEADING DEPARTMENT STORES, SLEEP SHOPS, AND MASS MERCHANDISERS.

IN 1995, THE COMPANY BEGAN DIRECT EXPORTING OF ITS FAMOUS SEALY POSTUREPEDIC SLEEP SETS, THE WORLD'S LARGEST-SELLING PREMIUM MATTRESSES.

THROUGH ITS SUBSIDIARIES, SEALY PRODUCES AND SELLS A COMPLETE LINE OF MATTRESSES, INCLUDING THE STEARNS & FOSTER BRAND.

CHARTER ONE'S NAME FITS THE ORGANIZATION WELL. ON THE surface, it means the former savings and loan was the first financial institution in the country to win a government charter to become a federal savings bank. In addition to its historical significance, the

name conveys a sense of innovation, growing size, and industry leadership.

Charter One originally was organized as First Federal Savings and Loan Association of Cleveland in 1934 at East 55th Street and Broadway Avenue in Cleveland, primarily serving the area's Czechoslovakian community. The bank's founder, Charles Frank Koch, ran the institution as a small neighborhood thrift until the late 1960s. At that time, his son, Charles Joseph Koch, who had spent 30 years in the aerospace industry as an engineer, made a career change, becoming chairman of the family business

with a charge to grow the company. By expanding First Federal's branches to Cleveland's suburbs, he grew its assets to nearly $200 million by the mid-1970s.

Later, with the help of his sons—Charles John "Bud" Koch, who became president and chief operating officer in 1980, and John D. Koch, head of lending operations, who joined the bank in 1982—First Federal's growth exploded. By the mid-1990s, its assets totaled $14 billion, it had become the fifth-largest federally insured financial institution in Ohio, and it ranked among the top 10 savings banks in the country.

BUILDING A HERITAGE OF GROWTH

The growth of Charter One has not been without glitches—such as the national savings and loan crisis of 1980 and the stock market crash of 1987. Yet this Cleveland institution has managed to weather the storm through smart strategies and keen investments. Bud Koch, now chairman and CEO, says that in 1980, the bank adopted a strategic plan calling for geographic expansion and product diversification. "We wanted to avoid being too dependent on one market and product," he says, referring to the need to offer products and services beyond traditional savings accounts and home mortgages. To help achieve that objective, the original savings institution obtained the first federal savings bank charter in the United States.

In the early 1980s, the bank merged with small Ohio institutions in Youngstown, Columbus, Chillicothe, and Willoughby. By 1982, thanks to its diversification efforts, "the savings and loan crisis was over for Charter One," recalls Koch. "Every year since then, we've had an impressive earnings year." In the late 1980s and early 1990s, Charter One acquired such local entities as First Federal Savings and Loan of Akron, Broadview Federal Savings Bank, Women's Federal Savings Bank, First Federal Savings and Loan Association of Toledo, and First American Savings Bank in Canton. In an effort to raise funds for further expansion, Charter One converted to a public stock company in 1988 and created a holding company, Charter One Financial, Inc. In

CHARLES JOHN KOCH IS CHAIRMAN AND CHIEF EXECUTIVE OFFICER OF CHARTER ONE BANK AND ITS PUBLICLY HELD PARENT, CHARTER ONE FINANCIAL, INC.

◀ BARNEY TAXEL

1995, the bank doubled its size by merging with First Federal of Michigan.

Charter One today bears little resemblance to the small neighborhood thrift of 1934—except perhaps in its tradition of family leadership and commitment to Cleveland. As of early 1997, the bank had some 2,500 employees, with 95 offices in Ohio and 80 in Michigan. Its market capitalization was the sixth largest in the country, and its share price appreciation had grown 33 percent annually since going public. Charter One's stock, which was offered for an adjusted $3.38 per share in 1988, was trading at $43 per share just nine years later. "It's been a terrific investment for everybody," says Koch.

True to its strategic plan, Charter One offers a great diversity of products. In 1996, for example, the bank originated $3.8 billion in residential, consumer, and business loans and leases. Other products and services include free checking, supermarket banking, mutual funds, tax-deferred annuities, and debit cards.

AN INVALUABLE CORPORATE CITIZEN

Despite its exponential growth, Charter One has maintained a sense of its heritage. "We have a corporate desire to support the city of Cleveland to the extent that we can," says Koch, noting that all of Charter One's back office operations, such as check processing and other administrative functions, have been combined in Cleveland. As part of that consolidation, the bank spent $3 million rehabilitating an old library building in the Memphis-Fulton area and moved 200 employees there. "We could have taken the easy way out and relocated the center to an industrial park in the suburbs; instead, we kept an income tax base of 200 employees in the city," Koch explains.

Koch himself is involved in Cleveland Action to Support Housing, which provides services such as below-market-rate loans to urban dwellers to help rejuvenate the city's neighborhoods. He also is a trustee of Cleveland Tomorrow, an organization of local executives who work on redevelopment issues, and Village Capital Corp., one of Cleveland Tomorrow's spin-off groups. Village Capital also works to rehabilitate older housing in Cleveland. Koch notes that, as a corporate citizen, "Charter One has a commitment to stabilize the neighborhoods of its core city."

The future bodes well for Charter One, which has been positioning itself to stay one step ahead of the many changes in federal banking legislation. Today, it may not look like a small thrift on Broadway, but Charter One is securing for itself a long future and a prominent place in Cleveland's business history.

FOUNDED IN CLEVELAND IN 1934, CHARTER ONE BANK OPERATES NEARLY 180 BANKING CENTERS IN OHIO AND MICHIGAN.

WITH ITS STRATEGIC POSITIONING AS A CONSUMER-ORIENTED RETAIL BANK, CLEVELAND-BASED CHARTER ONE BANK DELIVERS A RANGE OF COMPETITIVELY PRICED, ATTRACTIVELY PACKAGED FINANCIAL SERVICES.

KICHLER LIGHTING GROUP IS ONE OF THE BRIGHTER LIGHTS IN Cleveland's renaissance crown. The company's growth has paralleled Cleveland's, emerging from its humble origins to become one of the largest and most respected players in the decorative lighting industry.

Privately held, Kichler is widely known as the leader in product designs and customer service, as well as in advanced marketing programs for its lighting customers.

The company is the talk of the trade, winning back-to-back A.R.T.S. Manufacturer of the Year awards in 1994 and 1995, as well as a lighting industry Academy of Achievement award for Chairman Sam Minoff, recognizing his lifetime of accomplishments. In 1996, Sam and CEO Barry Minoff won the prestigious Entrepreneur of the Year award for northeast Ohio as sponsored by Ernst & Young, *USA Today,* and the NASDAQ market system. The company was also inducted into the Family Business Hall of Fame at Case Western Reserve University's Weatherhead School of Business.

For all its success, Kichler Lighting is the kind of organization that has not forgotten the values that propelled it to its current leadership position. Kichler's customers rate the company as one of the easiest to do business within the industry. They also report that Kichler management remains close to the business. "They understand the business, they are the best at what they do, and they care about us as customers," said one individual.

Much of this attitude can be attributed to Sam Minoff and to the humble origins of the company. Kichler Lighting was established in 1938. In 1954, Sam purchased the nearly defunct company for $5,000 and, in the first month of his ownership, sold only $1,000 worth of lighting.

Today, the company has

CHAIRMAN SAM MINOFF (CENTER) NOW SHARES THE LEADERSHIP OF KICHLER LIGHTING GROUP WITH SONS ROY (LEFT), WHO SERVES AS VICE PRESIDENT, AND BARRY (RIGHT), WHO SERVES AS CEO.

CLEVELAND-BASED KICHLER LIGHTING IS WIDELY KNOWN AS THE LEADER IN PRODUCT DESIGNS AND CUSTOMER SERVICE, AS WELL AS IN ADVANCED MARKETING PROGRAMS FOR ITS LIGHTING CUSTOMERS.

more than 1,000 employees around the world, including 350 at its Cleveland headquarters. Kichler Lighting's sales volume places it number one in residential decorative lighting in the United States and Canada, and perhaps in the world.

The Kichler Lighting Group is made up of six product divisions. The largest is Kichler Lighting, which manufactures a complete line of decorative lighting fixtures for the home. The product line covers the full spectrum of residential lighting, from outdoor lighting to bathroom lighting fixtures to dining room chandeliers, with prices ranging from under $10 to more than $4,000. Westwood Lighting, a recent acquisition located in El Paso, Texas, is noted for its top-quality, yet moderately priced, brass table and floor lamps. Another acquisition, Hartford Prospect, based in Manchester, Connecticut, manufactures lamps, as well as a full range of Tiffany-style fixtures. Minoff Lamp grew from within the Kichler organization and specializes in high-end designer portable lamps. The Kichler Landscape Lighting line was also an internal start-up and has grown to become one of the nation's top producers of professional quality landscape lighting. And, finally, Glass Industries of Wallingford, Connecticut, is a supplier of glass to lighting industry manufacturers.

Barry Minoff attributes the strength of the firm to its emphasis on design, service, quality, and marketing. In an interview with a lighting trade magazine, Minoff proclaimed, "What Kichler does best is design innovative products—we create a salable product at a value price. We service better than anyone, and our marketing programs are leading edge."

Kichler's 631,000-square-foot, 40-acre headquarters in Cleveland is home to its adminis-

trative and manufacturing operations, as well as a central warehouse and distribution center. The company, which purchases materials from all around the world and sells its products on a global basis, has six outlying warehouse locations, three manufacturing facilities in Mexico, and multiple purchasing offices overseas.

Sam now shares the leadership of the family-owned company with sons Barry and Roy. He insists on extending that family atmosphere to all Kichler employees. In fact, one of Sam's core values as a businessman is to know the importance of treating employees like family. To that end, Kichler Lighting Group boasts the industry's strongest team of employees and nearly constant employment in Cleveland.

That sense of extending the family also translates to the company's support of the Greater Cleveland community, where the Minoffs support the zoo, several Cleveland museums, and a variety of local charities.

Since its founding nearly 60 years ago, Kichler Lighting Group has achieved a status that most young entrepreneurial organizations rarely attain. The company leads its industry in the United States, yet is geared for even greater future growth. In addition to internal development, Kichler plans to seek out acquisitions that will add to its existing manufacturing skills or create additional product lines. The company's goal is to become the largest and most profitable supplier of residential decorative lighting and accessories in the world. And if corporate history is any indication, Kichler Lighting will do just that.

CLOCKWISE FROM TOP LEFT: KICHLER LIGHTING PRIDES ITSELF ON MANUFACTURING SUCH DISTINCTIVE PRODUCTS AS CHANDELIERS THAT ARE MADE OF 24 PERCENT LEAD CRYSTAL AND ARE 24K GOLD PLATED.

HARTFORD PROSPECT, BASED IN MANCHESTER, CONNECTICUT, MANUFACTURES LAMPS, AS WELL AS A FULL RANGE OF TIFFANY-STYLE FIXTURES.

KICHLER OFFERS AN ARRAY OF OUTDOOR LIGHTING, INCLUDING LANDSCAPE PATH LIGHTS.

KICHLER'S CONTEMPORARY LINE OF CHANDELIERS FEATURES HALOGEN LIGHTING IN A NICKEL FINISH.

THE COMPANY MANUFACTURES A SIGNATURE MINOFF LAMP, A HALOGEN LAMP ACCENTED WITH BRASS AND CRYSTAL.

HOME OWNERSHIP HAS LONG BEEN AN IMPORTANT PART OF THE American dream. The goal of raising a family in a safe, secure neighborhood with good schools and access to convenient shopping has prompted newlyweds, young families, and recent immigrants

to work hard and save money for their first home. During the Depression in the 1930s, many Americans feared they would lose their homes due to lost jobs and low wages. Mortgage foreclosures nationwide rose from 75,000 in 1928 to more than 275,000 in 1932. In response, Congress passed the National Housing Act in 1934, which created the Federal Housing Administration (FHA) to insure home mortgages through the establishment of the Federal Savings and Loan Insurance Corporation.

In Cleveland, nearly one-third of city residents were unemployed or underemployed during the Depression. To keep the dream of home ownership alive, Ben S. Stefanski; his wife, Gerome; and a group of civic-minded investors applied for a federal charter in

1938 to create a savings and loan association in the vicinity of East 70th Street and Broadway Avenue.

Stefanski and his colleagues were challenged by the economic uncertainty of the time. However, the group persisted and finally won the charter. With initial capital of $50,000, Third Federal Sav-

ings and Loan Association opened its first office on Broadway Avenue on May 7, 1938.

YEARS OF GROWTH

*S*tefanski started small, serving many of the struggling immigrant families from Poland and other parts of eastern Europe who had settled in the area. Business activity grew, and the savings and loan association thrived.

Near the end of World War II, the Servicemen's Readjustment Act (also known as the G.I. Bill of Rights) gave each veteran the opportunity to acquire a low-cost mortgage loan. Local real estate activity boomed after the war as veterans took advantage of the loan program to buy homes in Cleveland and nearby suburbs. Third Federal Savings grew as it helped veterans and their young families begin a new life.

In the mid-1950s, Stefanski decided to expand the savings and loan by opening branch offices in growing Cleveland suburbs. By its 25th anniversary in 1963, Third Federal Savings had eight branches in addition to a new headquarters facility at 7007 Broadway Avenue. The assets of the savings and loan association had grown to $150 million, and its deposits were insured up to $10,000 each, a considerable reserve for the period.

Third Federal Savings continued to grow steadily through the sixties and seventies. By the end of 1982, its assets topped $1 billion. Around this time, federal legislation allowed the thrift industry to venture into new areas of business, such as commercial loans, demand deposit accounts,

MARC A. STEFANSKI (TOP) HAS BEEN CHAIRMAN AND CEO OF THIRD FEDERAL SINCE OCTOBER 1987. HE SUCCEEDED HIS FATHER, WHO RETIRED AFTER 50 YEARS OF SERVICE.

GEROME R. AND BEN S. STEFANSKI WERE COFOUNDERS OF THIRD FEDERAL SAVINGS (BOTTOM).

investing in government securities, and more. However, Stefanski decided Third Federal Savings would remain true to its original mission: to provide home mortgages for the residents of northeast Ohio. By staying its course, the savings and loan association could minimize risks and keep its overhead low for customers.

THIRD FEDERAL SAVINGS TODAY

*U*nder the direction of Ben and Gerome Stefanski's son, Marc, who assumed the post of chairman and CEO in 1987, Third Federal Savings now has assets exceeding $5 billion. Today, it issues more home mortgages than any other lending institution in northeast Ohio. The company retains its rich heritage by remaining headquartered in the same Cleveland neighborhood where it began.

"My father grew up in this area, now known as Slavic Village, and my parents wanted to help maintain a viable, vibrant community built on the pride of home ownership," says Marc Stefanski. "We've long been an important part of this neighborhood, and we remain committed to Cleveland—its neighborhoods and suburbs."

Today, Third Federal Savings is synonymous with personal service, stability, and sound financial management. With more than $5 billion in assets, 26 branch offices in northeast Ohio, and 600 associates, Third Federal Savings continues to enjoy solid growth by controlling costs and constantly looking for new ways to improve service. Updated technologies, such as immediate on-line loan approval, have made it even easier for Third Federal Savings customers to achieve their goal of home ownership. One innovative way the savings and loan promotes home ownership is by offering home buyers no-cost loans with

no up-front closing costs. Additionally, Third Federal home loans with only 15 percent down require no private mortgage insurance.

True to its local heritage, Third Federal Savings has joined efforts to increase the rate of home ownership in Cleveland neighborhoods. It has made home ownership more accessible and affordable to low-income residents through initiatives such as the Cleveland-Akron-East Cleveland Program that offers lower-interest-rate mortgages with only 5 percent down.

A close relationship with the communities, families, and individuals it serves has always been a hallmark of Third Federal Savings. Customers who walk into any branch today are greeted by a friendly hello from neighborhood loan officers. Marc Stefanski says that the savings and loan will never lose the personal touch that sets it apart from other financial institutions. Third Federal Savings looks forward to providing its special brand of friendly, personal service to future generations of home buyers in northeast Ohio.

CHAIRMAN MARC A. STEFANSKI AND PRESIDENT GEROME R. STEFANSKI, ALONG WITH BOARD MEMBERS, BREAK GROUND FOR THE MAIN OFFICE HEADQUARTERS LOCATED ON BROADWAY (TOP).

SURROUNDED BY FAMILY AND BOARD MEMBERS, THE STEFANSKIS CUT THE RIBBON TO SIGNIFY THE GRAND OPENING OF THE MAIN OFFICE IN SEPTEMBER 1994 (BOTTOM).

SINCE 1940, THE FLEDGLING PARTS BUSINESS THAT BROTHERS JACK, Joe, and Morton Mandel started with only $900 has grown into a multinational corporation with combined sales of more than $1.6 billion. And, as it heads into the 21st century, Premier Farnell

Corporation is well on its way to accomplishing its mission of becoming one of the world's leading industrial distributors.

The company's goal became attainable in April 1996, when Farnell Electronics, PLC, of Leeds, England, merged with Premier Industrial Corporation. With a focus on the United Kingdom and Europe, Farnell distributes electronic and electrical components in 16 countries. Premier distributes electronic components and industrial maintenance and repair products, primarily in North America.

Each reported more than $800 million in gross revenues during their last year as separate entities. Together, they represent the third-largest electronics distributor in the world.

"This compelling strategic combination offers tremendous opportunity for our shareholders, customers, and employees," says Morton Mandel, who served as CEO of Premier for 38 years until the merger and who now serves as Premier Farnell's deputy chairman. "The complementary geographical coverage of our respective organizations will form a strong foundation for enhanced growth in both electronics and industrial distribution."

AN AMERICAN SUCCESS STORY

In 1940, the Mandels purchased their Uncle Jacob's defunct auto parts business. The brothers' first inventory included $3,000 in parts sent by their Uncle Conrad in shiny yellow

boxes labeled with the trademark "Premier." With Conrad's permission, the Mandel brothers adopted the Premier name and began their relentless climb to success.

The early years were a struggle, as much of the nation's industrial production was devoted to World War II. Premier survived partly by selling make-do parts. For example, the company replaced steel grills with wooden ones painted silver to resemble the real thing.

By the 1950s, however, Premier had grown into a large, independent supplier of automotive replacement parts. Meanwhile, it entered the industrial maintenance market—the first in a string of strategic moves into promising niche markets. The company's growth triggered the purchase of additional space for shipping, warehousing, and offices in 1952. Two years later, Premier bought two nearby parcels for further expansion and opened its first facility outside Cleveland in Los

CUSTOMERS RELY ON PREMIER'S VAST PRODUCT SELECTION, DEEP INVENTORIES, AND EXCEPTIONAL SERVICE TO MAINTAIN AND REPAIR THEIR EQUIPMENT (LEFT).

REPAIR SHOPS DEPEND ON PREMIER'S INNOVATIVE PRODUCTS FOR FASTER AND BETTER REPAIRS (RIGHT).

BARNEY TAXEL

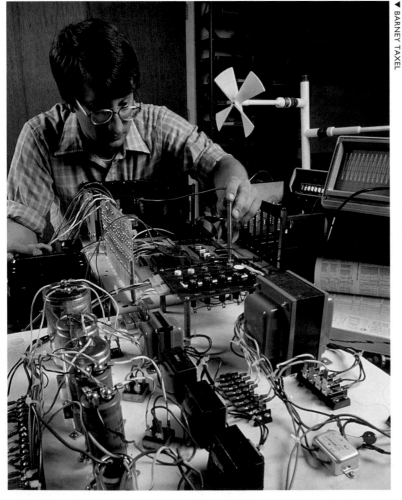

Angeles. In 1957, the company installed its first electronic data processing system.

The 1960s began with a move into Canada and the public offering of Premier's stock. In 1961, the company began a long tradition of providing fasteners to race cars in the world-renowned Indianapolis 500, and in 1962, Premier made its first acquisition. Prior to the 1996 merger, Premier acquired a total of 12 companies in complementary markets.

Despite a worldwide recession, Premier prospered during its fourth decade as a distributor of parts used in industrial maintenance, fire fighting, and electronics. In 1973, the company moved into international markets, primarily western Europe, while seeking out exclusive distributors in other, smaller countries. In addition, Premier opened a research and development center in Cleveland. By the 1980s, annual revenues had topped $300 million, the company had opened a distribution facility outside Cleveland in Warrensville, and it had established wholly owned operations in six countries and exclusive distributorships in 27 others.

Premier's success has not gone unnoticed. The company's devotion to customer service was chronicled in a 1990 *Business Week* cover story, and in 1995, Premier was among the companies profiled in the book *Making It in America: Proven Paths to Success from 50 Top Companies.*

TURNING TO PHILANTHROPY

*W*hen explaining the family philosophy, the brothers turn to their upbringing in a poor Cleveland neighborhood and the lessons learned from their parents. "When our values were being formed, we understood that helping someone who's hurting is part of what you do," they say.

The Mandels have always

MARTIN REUBEN

MARTIN REUBEN

been committed to civic improvement. The MidTown Corridor is a community development group launched by the brothers to help revitalize the neighborhood around Premier's headquarters. Morton Mandel played a leading role in forming Cleveland Tomorrow, which puts top CEOs to work helping to strengthen Cleveland and improve the quality of life for all citizens. For years, the Mandels have worked to build and strengthen the Jewish communities in Cleveland and Israel.

The Mandels' commitment to philanthropy is very apparent at Case Western Reserve University. Alongside the Mandel School of Applied Social Sciences, for

example, the Mandel Center for Non-Profit Organizations provides specialized management training for leaders of nonprofit agencies, who are often more in tune with their particular cause than operational issues and the bottom line. Since the Mandels supported the creation of the center, more than 15 other universities, including Harvard, have followed suit.

"There are always too few dollars to go around," the Mandels say. "What one wants to do is use those dollars to maximize the impact of nonprofit institutions on society." Today, the Mandels have focused on funneling much of their time and money into nonprofit causes. "What we really want to do is build a systematic philanthropic program that is focused on a few areas of concentration—and alongside that focus is also a sense of obligation to the whole community," they add.

That kind of commitment has ensured both Premier Farnell and the Mandels a strong presence in the Cleveland area for nearly six decades. Their legacy will continue to serve the community for years to come.

PREMIER FIELD REPRESENTATIVES ARE TRAINED TO SHOW HOW A CHANGE IN PRODUCT CAN REDUCE REPAIR COSTS.

THE COMPANY SUPPLIES A BROAD ARRAY OF ELECTRONIC AND ELECTRICAL PRODUCTS FOR USE IN PRODUCT DEVELOPMENT, MANUFACTURING, AND MAINTENANCE AND REPAIR.

OR MORE THAN 50 YEARS, AlliedSignal Truck Brake Systems Co. and its corporate predecessors have helped stop the trucks, tractor trailers, and buses navigating America's roads and highways. ❖ From its headquarters in Elyria, fewer than 30 miles west

of Cleveland, the company continues to wield a strong hand in the evolution of the brake systems used on air-braked vehicles around the world—not only on heavy trucks and tractor trailers, but also on buses, fire trucks, and off-highway vehicles. Already the industry leader in North America, AlliedSignal has responded to the globalization of the economy by moving overseas to serve foreign markets as part of an international joint venture. Simply put, the world is a safer place because of the company's line of Bendix® truck brake systems and components.

While remaining focused on its core business, the Elyria-based operation can rely on the management and financial support of AlliedSignal Inc., its diversified, multinational parent corporation. With annual earnings of more than $14 billion; extensive operations in aerospace, automotive, and engineered materials; and more than 76,000 employees, AlliedSignal is primed for the 21st century.

"We invite you to take a closer look at the continuing transformation at AlliedSignal and to follow our progress as we strive to fulfill our vision of becoming one of the world's premier companies," says Larry Bossidy, chairman and chief executive officer of AlliedSignal Inc.

PUTTING THE BRAKES ON HEAVY TRUCKS

Today, AlliedSignal Truck Brake Systems Co. directs all of its North American operations from Elyria, while manufacturing products in Kentucky, North Carolina, Indiana, and Mexico. Elsewhere in the world, the company is represented by its joint venture partner, Munich-based Knorr-Bremse AG, and operations in Italy, France, England, the Czech Republic, Hungary, Turkey, Brazil, Korea, Hong Kong, and China.

The company's mainstay products are Bendix AntiLock braking systems (ABS), Bendix air compressors, Bendix air dry-

FROM ITS HEADQUARTERS IN ELYRIA, FEWER THAN 30 MILES WEST OF CLEVELAND, ALLIEDSIGNAL TRUCK BRAKE SYSTEMS CO. CONTINUES TO WIELD A STRONG HAND IN THE EVOLUTION OF THE BRAKE SYSTEMS USED ON AIR-BRAKED VEHICLES AROUND THE WORLD. PRODUCTS FEATURED BY THE COMPANY INCLUDE BENDIX AIR DRYERS, COMPRESSORS, AND VALVES AS WELL AS FRAM HEAVY-DUTY FILTERS AND AUTOLITE SPARK PLUGS.

ers, and Bendix air brake valves installed by heavy-duty truck manufacturers or available from aftermarket dealers and distributors. The company also produces and sells a full line of heavy-duty FRAM® filters in the aftermarket.

While heading down the highway, motorists can be assured of the reliability of AlliedSignal braking systems on many heavy-duty trucks manufactured by Freightliner/Mercedes-Benz, Peterbilt and Kenworth, Navistar, Mack/RVI, Ford, Volvo, GMC, and Western Star. In addition, Bendix braking systems and components are used by many trailer and bus manufacturers.

A TECHNOLOGICAL STANDARD

The history of AlliedSignal Truck Brake Systems Co. parallels the gradual acceptance of air brakes as the technological standard for safety and reliability in vehicular travel. On April 13, 1869, when he was only 23 years old, George Westinghouse was awarded a patent for his latest invention: air brakes for use on railroad cars. Eventually, air brakes were also installed on logging trucks, tractors, cars, and other types of trucks. In 1930, the Bendix-Westinghouse Air Brake Company was formed by Westinghouse and Vincent Bendix, an automotive entrepreneur.

Bendix-Westinghouse moved its headquarters in 1941 to Elyria—today the site of AlliedSignal Truck Brake Systems Co.'s North American headquarters and engineering technical center. Spurred by World War II and a disastrous highway accident in 1955, virtually every tractor trailer in America is now outfitted with protection valves, such as the Bendix TP-1.

In 1982, after several shifts in corporate ownership, Bendix merged with Allied Corporation. The company became an operating unit of Allied Automotive, an independent supplier of Bendix, FRAM, and Autolite® products worldwide.

In 1986, Allied acquired the Signal Corporation and established AlliedSignal Inc. Since that time, all of AlliedSignal has been transformed by a restructuring effort and a renewed commitment to total quality. From 1991 to 1995, shareholders enjoyed growth in earnings per share at a compound average rate of 25 percent. Operating margins for the same period nearly doubled.

BRAKING INTO THE FUTURE

Today, AlliedSignal Truck Brake Systems Co. and its partner, Knorr-Bremse AG, form an international joint venture that is the world leader in air brake systems and components for heavy trucks. Driving toward the next century, the company is developing new technologies that will allow heavy truck operators enhanced braking, as well as improved traction control during acceleration. Someday, wires and electronic components will replace many mechanical and hydraulic components—helping reduce cost and improve safety and reliability for heavy-duty truck brake systems.

AlliedSignal continues to acquire attractive companies, move into untapped markets, and develop innovative products. Likewise, its Operation Excellence program will bring improved productivity, while rooting out even the slightest imperfections in manufacturing processes, thus allowing the company to compete more effectively in world markets.

Displayed prominently at facilities in 40 countries around the world is AlliedSignal's vision for the future in northeastern Ohio and beyond: "To be one of the world's premier companies, distinctive and successful in everything we do." If history is any indication, AlliedSignal Truck Brake Systems Co. is sure to stay on the road to success.

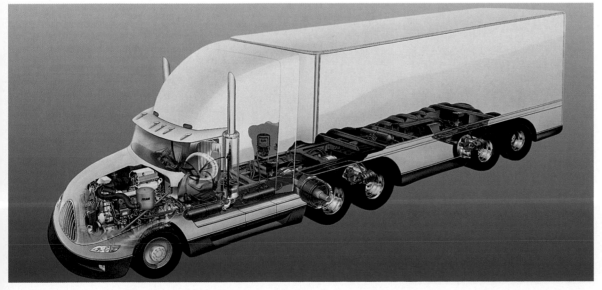

FOR MORE THAN 50 YEARS, THE COMPANY AND ITS CORPORATE PREDECESSORS HAVE HELPED STOP THE TRUCKS, TRACTOR TRAILERS, AND BUSES NAVIGATING AMERICA'S ROADS AND HIGHWAYS.

SINCE 1941, THE NATIONAL AERONAUTICS AND SPACE ADMINISTRATION's (NASA) Lewis Research Center has worked to develop technologies that send Americans into space and aircraft engine systems that quickly jet military pilots and travelers around the world. From its 350-acre,

FROM ITS 350-ACRE SITE, ADJACENT TO CLEVELAND HOPKINS INTERNATIONAL AIRPORT, NASA LEWIS CARRIES OUT ITS AERONAUTICAL, SCIENCE, AND TECHNOLOGY PROGRAMS IN 24 MAJOR FACILITIES AND MORE THAN 500 SPECIALIZED FACILITIES.

140-building complex adjacent to the Cleveland Hopkins International Airport, NASA operates and performs research in facilities as diverse as engine test cells, wind tunnels, and microgravity drop towers. In fact, NASA has designated the Cleveland facility as its lead center for aeropropulsion and its center of excellence in turbomachinery.

But NASA Lewis has also made contributions to everyday life. It has provided the technology behind the coatings on Bausch & Lomb's Ray-Ban® (Diamond® Survivor®) sunglasses, as well as software tools that helped develop the fans that will make the next generation of Kirby vacuum cleaners the quietest in the company's history.

In addition, NASA Lewis has transferred technologies developed at the center to companies involved in a wide variety of ventures. Through partnerships with the Cleveland Clinic and other organizations, NASA Lewis has contributed to developments in telemedicine, which allows doctors and patients in isolated or disaster-stricken areas access to consultation with world-renowned medical experts, and has brought its knowledge of pump design to an innovative heart pump that can assist patients awaiting a transplant. "Ultimately, we want the public to benefit from what we do," says Donald J. Campbell, director, NASA Lewis Research Center.

NASA operates the Advanced Communications Technology Satellite (ACTS), which provides solutions to a wide range of high-tech communication needs. "Through ACTS, we have given companies the ability to go into remote sites with a small antenna and real-time television. And we can connect them to some of the major medical facilities in the nation," Campbell says.

REWRITING THE SCIENCE BOOKS

NASA Lewis researchers conduct a variety of experiments in facilities sought after by companies and countries worldwide for their unparalleled capabilities in approximating zero gravity conditions in combustion and fluids. An outcome of these ground-based experiments was when the U.S. Microgravity Laboratory, launched in 1997, carried into space 11 experiments that were designed and managed by 10 investigators from both NASA Lewis and the Greater Cleveland community.

"Through this mission and others, we will gain a greater understanding of science in space that will better prepare us for liv-

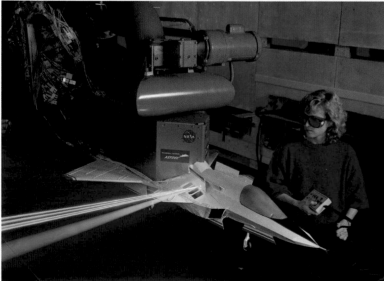

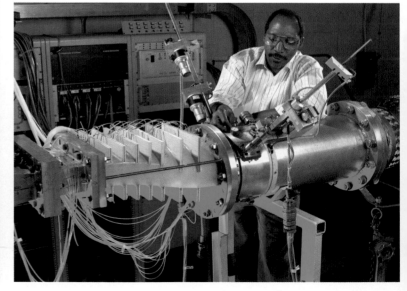

ing in space, while allowing us to rewrite some of today's chemistry and physics books," Campbell says.

MAKING FLYING SAFER

Established in 1941 as the Aircraft Engine Research Laboratory by the National Advisory Committee for Aeronautics (NACA), NASA Lewis was one of only three such centers nationwide. In October 1958, the NACA centers became the nucleus of the National Aeronautics and Space Administration. The Cleveland center developed an international reputation for its research on jet propulsion systems and pioneered changes in the manufacturing of jet engines to make flying safer. "The engine components on airplanes today are the result of research we conducted throughout the last 50 years," Campbell says. While making engines quieter, safer, and more environmentally friendly, NASA Lewis also has worked to develop ice protection devices that are now standard equipment on all commercial airliners.

By the year 2001, NASA Lewis researchers expect to have ready for commercial development a generation of low-cost, intermittent combustion engines and mod-

ern turbine engines for general aviation light aircraft. Shortly after the turn of the century, the center expects to unveil engines that will power the next generation of supersonic airliners, enabling travelers to go from Los Angeles to Tokyo in little more than four hours, instead of the 10 hours required aboard today's subsonic airliners.

TRANSFERRING TECHNOLOGY FOR PUBLIC USE

In recent years, transferring technology to companies for public use has become a primary focus of the center. "It's an important way taxpayers get a return on their investment," says Ann O. Heyward, chief of the Commercial Technology Office.

Applying aerospace know-how to other applications resulted when NASA Lewis surface experts developed a technique that can restore paintings damaged by smoke and fire. Through exposure to an environment originally developed to simulate that of low earth orbit in space, museum paintings can be restored without affecting the masterpiece itself. NASA Lewis has also worked with the U.S. Forest Products Laboratory to develop a thinner saw blade

capable of withstanding extreme heat without warping. The blade will allow lumber companies to get more wood from fewer trees with less waste, thereby accommodating loggers and environmentalists alike.

When Cleveland-based Tenatronics worked with NASA Lewis to test a cellular antenna designed for automobiles, a new product for the European market was developed. The NASA Lewis CARES/LIFE (Ceramics Analysis and Reliability Evaluation of Structures LIFE prediction) software program, originally designed to analyze engine structures made of ceramic materials, was modified to assess brittle materials ranging from hip joints to television picture tubes to dental crowns.

NASA Lewis employs more than 3,700 civil service and support service contract personnel. Through contracts, grants, utilities, salaries, and benefits, it adds more than $400 million to Ohio's economy, with an accumulated economic output exceeding $1 billion.

From infusing dollars into the economy to exploring new scientific ways of thinking, NASA Lewis has proved time and again that its presence in Cleveland is invaluable.

THE MORE THAN 3,700 CIVIL SERVICE AND SUPPORT SERVICE CONTRACT EMPLOYEES AT NASA LEWIS RESEARCH CENTER STRIVE TO DEVELOP NEW TECHNOLOGIES AND TRANSFER THEM TO COMPANIES FOR PUBLIC USE.

CENTRAL CADILLAC

THE RENAISSANCE OF CLEVELAND HAS BROUGHT A RESURGENCE OF business back to downtown. But Central Cadillac, downtown Cleveland's only automobile dealership, is a business that began there and stayed there. Central Cadillac was established in Cleveland in

1942 by George H. Lyon, owner of Central Chevrolet, one of the largest Chevy dealerships in Ohio. That year, General Motors (GM) appointed Central Chevrolet the Cadillac distributor for northeastern Ohio. Today, more than 55 years later, Central Cadillac's sales and service continue to thrive in the heart of downtown Cleveland, right where it all began.

Back in the early days of Central Cadillac, distributors sold Cadillacs to other dealers, acting as the wholesaler between the factory and the dealership. Lyon started Central with a loan from GM's Motors Holding Division, which was repaid over the years from company profits. The original dealership was located at 2040 East 71st Street, within the Central Chevrolet service facility.

THE END OF THE WAR BEGINS A NEW ERA FOR CENTRAL

During the years of World War II, no automobiles were produced in the United States. With the end of the war, production resumed in 1945. That year, Frank H. Porter Sr., Lyon's son-in-law, joined the company after serving in the war.

Three years later, construction began on the existing facility at 2801 Carnegie Avenue. Late in 1949, Central Cadillac opened at this location, with a distinctive building featuring a unique architectural design.

With the economic growth of the country after the war, Central Cadillac prospered as well, rising quickly to become one of the largest Cadillac distributorships and dealerships in the United States.

INNOVATORS IN AUTO SALES AND SERVICE

Central Cadillac's success can be attributed to instituting many new, innovative approaches in sales and service, according to Porter. "In the mid-1950s, we started the Prudential Finance Company, which helped finance cars sold by Central Cadillac, as well as other automobile dealers," he explains. "Buying an automobile on time was a new concept, and Central was one of the first companies in the area to offer this service.

"We were also in on the ground floor of the fledgling leasing industry when we formed Executive Leasing back in 1959," adds Porter. "Today, it continues to be one of the most successful leasing companies in the area, leasing Cadillacs, as well as all other makes and models, both new and used."

Likewise, Central Cadillac was an innovator in its approach to service. In 1954, the dealership instituted Central's Mobile Service, sending mechanics to customers' homes in special trucks—equipped with radio phones—to service customers' automobiles. Today, Central continues this service, along with 24-hour emergency roadside service.

Customers bringing their cars to Central's service facilities also enjoy a number of conveniences. The on-premise coffee shop enables customers to sit down, relax, and order a tasty breakfast, lunch, or snack while their autos are serviced. Central Cadillac also provides a courtesy car that drops off customers at their downtown offices when their cars are being serviced.

MORE THAN 55 YEARS AFTER ITS INCEPTION, CENTRAL CADILLAC'S SALES AND SERVICE CONTINUE TO THRIVE IN THE HEART OF DOWNTOWN CLEVELAND, RIGHT WHERE THE DEALERSHIP BEGAN.

◄ BARON PHOTOGRAPHY

THREE GENERATIONS
OF FAMILY OPERATIONS

*I*n 1965, Cadillac Motor Car eliminated its distributorship system, and Central Cadillac no longer sold cars to other dealers. That same year, Lyon retired from the business and Porter became president. In the early 1970s, two of Porter's sons, Frank H. Porter Jr. and George H.L. Porter, joined the dealership, bringing a third generation of the family into Central's operations.

Throughout the 1970s, 1980s, and 1990s, Central Cadillac has continued to serve the needs of Cadillac owners through excellence in sales and service. According to Frank Porter Jr., "Since we began, Central has sold and delivered over 130,000 cars. Historically, we sell close to 50 percent of the Cadillacs purchased in northeastern Ohio. We attribute this sales success to our solid management policies and our employees' strong commitment to excellence."

Today, Central Cadillac employs 95 people in various sales, service, clerical, and maintenance positions. A number of these employees have worked for Central for 20 years or more.

Mechanic Bob Smart has been with Central Cadillac since 1952. He credits his longevity with Central Cadillac to the fine people he works with and the strong management of the company. "You couldn't ask for better people to work with and for. Central is a very well-managed company," says Smart. "If we make a good impression, customers come back."

A COMMITMENT TO THE FUTURE

*L*ooking back on nearly 60 years of success, George Porter envisions an even brighter future for Central Cadillac. "We believe the future for Cadillac dealers is very bright, indeed," he says. "Over the past few years,

▶ BARON PHOTOGRAPHY

▶ BARON PHOTOGRAPHY

CUSTOMERS BRINGING THEIR CARS TO CENTRAL'S SERVICE FACILITIES ENJOY A NUMBER OF CONVENIENCES, INCLUDING AN ON-PREMISE COFFEE SHOP AND A COURTESY CAR THAT DROPS OFF CUSTOMERS AT THEIR DOWNTOWN OFFICES WHEN THEIR CARS ARE BEING SERVICED.

FAMILY MANAGEMENT CONTINUES WITH VICE PRESIDENT GEORGE H.L. PORTER (LEFT) AND EXECUTIVE VICE PRESIDENT AND GENERAL MANAGER FRANK H. PORTER JR. (RIGHT).

the Cadillac Division of GM has regained the reins of technological leadership with the North Star System and the all-new entry luxury sport sedan Catera.

"People are coming in to see these cars, and they are buying them. We're seeing a new, younger generation of customers," George Porter adds. "In many cases, they are the second or third generation of families who've been Central customers. We have a winning combination—the new Cadillac styling and Central's 55-year reputation for outstanding quality and service."

ELL KNOWN IN THE CLEVELAND AREA FOR MORE THAN 50 YEARS AS the leader in the fabric and crafts industry, Fabri-Centers operates more than 900 stores in 48 states, employing more than 18,000 creative people whose vision is "to serve and inspire creativity."

A look inside most American homes reveals creative people eagerly at work; some are carrying on a family tradition, while some only recently have discovered the pleasure of make-it-yourself activities. Fabri-Centers nurtures these creative spirits, providing a community gathering place where people find resources, tools, assistance, and inspiration. Whether their vision is to create decorator curtains, a hand-sewn doll, or a lush arrangement of silk flowers, customers know Fabri-Centers can help them turn a limited budget into unlimited creativity.

A MODEST BEGINNING

The story of how Fabri-Centers became the nation's largest fabric and craft retailer is a vivid example of the American dream in action. Started by two immigrant families who escaped from Nazi Germany, the company began in 1943 with a single, modest storefront, The Cleveland Fabric Shop, on the east side of the city. For more than 54 years, the company grew from storefronts to strip shopping centers to regional malls and back to strip centers as superstores.

Although Fabri-Centers is now publicly held, it has remained primarily a family-owned enterprise. Chairman, President, and CEO Alan Rosskamm, grandson of one of the founding families, provides the link to the company's past and is intent on successfully leading it into the 21st century. Today, Fabri-Centers stores, operated under the names Jo-Ann Fabrics & Crafts and Cloth World, offer more than 60,000 products and sell more than 100 million yards of fabric annually.

STRATEGY FOR GROWTH AND PROFITABILITY

In an effort to continue to serve and nurture its customers' creativity, Fabri-Centers is well poised for future growth and improved profitability, with specific strategies in place.

FOR MORE THAN 50 YEARS, FABRI-CENTERS OF AMERICA HAS ENCOURAGED CUSTOMERS TO DISCOVER AND DEVELOP THEIR CREATIVE SPIRITS THROUGH SEWING AND CRAFTING.

The company has repositioned itself from a group of small, mall-based stores to a chain of superstore destinations. This larger format has allowed Fabri-Centers to capitalize on the growing craft market by expanding its products to include craft, floral, seasonal, and home decor categories during a period when demand for these products is increasing.

Continuing its strategic transition to larger-format stores, the company opened 62 superstores and closed 90 smaller stores during the 1996 fiscal year. Management anticipates opening 50 to 60 new stores in fiscal 1997 and closing another 60 to 70 smaller stores.

Fabri-Centers also has invested in technology, which gives it a competitive advantage. Its industry-leading systems produce SKU-level merchandise tracking, permitting better purchasing and allocating decisions with fewer markdowns. These systems enhance customer service by providing scanning capabilities for faster checkouts, as well as improving store productivity by automating tasks.

Fabri-Centers is strategically committed to exceeding customer expectations with a focus on retailing fundamentals: having the merchandise the customer wants—well displayed and in stock—and providing friendly, knowledgeable service.

The company's traditional emphasis on quality ensures that customers will find the best materials for their creative efforts. Surveys indicate that customers are drawn to Fabri-Centers' variety of first-quality fabrics, and the company confirms its customers' confidence with a continually refreshed line of products. Its buyers travel the world, exploring the latest craft and fabric trends and seeking new sources for the materials that will encourage customers to pursue these

and other creative ideas. The superstore format, with more than 60,000 individual products, allows Fabri-Centers to be the one-stop shopping destination for sewers and crafters.

NURTURING CREATIVITY

One of the reasons people love sewing and crafting is that these interests often lead to interaction with others—friends, family, and even strangers—as they share ideas, experiences, and the passion to create. Recognizing this motive, Fabri-Centers has established its stores as community gathering places that encourage customers, even first-time visitors, to discover and develop their creative spirits.

A SPRINGBOARD FOR NEW IDEAS

In November 1995, Fabri-Centers opened Jo-Ann etc (experience the creativity), a 45,000-square-foot "lab" adjacent to its corporate headquarters in Hudson, Ohio, designed to test new concepts in sewing and craft merchandising.

This creative lab is three times larger than the standard superstore, with ample space to experience creativity through hands-on "try me" centers, ongoing classes, and demonstrations. Custom services include floral design, custom furniture, professional home decor sewing services, custom quilting, and custom framing. This new store is proving to be the ideal setting for the company to combine

its experience and expertise in fabric and craft retailing with new approaches to meeting customers' needs.

BREAKING NEW GROUND

Fabri-Centers continues to break new ground in the fabric and craft industry with an enhanced product mix, a clearer understanding of customer needs and shopping patterns, and fresh concepts for making its superstores better than ever.

The company intends to maintain a position of leadership in its industry by offering customers everything they need—materials, tools, assistance, and inspiration—to fulfill their creative dreams. As it continues to find new ways to nurture its customers' creativity, Fabri-Centers also is creating more value for everyone connected with the company.

WHETHER THEIR VISION IS TO CREATE DECORATOR CURTAINS, A HAND-SEWN DOLL, OR A LUSH ARRANGEMENT OF SILK FLOWERS, CUSTOMERS KNOW FABRI-CENTERS CAN HELP THEM TURN A LIMITED BUDGET INTO UNLIMITED CREATIVITY.

BORN THE YOUNGEST OF NINE CHILDREN, JOSEPH E. COLE, FOUNDER of Cole National, lived the American dream, rising from the poverty of the Great Depression to become a man who hobnobbed with U.S. presidents. Beginning his career at Cleveland's National Key

Company in 1935, the firm he would eventually purchase in 1944, Cole expanded the vision of this key-manufacturing business and, under his leadership, Cole National Corporation became a national specialty retailer of eyewear and giftware with more than 3,000 stores.

Cole believed in working hard, having high aspirations, and setting goals, a philosophy that he integrated throughout his business career. When he died in 1995, a small notebook with pages dated from the late 1930s was found among his personal papers. The notebook revealed Cole to be a highly ethical and goal-oriented individual. Some of his notations include: "Assert yourself with knowledge and confidence," "Develop a definite, active, and likeable personality," and "Look anyone in the face and honestly and fearlessly know that you have done what you thought was right

and best." Cole's philosophy for living translated into success for his business.

A RETAIL GIANT

The company's Cole Vision segment is the largest optical retailer in the world, operating approximately 2,000 locations under the names Sears Optical, Pearle Vision, Montgomery Ward, B.J.'s Wholesale, and Target Optical. These optical stores offer the personal touch of a private consultation with a doctor of optometry, combined with the advantages of purchasing frames from a large chain store. Customers can choose quality eyewear from a wide selection at great prices. In order to keep pace with the changing face of health care, the company recently launched the Cole Managed Vision Care program, which provides exclusive eye care benefits to more than 25 million people.

Cole also operates optical stores in Canada, Puerto Rico, and the Virgin Islands, and owns 20 percent of Pearle B.V., which operates 200 optical stores in Holland and Belgium, and is looking to expand to more countries throughout Europe.

Cole's other business is Cole Gift, the only national chain of personalized gift stores in the United States. The company's 1,302 stores include Cole Gift Centers, a chain of 505 leased gift departments located primarily in Sears, and more than 800 Things Remembered stores in major enclosed shopping malls.

Cole National pioneered the successful combination of retail and service formats that has earned the company a leadership position in the personalization business. The merchandise offered at the Cole Gift Center in Sears includes engraved gifts; such seasonal merchandise as gift baskets,

THE MERCHANDISE OFFERED AT COLE GIFT CENTERS IN SEARS STORES INCLUDES ENGRAVED GIFTS AND SEASONAL MERCHANDISE (BOTTOM LEFT), AS WELL AS BLANKET THROWS, STATIONERY, AND PICTURE FRAMES (BOTTOM RIGHT).

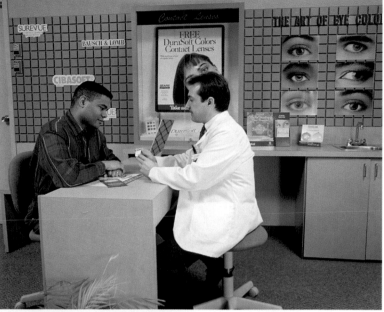

blanket throws, and greeting cards; and such services as key duplication.

Things Remembered and Things Remembered Superstores provide the consumer with a larger selection of personalized gifts. These stores offer while-you-shop engraving, key duplicating, monogramming, and glass etching, as well as private-label and brand-name merchandise.

A CORPORATE MAINSTAY IN CLEVELAND

*E*ver aware of its founder's humble origins, Cole National displays a steadfast commitment to its employees, its customers, and the city of Cleveland. The company takes strides to promote across-the-board employee appreciation and counts its dedicated workforce as its finest resource. Cole National also views itself as a place that offers opportunity for career growth for those willing to put forth the effort required to provide customers with the finest products, value, and service.

Founded and based in Cleveland, Cole National has been providing jobs to citizens of northeastern Ohio for more than 50 years. The company incorporates Cleveland's old-fashioned

values of hard work, foresight, and quality—values that will always remain ingrained in Cole's philosophy and culture.

Joseph Cole was truly a man with a clear vision for the future. He realized that with the right opportunity, a small venture had the potential to become an important player in the national and world markets. He understood that in order to support the ventures of a growing company, employees must be appreciated and allowed to express their ideas and concerns. Tapping Cleveland's

resource of hardworking people, Cole lived out the American dream and created a corporate giant with nearly 20,000 full- and part-time employees.

The Cole National culture continues to thrive under the leadership of Joseph Cole's son, Chairman Jeffrey Cole, who has overseen the company's growth since the early 1980s, and President Brian Smith, who with Cole is preparing the company to be a successful and important business and a quality place to work in the 21st century.

CLOCKWISE FROM TOP LEFT: AT ANY OF THE COLE VISION LOCATIONS, CUSTOMERS CAN CHOOSE QUALITY EYEWEAR FROM A WIDE SELECTION AT GREAT PRICES.

COLE VISION'S OPTICAL BOUTIQUES OFFER THE PERSONAL TOUCH OF A PRIVATE CONSULTATION WITH A DOCTOR OF OPTOMETRY, COMBINED WITH THE ADVANTAGES OF PURCHASING FRAMES FROM A LARGE CHAIN STORE.

THINGS REMEMBERED AND THINGS REMEMBERED SUPERSTORES PROVIDE THE CONSUMER WITH A LARGER SELECTION OF PERSONALIZED GIFTS. THESE STORES OFFER WHILE-YOU-SHOP ENGRAVING, KEY DUPLICATING, GLASS ETCHING, AND MONOGRAMMING, AS WELL AS PRIVATE-LABEL AND BRAND-NAME MERCHANDISE.

NIVERSAL GRINDING CORPORATION (U.G.C.), A PRECISION GRINDING facility, was founded in 1944 in downtown Cleveland across from what is now Jacobs Field. With the need for grinding on the rise following the end of World War II and the boom in the automotive

industry, business flourished. In the early 1950s, the Flats became the second home for the company. An increase in business brought about U.G.C.'s move in 1979 to its current, 80,000-square-foot building on Cleveland's near west side.

Like other manufacturers in the area, the company experienced tough times in the otherwise high-flying 1980s. Return on investment was low and competition was high. In 1986, the former owners of U.G.C. announced that the company would shut its doors for good.

This announcement changed the lives of many, including Donald R. Toth, who had gone to work at the U.G.C. plant where his father had once been a grinder. Don Toth began working at the company as a shipping clerk in 1958. While his coworkers contemplated their future unemployment, Don refused to throw in the towel. He recognized opportunity where others saw only despair. He believed that the quality of the products, the

commitment to service, and the dedication of its employees had kept U.G.C. afloat in previous hard times, and that the company could have future success if managed well. After the announcement, Don approached U.G.C.'s owners and negotiated the purchase of the company. Upon successful nego-

tiation, U.G.C. reopened and was back in business. In a matter of days, Don had become the company's owner.

Don made the decision to maintain U.G.C. in Cleveland. "We have access to skilled metal-working personnel, a superior transportation system, and a his-

TOP: THE MANAGEMENT TEAM OF UNIVERSAL GRINDING INCLUDES (STANDING, FROM LEFT) MARSHALL TOTH, BOB DRING, MONICA TOTH, MARK HOYT, (SITTING) MICHAEL HOYT, NANCY TOTH, DON TOTH, AND ED CINADR.

BOTTOM: THE PRODUCTS THAT U.G.C. MANUFACTURES ARE UTILIZED IN MANY INDUSTRIES, SUCH AS AUTO-MOTIVE, FOOD, AND MEDICAL.

our customers to obtain the end result they want."

Don adds, "From the standpoint of diversity in services offered, U.G.C. maintains a leading edge in the industry. Our capability to perform most all grinding operations makes our service very marketable." Among the grinding services offered are blanchard, centerless (infeed and thrufeed), double disc, hypro lapping, internal/external, and surface. In addition to grinding, U.G.C. can furnish items complete to blueprint specifications. "In lay terms, that means a customer provides a blueprint and U.G.C. will work with the necessary vendors to create a quality product. This is only possible by using some of Cleveland's other quality companies and resources to get the best final product possible," Don explains.

U.G.C.'s dedication to service is reflected throughout the organization in the personal pride its staff take in performing their jobs. "My goal is to improve my service every day. The better I perform, the more efficient we become," comments an employee. That attitude, Don explains, helps the company produce better products. U.G.C. also continues to upgrade as it grows, taking advantage of opportunities to enhance its reputation for providing high-quality products and superb service. Recent additions include a new computer system and a laser that marks, or etches, metals.

"Universal Grinding Corporation—as a company and a family—is firmly committed to Cleveland. We will continue to address new ways to improve our service and customer relations, to show the pride of a Cleveland-based company," concludes Don. "Our customers as well as our employees are the ones to be congratulated for the continued success of Universal Grinding Corporation."

U.G.C.'S PRODUCTS LIVE UP TO THE COMPANY'S MOTTO: "WHEN IT'S UNIVERSAL, IT'S GROUND TO BE GOOD."

tory of business in Cleveland that enables us to get our completed products to our customers on time. Cleveland is conveniently located in the Midwest and gives us the ability to serve our customers no matter where they are," comments Don. Although the majority of its customers are from Ohio and the surrounding states, U.G.C. also serves customers from coast to coast, as well as some international businesses.

Don is the owner/president and his wife, Nancy, serves as vice president. Four of their six children play a significant role in U.G.C.'s day-to-day operation. Don explains, "We not only have a business commitment to our customers, but a family commitment to U.G.C. and Cleveland as well."

While many industrial companies have left the city, U.G.C. has stayed and continued to succeed. A solid marketing plan, quality products, and timely deliv-

eries have helped the company become one of the largest job shop grinding facilities east of the Mississippi. The products that U.G.C. manufactures are utilized in many industries such as automotive, food, and medical.

In the past decade, U.G.C. has gone from hard times to a successful, thriving company. From 1993 through 1996 alone, 14 new pieces of equipment were added to handle the increase in volume. Monica Toth, U.G.C.'s sales/marketing manager, maintains, "The trust the company has inspired and the partnerships it has developed with its customers are responsible for the continued growth. U.G.C.'s motto is 'When It's Universal, It's Ground to Be Good,' and we truly believe that. Our customers look to us to produce the very best product and we continue to strive for excellence. We are willing to help with the research and development for

OM GROUP, INC.

A COMMON GOAL AND A CAN-DO ATTITUDE DISTINGUISH THE culture at OM Group, Inc. (OMG), a company without peer in the specialty chemicals field. "People like to work for a company that has a vision," says James P. Mooney, chairman and CEO. "But that

vision has to be one in which many people in the organization have reached the same conclusion as to where the company can be in five years."

OMG currently supplies more than 300 different product offerings to more than 1,500 customers in 50 countries. Of the company's 1996 revenues of $388 million, 75 percent was derived from cobalt-based products, with another 14 percent from nickel-based products. Customers in North and South America account for 40 percent of sales; European customers, 40 percent; and customers in the Asia-Pacific region, 20 percent. OMG products are used to manufacture everything from toner for copiers and printers to magnets, magnetic tapes, rechargeable batteries, and mining and machine tools.

"Our markets are key to our success because we sell additives for use in other chemical processes where the products are essential to the way people live throughout the world," says James M. Materna, CFO. "Our products typically represent a small portion of the total cost, but are critical to product performance."

FROM MOONEY CHEMICALS TO OMG

Founded as Mooney Chemicals, Inc. in 1946 by Mooney's father, James B. Mooney, the international metals-based company has experienced great success in its 50-plus years of business. Named president and CEO in 1975, the younger Mooney joined the organization in 1971, when annual sales totaled $2 million, and guided it to sales of $60

million by 1991, when the company merged with Outokumpu Chemical Oy of Finland.

Today, Mooney credits the exceptional development during that time to three key figures who shaped OMG's values, which remain the foundation for its continued success. First among those is his father, who instilled an emphasis on associate stewardship. Next is Leon Danco, who provided guidance on how to run a privately held company like a publicly held business. Finally, Dr. W. Edwards Deming and his lessons in quality helped OMG move from 10th to first among 13 primary competitors and become the first chemical company to receive Ford Motor Company's Q1 rating. "If we didn't have the principles of those three to operate with right from the start, I don't

OMG's APEX RECYCLING FACILITY IS LOCATED IN ST. GEORGE, UTAH.

think our future would be as bright as it is today," Mooney says.

The Outokumpu Mining division of Outokumpu Chemical Oy was seeking to divest itself of its cobalt chemical business in order to focus on its mining operations. In 1991, the parent company acquired all of the Mooney family's interest in the Cleveland business—except for the 5 percent retained by James P. Mooney—and combined it with Outokumpu Mining's cobalt chemical operations to form OM Group. The new OMG created a backward vertical integration that furnished the Cleveland operation with its own raw material supply and manufacturing facilities in Kokkola, Finland, as well as a smaller manufacturing operation in Ezanville, France. OMG quickly became the largest consumer and second-largest refiner of cobalt in the world.

AN ENLIGHTENED PHILOSOPHY

OMG backs up its enlightened philosophy of associate stewardship with concrete programs. In addition to extensive training initiatives that are available to everyone throughout the company, all associates have the opportunity to take courses in business graduate schools. OMG's health plan offers 100 percent hospitalization and is self-funded so that associates never have to worry about coverage. Additionally, the company's profit-sharing plan contributes up to 15 percent of the associates' earnings.

The combination of safety training and OMG's commitment to safety programs has also paid off tremendously. "Our Franklin, Pennsylvania, facility has gone 24 hours a day, seven days a week for eight years without one lost-time accident," says Eugene Bak, OMG's president and COO. "Our Kokkola plant, which used to have 10 lost-time accidents a month, has dropped to about three a year."

Another indicator of OMG's far-reaching dedication to its people is the company's annual sales-per-associate figure of more than $850,000, which equals at least twice the national average for the specialty chemicals industry. Presently, more than 95 percent of OMG's U.S. associates are shareholders, and the company is also developing a stock program for its European sector.

Targeted growth areas for the future include continued geographic expansion—in Central and South America and particularly in the Asia-Pacific region, which five years ago accounted for only 5 percent of OMG's sales and today claims 20 percent. The company will also continue to rely on growth from new products, which historically have represented 10 percent of its annual sales.

In fact, growth potential for OMG is so explosive that the company is poised to become one of only eight New York Stock Exchange or NASDAQ businesses to achieve 15 percent growth in earnings per share for five years in a row. Mooney concludes, "We have a lot more changes coming, and that's exciting."

OMG's ENLIGHTENED PHILOSOPHY OF ASSOCIATE STEWARDSHIP CAN BE TRACED TO FOUNDER JAMES B. MOONEY.

RPM, Inc.

RANK C. SULLIVAN FOUNDED HIS COMPANY IN 1947 WITH THE simple philosophy that people are an organization's best asset. His motto—"Hire the best people you can find, create the best environment to keep them, and let them do their jobs"—has served

Republic Powdered Metals, the forerunner of RPM, Inc., well for five decades. Not only has that approach created a company with a reputation for quality, but it has garnered record annual sales and earnings for 50 consecutive years. Today, under the helm of Frank's son, Chairman and CEO Thomas Sullivan, RPM has become a $1.3 billion holding company and an industry leader.

RPM was founded on Cleveland's west side to produce a heavy-duty protective coating known as ALUMANATION. Today, this product remains the largest-selling aluminum coating in the world, while the company has diversified its offerings to include more than 100 products that maintain and enhance buildings and structures. RPM produces coatings, sealants, and specialty chemicals that command top positions in industrial and consumer markets. Brand names include Rust-Oleum, B-I-N sealer, Bondo, Mar-Hyde auto body paints, Carboline, and Day-Glo. RPM products are used in waterproofing, general mainte-nance, corrosion control, and

other chemical applications. The company also makes do-it-yourself products for the home maintenance, automotive repair, consumer hobby, leisure, and marine markets.

SMART ACQUISITIONS

RPM's tremendous success is the result of smart acqui-sitions and internal growth. Says Sullivan, "We buy only good com-panies, serving niche markets, where the management is willing to stay on and work with RPM. We took my father's approach and turned it into an acquisition philosophy."

RPM reached its first $100 million sales year in 1979, and in 1995, it hit the landmark $1 bil-lion sales mark. The company has 75,000 shareholders and 5,000 em-ployees, 500 of whom work in Greater Cleveland, including 32 at its corporate headquarters in Medina. RPM also employs 600 sales representatives and maintains approximately 60 plants in the United States, Canada, and Europe.

RPM's largest acquisition was completed in February 1997—Tremco Inc., a BFGoodrich sub-sidiary that manufactures and sells sealants and coatings. Based in

Cleveland, Tremco employs more than 1,000 people at office and plant locations in the United States and 16 other countries. Its sales in 1995 exceeded $300 million. "The Tremco acquisition," says Sullivan, "allows RPM to accelerate the expansion of our core maintenance businesses." It also enhances RPM's continuing involvement in overseas markets. In the mid-1990s, foreign markets accounted for $200 million in annual sales. Another $100 million in annual sales came from licensees and joint venture agreements in other countries.

A key factor in RPM's development is James A. Karman, who joined the company in 1963 and became its president in 1978. Together, Karman and Sullivan have taken RPM, since its inception in 1971 after the death of Frank C. Sullivan, from annual revenues of $11 million to an estimated $1.3 billion for the fiscal year ending May 31, 1997.

A STRONG FUTURE

Over the years, RPM has consistently been a Wall Street favorite and one of the top 100 stock picks among investment clubs. In fact, the company has averaged a 21 percent annual rate of return for nearly 20 years. Sullivan believes the future looks even brighter.

"I think we're in a better position to grow than at any time in the past," Sullivan says, noting that RPM now has key young management working at both the operating and corporate levels. "This is a company where perseverance has really paid off—not only for our people, but for our stockholders." He notes that more than half of the company's earnings are typically paid out as dividends. "We have an unusually high dividend for a growth company," Sullivan adds. RPM has increased its annual cash dividend for 22 consecutive years.

RPM's success also has meant dividends for nonprofit organizations in the city of Cleveland. For example, the company's CEO is involved in Malachi House, a hospice for terminally ill homeless and indigent people on the near west side; May Dugan Service Center in the same area; and Urban Community School, a private, inner-city school serving the residents of the near west side. Sullivan also cochairs the Advisory Board of City Year. RPM has membership in Cleveland Tomorrow, an economic development group comprised of local chief executive officers, and has participated in the Commission on Poverty convened by the mayor's office.

Although RPM is representative of Cleveland's past, when the city was a hotbed of the nation's coatings industry, the company has successfully translated that heritage into a thriving present and a solid rank among the largest coatings companies in the world. With its energetic management and strong, sure business philosophy, RPM will continue to ensure Cleveland's role in the manufacturing world of today and tomorrow.

THE DATE WAS DECEMBER 17, 1947. AT 8 P.M., 300 HOMES EQUIPPED with new television receivers tuned in to see a ghostly test pattern flicker across the screens in their living rooms. The first image was a station identification: It read WEWS Cleveland. And so

began the era of local television broadcasting. Following that image, viewers in northeast Ohio were treated to their very first television remote broadcast, the "*Cleveland Press* Christmas Show" starring actor Jimmy Stewart.

WEWS marked the first venture into television by the Cincinnati-based Scripps Howard Company. In fact, the station's call letters were chosen in honor of Edward Willis Scripps, the company's founder. Scripps had strong ties with Cleveland, having founded his first newspaper, the *Penny Paper*, in the city. Its name would later be changed to the *Cleveland Press*.

FROM HUMBLE BEGINNINGS

When WEWS was originally established, its offices, studios, and storage space were all located in an old dance hall on East 13th Street near Chester Avenue in downtown Cleveland. There were few network or syndicated shows to use in programming the station, so the television pioneers of that time relied upon their creativity and talent to fill the airwaves with locally produced—mostly live—shows. The original WEWS studio on East 13th Street would alternately be turned from a classroom to an ice rink, to a dance hall, to a roller rink, to a boxing ring, to a bowling alley, and then back to a news studio.

Many of the early shows would be considered simplistic these days. One, *Arriving and Leaving*, featured host Paul Hodges walking up to unsuspecting travelers at Cleveland's bus station. Hodges would pop them a question, using the show's title. During slow periods, he was also known to talk with the drifters sleeping at the bus stop.

In the 1940s, programming was often considered secondary to the event of television itself. That there was television at all seemed far more important than what programs were available.

Sporting events lent themselves to live coverage, and WEWS proudly broadcast the 1948 World Series. Football, baseball, and hockey games made for popular television broadcasts, as did ribbon cuttings and parades. As the industry grew in size and audience, new and different kinds of shows were offered. WEWS continued to be an innovator in producing its own programs. There was the *One O'Clock Club*, a forerunner of today's talk shows, which was hosted by veteran Cleveland broadcasters Dorothy Fuldheim and Bill Gordon. Then there were

FRED GRIFFITH AND JAN JONES ARE SHOWN HOSTING *The Morning Exchange* IN 1977. THE SHOW WAS THE PROTOTYPE FOR *Good Morning America* AND HAS BEEN ON THE AIR SINCE 1972.

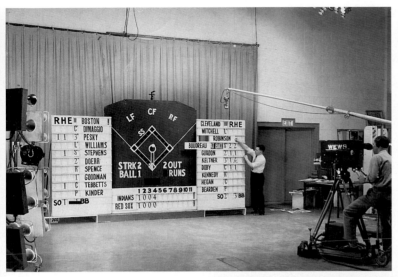

programs like *Bill Veeck Reports*, a sports commentary show, and talent showcases with Gene Carroll and the Polka Review, which later became known as *Polka Varieties*. Both *Polka Varieties* and *Upbeat*, a teen dance and music show hosted by Don Webster, would later become syndicated nationally and reach thousands of people throughout the United States.

In 1972, WEWS again took an unprecedented step into the future, introducing *The Morning Exchange*. The show's two-hour, live format was unique, and many national television programs, including *Good Morning America*, were patterned after it. In 1996, *The Morning Exchange* celebrated its 25th anniversary, and is now the longest-running program of its kind in the country.

WEWS TODAY

Fast-forward just over 50 years from the station's founding, and you will find an ultramodern, technologically advanced, full-service television facility located at East 30th Street and Euclid Avenue. Today known as NewsChannel 5, WEWS produces more local news and programming than any other station in northeast Ohio and, due to tremendous viewer support,

holds the exclusive title of "Ohio's Most Watched Newsteam."

In the fast-paced media world, where buyouts and mergers are standard fare, WEWS proudly remains as the anchor broadcasting station of today's E.W. Scripps Company. Despite the changes in

technology and the staggering growth of the television industry, WEWS remains firm in its commitment to quality broadcasting and to serving the communications and community needs of northeast Ohio.

CLOCKWISE FROM TOP LEFT: IN 1948, NORTHEAST OHIOANS TUNED IN TO NEWSCHANNEL 5 TO WATCH THE CLEVELAND INDIANS, ON THE WAY TO WINNING THE WORLD SERIES, PLAY THE BOSTON RED SOX IN A REGULAR SEASON GAME.

THE LATE DOROTHY FULDHEIM, PICTURED HERE HOSTING THE *Duquesne Report* CIRCA 1955, BEGAN HER TELEVISION BROADCAST CAREER IN 1947 AT AGE 55.

FIFTY YEARS AFTER ITS FOUNDING, NEWSCHANNEL 5 CONTINUES TO BE THE MARKET LEADER IN PROVIDING NEWS, INFORMATION, AND ENTERTAINMENT TO THE PEOPLE OF NORTHEAST OHIO. TED HENRY AND LORNA BARRETT ANCHOR A TEAM OF AWARD-WINNING PROFESSIONAL JOURNALISTS.

WYSE ADVERTISING

W hen ad buyer Marc Wyse teamed up in 1951 with copywriter Lois Wyse to publish a weekly column called *Wise Buys* for the *Plain Dealer*, neither dreamed that they would make advertising history in Cleveland. ❖ Yet that's exactly what they did. Today, more

than four decades later, Wyse Advertising not only ranks as Cleveland's largest ad agency, but also is one of the 100 largest in the United States and one of the 25 largest in the Midwest, with five divisions and 175 employees. Across the country, Wyse is known for its unique ability to combine solid strategic planning with high-impact creativity to develop fresh, intelligent, and memorable ads. The company's client list includes such impressive names as TRW, KeyCorp, Sherwin-Williams, American Greetings, and Applebee's Restaurants.

Impressive as its client list is, Wyse's ads are what catch people's attention. Whether promoting greeting cards or ball bearings, the agency consistently creates award-winning ads that get results.

That's due in part to the unique management structure of the company. President Michael Marino is an award-winning copywriter. Chief Operating Officer Howard Zoss offers an extensive background in strategic planning. And Chairman Marc Wyse says it's the blend of the two disciplines that is responsible for the company's success.

"We take tremendous pride in our creative product and feel that advertising is the art form of business," says Wyse, "but it's our attention to strategic planning that yields such good creative output."

That strategy has not only helped the company grow to a $140 million agency, but it has also helped grow Wyse's client

companies. In fact, growing clients has become something of a Wyse specialty. The company's "With a name like Smucker's, it has to be good" campaign helped turn a tiny jam and jelly manufacturer into a category leader. Today, that trend continues, as Wyse has seen its client Applebee's grow from 125 locations in 1992 into a nationwide chain of restaurants with 900-plus locations.

Throughout the years, Wyse has kept pace with the needs of its clients, adding five divisions to offer a comprehensive menu of services. Among them are iCatcher, which produces collateral material and sales promotions; Wyse Direct, specialists in direct marketing, including Internet communications; PinnAcle Media, a media buying service; Wyse-Landau Public Relations; and North Coast Behavioral Research. Each division serves not only Wyse Advertising clients, but its own as well.

Recently, the fast-growing company moved to impressive new quarters, with all divisions housed under one roof in an elaborate, 50,000-square-foot space in the prestigious Landmark Office Tower, complete with a glass-walled penthouse that offers 360-degree views of Cleveland's Public Square, Cuyahoga River, and Lake Erie.

As Wyse, Marino, and Zoss prepare the company for long-term success, they are confident that Wyse Advertising's blend of strategy and creativity will continue to fuel the company's growth for years to come.

GARLAND FLOOR CO.

LIKE THE CAT WITH ITS PROVERBIAL NINE LIVES, GARLAND FLOOR CO. has reinvented itself many times throughout its proud history in order to adapt to changes in technology and the marketplace. And, like that same cat, this Cleveland-based company has always landed on its feet.

Today, Garland offers ever expanding product lines of epoxy and other polymeric floor coatings, joint sealants, and renovating materials. The company is also finding new markets, such as pharmaceuticals and electronics, to add to its industrial base and has signed agreements with sales firms that will market its products around the globe. "We have capitalized on our strategic alliances," says Jonathon Wise, Garland's president. "I'm very upbeat about the future. We will be a significant player in our market."

EXPANDING WITH THE MARKET

Wise is the son of Garland's founder, Edward Wise, and the grandson of J.B. Wise, who in the late 1800s established a lubricating oil and paint company in Cleveland. By the 1940s, this predecessor firm had turned to selling building maintenance supplies, such as roofing products, coatings, and concrete patchings. And by the late 1950s, Edward Wise realized the many potential applications of epoxy resins, including the repair and sealing of worn and damaged concrete floors. This discovery led to the creation in 1959 of today's Garland Floor Co.

Garland sold its epoxy resurfacing compound by the drum, but Edward knew that in order for the compound to work effectively, the customer's floor had to be prepared properly. As a result, he developed the "total responsibility" concept, through which Garland prepared the floor and formulated, manufactured, and installed the epoxy flooring ma-

terial. Throughout the 1960s, 1970s, and 1980s, the company pioneered new methods of cleaning and resurfacing floors, and held its own as a major competitor in the marketplace.

In more recent years, as the market for floor installation contractors became flooded, Garland decided to focus on one of its strongest roots—the development of new technologies and markets. In 1988, the company's employees bought 25 percent of its stock, and in 1994, the contracting end of the business was sold when Garland acknowledged that it could no longer serve as both manufacturer and installer. "We had to face up to the realities of the marketplace," says Jonathon. The results of that decision, he adds, are starting to pay off. In 1996, for example, the company introduced 12 new products at an industry trade show.

Garland has invested a great deal of its resources in research and development. Among the company's most promising new products are a floor coating that provides protection from electrostatic discharge (an important find for customers who manufacture and assemble electronic components) and a variety of urethane coatings. In addition, Garland has entered into sales agreements with marketing representatives in the northwestern United States, Canada, and Mexico. Thanks to these developments and more to come, Garland Floor Co. expects to continue its heritage of success, with sales growing between 10 and 15 percent each year for the foreseeable future.

GARLAND FLOOR CO. OFFERS EVER EXPANDING PRODUCT LINES OF EPOXY AND OTHER POLYMERIC FLOOR COATINGS, JOINT SEALANTS, AND RENOVATING MATERIALS. WITH A STRONG, FLEXIBLE STAFF, THE COMPANY WILL CONTINUE ITS HERITAGE OF SUCCESS IN THE FLOORING BUSINESS.

EADQUARTERED IN CLEVELAND, REALTY ONE IS OHIO'S LARGEST real estate company, with annual residential sales of more than $2.5 billion. The company traces its origins to 1953, when Vincent T. Aveni founded Hilltop Realty in Lyndhurst, Ohio. After being joined

by his brother Joseph in 1959, the two men expanded the business through land development, as well as by building and managing condominiums, apartments, shopping centers, and office facilities.

The company grew in the 1970s when it added nine offices in Cleveland's eastern suburbs. In 1981, Hilltop acquired the 12 offices of HGM Realty, making HGM Hilltop the largest Realtor® in Ohio. In the next few years, many other independent companies would join HGM Hilltop. The 1987 merger of HGM Hilltop with Miller Bishop and Associates strengthened the firm's position as Ohio's leading Realtor. To mark this change, the organization was renamed Realty One on February 12, 1988.

Further growth came in 1989, when Realty One acquired Boebinger Realtors in the Akron/Canton area. Adding six counties

to Realty One's existing operations, these offices now form the firm's South Region.

Today, Realty One is a full-service real estate firm, with residential, commercial, property management, relocation and referral, and builder marketing divisions. The company enjoys stable and solid leadership, with Joseph T. Aveni as chairman of the board and chief executive officer, James C. Miller as president, and Vincent T. Aveni as chairman emeritus. This strong management is reflected in Realty One's enviable growth rate over the years: The firm is currently ranked as the top Realtor in Ohio and among the top 10 U.S. "megabrokers."

With more than 1,500 sales associates operating from more than 47 neighborhood offices, the firm averages more than 20,000 residential transactions each year. The company also serves more

than 700 relocation clients and represents more than 100 major residential builders in northern Ohio. Realty One's information HotLine has received more than 2 million calls since 1991.

PURSUING A PROGRESSIVE VISION

Realty One believes that its business principles—based on the core values of integrity, caring, excellent service, personal responsibility, and continuous improvement—set it apart from other real estate companies. Those principles are articulated in part by the firm's vision statement: "Our goal is to work together to meet and exceed our customers' expectations. We will treat our customers with the understanding that buying or selling a home is among the most important decisions one makes in a lifetime. As a result, we will develop long-term business relationships, and our customers will become Realty One's greatest champions."

The firm also believes that people are its greatest asset, and actively seeks input from its customers, employees, and sales associates. "We have a strong company culture at Realty One," says Joseph T. Aveni. "We value our people— employees and sales associates— tremendously." To help prepare those sales associates for the marketplace, the company created Realty One University, a 10,000-square-foot, state-of-the-art facility where the firm's customer-focused philosophy is taught.

Realty One attributes its current success to several factors. First and foremost, the company takes an innovative and proactive approach to its business with the

JOSEPH T. AVENI IS CHAIRMAN OF THE BOARD AND CHIEF EXECUTIVE OFFICE OF REALTY ONE (LEFT).

AT THE JUNCTURE OF I-77 AND I-480, THE REALTY ONE CORPORATE CENTER HOUSES THE FIRM'S 10,000 SQUARE-FOOT EDUCATIONAL FACILITY (RIGHT).

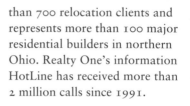

DAN DRY

▲ DAN DRY

unique Realty One Marketing System. "Extensive research has shown us where buyers come from, and we're marketing directly to them," says Joseph T. Aveni.

Responsiveness to customers is another Realty One principle. Consumer requests have led to home marketing innovations aimed at providing an information-generous experience for prospective buyers and sellers. Realty One was the first Realtor in the area to have a telephone hot line; the first to publish a picture-packed catalog of all the firm's listings, called the *Realty One Home Book*; the first to offer Total Representation, in which the firm represents both buyers and sellers in real estate transactions; and the first to augment its human resources staff with a multicultural coordinator, serving the needs of a diverse clientele. All Realty One listings can be accessed on the Internet at www.perfecthome.com, and the firm's latest innovation, On-Target Direct Marketing, pinpoints and markets to buyers with the greatest potential for purchasing a specific home.

A tribute to its decades of success, Realty One annually wins more marketing and sales awards than any other real estate company in Ohio. These include honors

▲ DAN DRY

from the Ohio Association of Realtors and the Genesis Relocation Network.

As it moves toward the 21st century, Realty One has no intention of slowing down. Indeed, the company is poised to expand its services more deeply into existing markets, while developing new markets and new customer services. "We also plan to enhance our services to our Realtors, making it easier for them to serve the buying and selling public," says Joseph T. Aveni.

Regardless of the company's future growth and success, however, Realty One remains firmly rooted in its hometown. "As a Cleveland-based company with a focus throughout northern Ohio, we have the opportunity to serve customers in a region that supports a quality of life that's unparalleled in most of America," adds Joseph T. Aveni. "With a manageable cost of living, good transportation options, and outstanding local amenities, Cleveland is a terrific place to call home."

COMBINING CUSTOMER FOCUS AND STATE-OF-THE-ART TECHNOLOGY, REALTY ONE LISTS AND SELLS MORE HOMES THAN ANY OTHER COMPANY IN OHIO (TOP LEFT AND RIGHT).

AN IMPORTANT COMPONENT OF THE REALTY ONE MARKETING SYSTEM, THE *Home Book* PROFILES EACH OF THE COMPANY'S APPROXIMATELY 4,000 LISTINGS WITH FACTS AND PHOTOGRAPHS (BOTTOM).

I T WAS MAY 1962, A TIME OF CONFRONTATION BETWEEN superpowers. On Black Monday, the Cuban missile crisis brought Wall Street to its knees. Undeterred by this unsettling event, which left the world on the verge of World War III, Midwestern National

Life Insurance Company of Ohio was setting up its business in Cleveland.

While remarkable, such timing hardly suggests anything but the most adroit management instincts. Like most new insurance companies formed during the "gold-chip era" of life insurance stocks, Midwestern was started on two foundations: a public stock offering that generated only $1 million in capital and surplus, and the notion that ". . . we could do it better, and we could become one of the gold chips."

BUILDING ON A TRIAD OF TRUSTS

With an eye toward managing steady growth, Midwestern's founders relied on a strategy emphasizing quality people, quality business, quality products, and quality growth.

This philosophy was central to the development of products, distribution, and the organization itself. Today, Midwestern continues to consider itself a partner in business with its customers, beneficiaries, shareholders, employees, and agents.

"In a life insurance company, our job as managers extends beyond the delicate balance of growth, profit, and stability," says Nicholas J. DiCicco Jr., president and CEO. "Midwestern National Life is in the business of insurance to fill the needs of individuals and businesses by relieving them of the burden of possible financial loss, thereby freeing them to pursue their individual visions of success. This places us in a genuine parity of relationships with our shareholders, our policyholders and beneficiaries, and our employees and agents."

This triad of trusts defines Midwestern's approach to doing business. Moreover, it remains embodied in the company's five operating principles: "To provide the most equitable contract of protection at reasonable rates with emphasis on initial and continuing service to both policyholders and their beneficiaries; to provide appreciating value to shareholders through careful control of expenses and continuous growth in sales, product distribution, and a concentration on conservative investments; to create for employees an environment for personal growth through education, training, and motivation, and for financial growth through fair compensation based upon individual merit; to accept our responsibilities as a corporate citizen by encouraging participation in community affairs and to conduct all activities with

ASSISTANT VICE PRESIDENTS BILL BIRD AND FRED TRUESDELL CHAT WITH UNDERWRITING/ISSUE MANAGER PATTI PHILLIPS IN THE LOBBY OF MIDWESTERN NATIONAL LIFE'S AWARD-WINNING HOME OFFICE BUILDING.

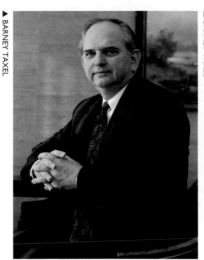

FROM LEFT:
NICHOLAS J. DICICCO JR., LLIF, IS
PRESIDENT AND CEO OF MIDWEST-
ERN NATIONAL LIFE INSURANCE
COMPANY OF OHIO, AS WELL AS
AN ORIGINAL INCORPORATOR OF
THE COMPANY.

FRANK J. RIHA, FLMI, SERVES AS
SENIOR VICE PRESIDENT AND CHIEF
FINANCIAL OFFICER.

VICE PRESIDENT AND CHIEF MAR-
KETING OFFICER ANTHONY G.
D'AGOSTINO, CLU, CHFC, HAS
BEEN WITH THE ORGANIZATION
SINCE THE 1960S.

the utmost regard for the public good; and to accept our responsibilities as a member of the insurance and financial services industry, presenting a favorable image and achieving recognition among our peers."

THE COMPANY BEHIND THE POLICY

Purchasing life insurance means buying more than a policy—it means investing in a company. With the triad of trusts in mind, Midwestern has stayed true to its strategy of stable, profitable growth. In this way, the company has seen its assets grow to more than $100 million. Meanwhile, in the first quarter of 1997, its capital and surplus increased significantly.

Midwestern maintains a high-grade investment portfolio. Less than one-tenth of a percent is devoted to stocks, while 45 percent is invested in government bonds and 55 percent in investment-grade corporate debt. Its ratios of surplus, liquidity, and solvency exceed those of the 25 largest insurance companies in the United States.

"We are dedicated to maintaining the strength and integrity of our investment portfolio. Therefore, our strategy has been to purchase only very high-quality investments," says Frank J. Riha, senior vice president and chief fi-

nancial officer. "This has resulted in consistently high and stable returns for the company and for our policyholders."

POSITIONING FOR THE FUTURE

Having outgrown offices in downtown Cleveland, Midwestern moved to its headquarters in the eastern suburb of Mayfield Village in 1986. There, the company has sufficient current office space, as well as land available for expansion.

At the close of the century, Midwestern is heading into new, exciting markets with the promise of even more rapid growth through strategic alliances within the financial services and insurance industries. To fund this rapid growth, the company has sought new capitalization that would support this expansion well into the new century.

In December 1996, shareholders approved a merger through which Midwestern became a wholly owned subsidiary of M C Equities, Inc. This agreement will increase the company's capital and surplus through a capital infusion by the parent company. As a result, Midwestern will be able to speed its expansion, while maintaining attractive surplus-to-assets ratios.

M C Equities backs Midwestern's growth plans with the ability to add new capital as needed. Now, the company can

venture into mergers and acquisitions, confident that M C Equities is prepared to absorb blocks of business, new partners, and new distribution channels.

Midwestern's strategic growth plan anticipates strategic alliances and partnerships, allowing the company to provide benefits and services to its partners' customers. "Middle- and upper-middle-income Americans are not receiving the same levels of service from the life insurance industry as they did in the past," says Anthony G. D'Agostino, vice president and chief marketing officer. "We intend to fill this gap in service to this vast market."

As chairman of the board and one of the founders, Fred A. Lennon identified DiCicco, Riha, and D'Agostino as the company's trio of leaders who have been with the organization since the early 1970s—and will chart its path into the 21st century.

Of course, Midwestern's growth depends on a continued adherence to its operating principles and its corporate will to maintain a balance of interest and concern for shareholders, policyholders, beneficiaries, employees, and agents. Only in this way can the company assure its strategic partners a degree of continuity in management rarely found among rapidly growing companies.

CENTRAL RESERVE LIFE INSURANCE COMPANY (CRL) WAS incorporated in 1963 and licensed in 1965. The company began operating its business as American Central Life Insurance Company, then reorganized in 1976 to become the primary subsidiary of

Central Reserve Life Corporation (CRLC). The company found its niche of providing high-quality, affordable life and health insurance to individuals and the small businesses of America by adhering to a simple philosophy: low-risk groups should pay lower premiums for their life and health insurance. In 1976, CRL recorded total revenue of just over $5 million. By 1989, the company had surpassed $100 million in annual premium income, and at the end of 1996, CRL had more than doubled that growth by reaching $250 million in premium.

Today, CRL specializes in meeting the varied insurance needs of small businesses and individuals. The company provides insurance products that include accident and health, individual and group life, group long-term disability, short-term major medical, and annuities.

CRL is best known for offering high-quality, affordable health insurance primarily for businesses with fewer than 50 employees. One of the main reasons behind the company's growth and the affordability of its health insurance plans is its innovative managed care programs. This integrated system of managed care controls helps keep claims costs down and rates significantly lower than the national average.

While many insurance companies have incorporated managed care in at least some capacity, CRL has developed a comprehensive system that encompasses nearly 30 areas, including selected individual case management, independent utilization review, and PPO arrangements. The company also continues to develop innovative initiatives, such as its Transplant Centers of Excellence Program for organ/tissue transplants, to provide the best coverage possible and assure a continually improving level of benefits.

At the heart of the company stands an uncompromising commitment to exceptional customer service. Geographically defined

LOCATED IN STRONGSVILLE, OHIO, CENTRAL RESERVE LIFE SPECIALIZES IN MEETING THE VARIED INSURANCE NEEDS OF SMALL BUSINESSES AND INDIVIDUALS, PROVIDING INSURANCE PRODUCTS THAT INCLUDE ACCIDENT AND HEALTH, INDIVIDUAL AND GROUP LIFE, GROUP LONG-TERM DISABILITY, SHORT-TERM MAJOR MEDICAL, AND ANNUITIES.

service teams process applications, answer questions, and handle claims quickly and accurately, keeping clients coming back through fast, efficient, and personal service. CRL's national network of general agents works with more than 13,000 independent agents to sell its plans. The company is presently licensed in 35 states, with primary markets in the midwestern, southeastern, and southwestern regions of the United States.

Over the past several years, Central Reserve Life Corporation has received recognition from the media for its accomplishments. *Forbes* magazine has twice placed CRL on its list of the 200 best small companies in America. For six years, *Equities* magazine named CRLC to its Dividends Champions List, recognizing the company as one of only 92 of the 4,500 NASDAQ listings to qualify for the honor. Central Reserve Life Corporation was named to the *Plain Dealer*'s 1995 list of the top 100 "Best Companies in Ohio." Qualifying companies were ranked according

to key measures, including revenue, return on equity, sales growth, and profit increase. CRLC was also included in the *Akron Beacon Journal*'s listing of the best-performing companies in Ohio for 1994. Companies that achieved this notoriety were ranked by profit margin, return on equity, sales growth, and total revenue.

SIMPLICITY AND PERSISTENCE

To address the recent challenges of the volatile health care reform environment, CRL maintains a fierce emphasis on its two guiding principles of simplicity and persistence. The company took several steps to consolidate its health plans into straightforward programs that are flexible, while complying with the various laws and regulations of each state. CRL has also standardized benefits wherever possible and has incorporated new benefits in order to remain a leader with a strong product portfolio.

Through the ongoing development of its people and the technology that supports its operations,

CRL continues to shape its future. The company has instituted a year-long management training program designed to generate a pool of highly qualified and motivated managerial candidates to fill future executive roles. A new claims and administrative information technology system will reduce the amount of paper required for processing information, while increasing the speed of information flow. This will significantly augment the speed and volume of transactions.

As CRL continues to refine its philosophies of simplification and persistence, it remains focused on the long-range goals of increased profit, value, and quality. The company also knows that future competitive advantages will arise out of the collective knowledge, expertise, and inventive approach to the business provided by its outstanding team of agents.

In the end, the total commitment of CRL's people toward meeting the needs of its customers ensures that the company will remain an innovative force in the health insurance industry.

▲ BILL PAPPAS

STUDENTS AT CUYAHOGA COMMUNITY COLLEGE ARE GOING places. "Tri-C is a place where people come to improve their lives," says Dr. Jerry Sue Thornton, president. "Student success is the focus of everything we do." ❖ Greater Clevelanders of all ages, from all

walks of life, look to Tri-C for the education they need to prepare them for the workplace. As the first and largest comprehensive community college in Ohio, Tri-C serves 60,000 students a year.

The college offers more than 70 career and certificate programs. Tri-C works directly with leaders in business, industry, and health care to ensure that the college's career programs and curricula prepare students to be productive members of tomorrow's workforce.

GREATER CLEVELANDERS OF ALL AGES, FROM ALL WALKS OF LIFE, LOOK TO TRI-C FOR THE EDUCATION THEY NEED TO PREPARE THEM FOR THE WORKPLACE.

More than a third of Tri-C's students take advantage of transfer programs, which allow them to earn the first two years of their bachelor's degree at affordable prices. Tri-C

maintains formal transfer and articulation agreements with many different institutions throughout Ohio and the nation.

Tri-C serves its students, as well as business and industry, at three campuses strategically located in the county. All campuses have fully equipped libraries, state-of-the-art technology, and cultural and athletic facilities. The college also serves the public and private sectors through its Business, Community and Economic Development unit. This unit focuses on economic development through programs to retrain employed workers and prepare people for the job market.

CULTURAL CONNECTION

In addition to outstanding academic programs, Tri-C is a vital community resource. Each year, more than 400,000 county residents visit the college's three campuses for cultural, civic, and sporting events.

The Tri-C JazzFest, the nation's premier educational jazz festival, draws top artists who perform for more than 40,000 adults and children each year. The Showtime at High Noon series attracts 13,000 people annually to extraordinary programs at Playhouse Square. Tri-C is also the educational component of the Rock and Roll Hall of Fame and Museum.

A GREAT PLACE TO START AND CONTINUE

Since opening its doors in 1963, Tri-C has served more than a half million students. The college's three campuses include the Eastern Campus in Highland Hills, the Metropolitan Campus

in downtown Cleveland, and the Western Campus in Parma. In addition, Tri-C offers classes at numerous off-campus sites.

Students can choose from more than 1,000 courses—ranging from arts and sciences to technical training—offered days, evenings, and weekends year-round. Although enrollment is high, class sizes average fewer than 20 students.

Tuition is about half that of state universities and a fraction of the cost of private schools. Fully accredited, Tri-C has a qualified, caring teaching staff, including a high percentage of doctoral-level faculty.

COMMUNITY OUTREACH

The college offers numerous programs that bring educational awareness, life skills, and motivation to underrepresented and underserved youths and adults.

Tri-C provides Educational Opportunity Programs to thousands of residents through partnerships with postsecondary institutions in Greater Cleveland, Cleveland Public Schools, and 52 agencies, including the Learning Disabilities Association of America, Cuyahoga County Department of Human Services, Urban League, and Veterans Affairs.

One of the college's most important roles in the community is fostering its partnerships with local business, industry, governmental agencies, and educational institutions.

Thornton adds: "We are proud of our active role in Greater Cleveland's rebirth and look forward to continuing these partnerships as we work together to meet the challenges of the 21st century."

FROM A PRIVATE, FAMILY-OWNED BUSINESS WITH ONLY A FEW Cleveland rental apartments, Associated Estates Realty Corporation today is a publicly traded real estate investment trust (REIT) that owns or is a joint venture partner in more than 80 apartment properties

with more than 16,000 suites strategically located throughout what the company calls "the vibrant Great Lakes region." Associated Estates is also responsible for another 7,000 suites in buildings under management contracts. The company's real estate assets exceed $500 million.

CLEVELAND ROOTS

Approximately two-thirds of Associated Estates' apartments are located in Cleveland, Akron, and Toledo, while 20 percent of the company's suites are situated in and around Columbus, which is currently considered one of the top 12 apartment investment markets in the country.

Many REITs have expanded into faster-growing markets, but for every boom, inevitably there is a bust. Associated Estates follows a more conservative strategy, one that trades the thrills of volatility for the assurances of steady, predictable growth.

"The Great Lakes region is alive and well," says Jeffrey I. Friedman, president and chief executive officer. "That is why we have chosen to grow and thrive here."

GROWTH THROUGH ACQUISITION AND DEVELOPMENT

While much of Associated Estates' growth has come through the acquisition of existing properties, the company has an in-house development staff that will oversee the construction of approximately 1,100 suites in 1997. The developments include 288 luxury town houses and garden apartments in Aurora, about 20 miles east of Cleveland. In

Streetsboro, another outlying Cleveland suburb, 112 apartments are being developed at The Village of Western Reserve, and in Columbus, 324 luxury suites are being built at Bradford at Easton, part of a $1.5 billion mixed-use development currently being undertaken by Les Wexner and The Limited.

Associated Estates has funded its expansion with cash generated from operations and through a combination of debt and equity financing. The company has chartered a steady growth path by maintaining a conservatively structured balance sheet. In addition, more than 80 percent of its properties are debt free.

"Our approach is a 'peck, peck, peck' one versus a 'gobble, gobble, gobble' strategy," says Friedman.

HARD-WIRED FOR THE FUTURE

In 1997, all of Associated Estates' properties became linked to the company's headquarters through a proprietary software system called Leasing Information System Assistant (LISA®). Developed in 1995 by the company's leasing consultants, business managers, and marketing staff, the program provides current, detailed information on each property, including vacancy and rental data and the status of leas-

ing applications. This information is downloaded daily to the main office where it is analyzed and incorporated into an expanding database used to assist in management decision making.

"LISA has become a tremendous help in terms of gathering marketing and leasing data," Friedman says, "as well as reducing the amount of paperwork at each property, leaving more time for leasing agents to service existing customers and attract new ones.

"To improve the management of our day-to-day operations, we have committed ourselves to adopting and fully utilizing those new technologies that will enhance our communications and provide a competitive marketing edge," Friedman adds.

CLOCKWISE FROM TOP: JEFFREY I. FRIEDMAN IS THE FIRM'S PRESIDENT AND CEO.

ASSOCIATED ESTATES HAS TAKEN UP RESIDENCE ON THE WORLD WIDE WEB AT WWW.AECREALTY.COM, ALLOWING POTENTIAL INVESTORS, SHAREHOLDERS, AND OTHER WEB SURFERS TO PERUSE SUCH COMPANY DOCUMENTS AS PRESS RELEASES, SHAREHOLDER REPORTS, AND SEC FILINGS. THE SITE IS ALSO LINKED TO SEVERAL OTHERS, INCLUDING RENT.NET, A SERVICE FOR APARTMENT HUNTERS.

ASSOCIATED ESTATES IS THE OWNER, MANAGER, AND DEVELOPER OF THE RESIDENCE AT BARRINGTON, A LUXURY APARTMENT COMMUNITY UNDER CONSTRUCTION IN AURORA, OHIO.

E NTRUSTED WITH EDUCATING THE CITIZENS OF OHIO'S NORTH-eastern urban area as an essential investment in the state's future, Cleveland State University fulfills its mission by providing a high-quality education. In developing the intellectual, social, cultural, and

technological growth of its students, the university enhances the quality of life and economic viability of the state and the region.

Today, 15,600 students from the metropolitan area bring diverse backgrounds, interests, and educational needs to this comprehensive urban university. Cleveland State University offers degrees in more than 70 undergraduate programs in business, arts and sciences, engineering, education, and urban affairs, complemented by a range of graduate courses offering 36 master's degrees and six doctoral-level degrees in fields that address Ohio's economic and social needs.

RESPONDING TO GLOBAL BUSINESS

P reparing students for work in the global marketplace is second nature to Cleveland State University. The university brings men and women from many cultural and ethnic backgrounds together in the classroom and in student activities, mirroring the diverse working environments that will predominate in the 21st century. "For several years," says Claire Van Ummersen, university president, "we have been concentrating on building strong relationships with universities in China, especially with Suzhou University." The two universities exchange graduate students for professional and cross-cultural education, facilitating the many business relationships between China and the United States.

Responding to the increasing challenges of the global economy, Cleveland State University has formed vital partnerships with metropolitan businesses and industries. One example is the Fenn College of Engineering's award-winning Advanced Manufacturing Center, where students receive hands-on instruction while solving manufacturing problems for local industries.

The university's cooperative education program, among the nation's 10 largest, helps students acquire career experience while obtaining a degree and earning income to pay tuition. More than 2,200 students currently participate in this program.

Cleveland State University's James J. Nance College of Business Administration, one of the largest business schools in Ohio, is accredited by the American Assembly of Collegiate Schools of Business (AACSB). Business students have received national accolades. In 1990, for example, a business school student achieved the highest score on the national CPA exam in a field of 75,000.

In 1996, Cleveland State students placed first in the annual Deloitte & Touche Accounting Challenge—the seventh time in the last 10 years that university students have won the event.

A PARTNER IN THE COMMUNITY

*W*e carry out our urban mission through partnerships with business and industry, with social service organizations, with other educational institutions and secondary school systems, and with health-related organizations," says Van Ummersen. "Our most recent partnership has been established with the new Great Lakes Science Center, where we created a program of environmental science for our students."

Cleveland State has established extensive partnerships within the community and serves as a valuable resource for Greater Cleveland. One example is its relationship with the Visiting Nurse Association (VNA), which provides health care staff for home health needs. Cleveland State student nurses work closely with VNA nurses in providing home health care services, and the university closely integrates instruction, research, and public service, including strong and growing student volunteer networks.

The university has addressed the social issues and needs of the surrounding urban environment through the Maxine Goodman Levin College of Urban Affairs. Ranked among the top 10 urban affairs programs in the country, the college is one of only 200 public administration programs in the nation that were reaccredited by the National Association of Schools of Public Affairs and Administration. The college furnishes students with opportunities for research and practical experience, including field work.

The College of Arts and Sciences prepares students for a broad range of life goals, from pursuing postgraduate and professional studies to working in the fields of public relations, advertising, music, and health sciences. Under a joint-use agreement, doctoral students in biology and chemistry work closely with Cleveland Clinic researchers to develop protocols in diagnosis and treatment. Completion of the university's new Health Sciences Building is scheduled for 1998.

The College of Education at Cleveland State is one of the top 10 producers of science teachers in the United States and a major source of culturally diverse graduates, who are in great demand throughout the nation. The Rockefeller Foundation has recognized the college as expert in the field of school restructuring. The college also aids local school districts in developing programs for teaching excellence.

With roots in the 19th century, the university's Cleveland-Marshall College of Law offers unique programs combining law with business and health care. The college collaborates with the Cleveland Clinic Foundation to offer the annual Medical Institute for Law. The largest law school in Ohio, Cleveland-Marshall serves the region's legal and judicial community with its comprehensive law library. Many of its graduates enter public service as judges, prosecutors, and public defenders. Ninety-two percent of Cleveland-Marshall's graduates passed the Ohio Bar exam on their first attempt in 1996.

Additionally, approximately 4,000 area residents annually take advantage of Cleveland State University's diverse adult continuing education offerings. Many graduate and other specialized programs are offered at employers' sites.

A RICH RESOURCE

*C*leveland State University contributes to area businesses and industry a pool of graduates who are distinguished by their strong work ethic, in-depth theoretical knowledge of their fields, and practical work experience. The university is an especially rich resource: 85 percent of its graduates remain in the area, prepared to work productively and ready to become responsible citizens, contributing to their families, employers, and communities.

Cleveland State University's new, 25-year master plan, Pathways to Learning, matches educational programs with superior academic classrooms, public spaces, and improved campus circulation—providing the foundation for continued educational excellence far into the 21st century.

STUDENTS AT CLEVELAND STATE UNIVERSITY HAVE THE ADVANTAGE OF BEING EXPOSED TO A WIDE VARIETY OF CULTURES AND IDEAS THAT WILL BETTER PREPARE THEM FOR THE GLOBAL MARKETPLACE AND DIVERSE WORKFORCE OF THE 21ST CENTURY (LEFT).

EVEN ON THE COLDEST WINTER DAYS, THERE IS PLENTY OF WARMTH IN "THE CAGE" FOR STUDENT EVENTS AND CELEBRATIONS. THE LARGE ATRIUM IN THE UNIVERSITY CENTER BUILDING PROVIDES A VARIETY OF RESTAURANTS AND STUDY AREAS FOR THE ENTIRE UNIVERSITY COMMUNITY (RIGHT).

*I*N ITS FIRST 50 YEARS, KAISER PERMANENTE PIONEERED A NEW WAY of delivering health care—the innovative prepaid group practice approach. In the years following the Great Depression, the organization that would become Kaiser Permanente began by

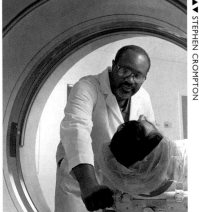

providing construction workers treatment when they were sick or injured, plus advice on how to stay well, all for a payroll deduction of five cents a day. With their doctors and hospitals within easy reach, the new approach to health care worked so well for members and their employers that Kaiser Permanente agreed to cover their families, too.

For more than 50 years, the word has spread. Kaiser Permanente membership has grown and the company is still pioneering innovations that give its members the quality health care choices they want and deserve. Today, Kaiser Permanente is the oldest and largest not-for-profit health maintenance organization (HMO) in the nation, with more than 7.5 million members in 16 states and the District of Columbia, including more than 200,000 members in nine counties throughout northeast Ohio. Kaiser Permanente has led the way through 50 years of change in health care by making quality medical care affordable and accessible. And the company today is still getting by on five cents: Out of every health care dollar collected, Kaiser spends only five cents on administration and related costs. The rest goes directly to patient care, research, medical equipment, and the like.

Kaiser Permanente is firm in its commitment to improve the health of the communities it serves and the belief that its mission-driven, not-for-profit enterprise can better meet the health care needs of individuals and communities than the for-profit plans with which it now competes. The first manifestation of this social purpose is market-

leading performance—defined by superior quality and affordability; competitive service, including care experience; and market sustainability. Only with market-leading performance can Kaiser Permanente do what is necessary to meet its social purpose. That includes being able to set the standard for the marketplace and to catalyze change in the industry by its performance, presence, and strength in the local communities Kaiser serves. Market-leading performance means refining the operation of its integrated national organization to find innovative and improved ways to serve

patients, members, and purchasers. Since its inception, Kaiser Permanente has played a critical role in defining the delivery of health care in America. In the years ahead, its social purpose and market-leading performance will only be intensified.

In northeast Ohio, Kaiser Permanente is the one health care delivery choice with a proven history of managing care by managing change—the only choice that combines local response with pioneering national leadership in managed health care delivery, innovation, and excellence. Kaiser Permanente's strong partnership

KAISER PERMANENTE HAS A TOTAL OF 13 MEDICAL FACILITIES LOCATED THROUGHOUT NORTHEAST OHIO (TOP).

KAISER PERMANENTE TAKES A "HIGH-TECH, HIGH-TOUCH" APPROACH TO DIAGNOSTIC PROCEDURES, AS WELL AS ROUTINE OFFICE VISITS AND HOSPITALIZATIONS (BOTTOM).

with the Ohio Permanente Medical Group is essential to the continuing growth and success of the organization. Successful group practices can most effectively deliver competitive advantage and quality care. The best opportunities for improving performance lie in reducing variation in clinical practice, thereby achieving lowered costs through improved quality. In northeast Ohio, Kaiser Permanente has enhanced its offerings to make it easier for more people to receive quality health care. This has been done by expanding its choice of doctors and the locations where members can see the doctor—combining Kaiser Permanente's traditional group model HMO with community-based, network-affiliated physicians, along with the transfer of its best practices.

to concentrate on patients and professional activities, including research and major clinical innovations. Electronic medical records give primary care and specialist physicians the vital medical information needed for plan members. And Kaiser's interactive PC network links its physicians with the country's leading specialists for consultation and research findings. That is why, as medicine changes, one thing stays the same: Kaiser Permanente keeps pace with the area's ever changing health care delivery system.

Culminating nearly 35 years as the pioneer in delivering organized health care in northeast Ohio, Kaiser Permanente has pursued a wide range of member-driven service enhancements and demonstrated substantial progress toward developing customized

Permanente understands that the changing face of health care delivery means one size does not fit all, so in addition to offering a broader choice of access to physicians, it offers flexibility in plan options. Kaiser Permanente offers health care for the way its purchasers and members want it— designed to give them the medical care they need for the way they live today—with choice, flexibility, and convenience.

In its first 50 years, Kaiser Permanente pioneered a new way of delivering health care. Now its focus is sharpened to execute a higher level of performance that catalyzes the marketplace. Kaiser Permanente understands that there is accelerating change in the local health care marketplace, while at the same time, there is escalating competition among health care

STEPHEN CROMPTON

When *Newsweek* magazine ran its June 24, 1996, story titled "America's Best HMOs," it featured a Permanente Group physician on the cover. That honor was no surprise to the more than 200,000 local members the HMO serves. The doctors are one of the most important reasons members choose Kaiser Permanente health care plans. Its doctors include top-notch, board-certified primary care physicians and specialists who have outstanding credentials and experience. And while Kaiser Permanente as a health care plan handles the business aspects of medicine, its physicians are free

programs to match the needs of patients, members, and purchasers. Nowhere is the phrase "high-tech, high-touch" more apt than in health care, where the evolution of new technologies is allowing Kaiser Permanente to improve service, boost access, and provide higher quality. All of today's sophisticated technological capabilities are converging on health care, creating a new and ever changing delivery environment. Integrating critical information with interactive technology results in better quality, appropriate care, broader access, and overall happier members and purchasers. Kaiser

provider organizations. Members can be confident that their HMO is the one performance-proven source of continuing leadership in health care delivery in northeast Ohio. Kaiser Permanente differentiates itself with confidence and credibility based on facts as it continues to move measurably ahead in quality, scope, and results.

With a focus on managing care by managing change, the organization continually lives up to its motto, "Kaiser Permanente. . .We Make Change Work for You."

*N*ESTLED IN THE WOODS AT A QUIET STREET CORNER ON CLEVELAND'S EAST side is the headquarters of Developers Diversified Realty Corporation (DDR), the nation's industry leader in the acquisition, development, ownership, and management of power-strip shopping centers. ❖ From

this Moreland Hills office building, known as the Heritage, Bert and Scott Wolstein manage not only DDR, a publicly traded real estate investment trust (REIT), but also a string of other private business ventures engaged in commercial and residential development across the country.

GROWING WITH CLEVELAND

*L*ocally the Wolsteins are probably best known as the owners of the Cleveland Force, a professional indoor soccer team that electrified the community and often filled the 21,000-seat Richfield Coliseum from 1979 to the league's demise in 1988. However, the family's business ties to the community go back to the 1950s when Bert developed more than 1,000 homes in Twinsburg, southeast of Cleveland, including Heritage Hills. The company's headquarters for the past 16 years takes its name from this early development.

Bert was also project manager back in 1958 for the original Great Northern Shopping Center, a mall and strip center development located west of Cleveland in North Olmsted, which, coincidentally, was recently acquired by DDR. More recently, a Wolstein venture developed and owns the Renaissance Building, the first new multistory office structure built around Playhouse Square in approximately 60 years and a towering benchmark for the rebirth of this entire district.

The company has also developed two upscale planned communities around Jack Nicklaus signature golf courses: Barrington, a $400 million, 800-residence

project in Aurora that includes a shopping center, and Glenmoor, a $200 million, 380-residence development that is located an hour's drive south of Cleveland in the city of Canton.

Heading toward the 21st century, the Wolsteins are in the midst of a $50 million multiple-phase development on seven acres along the east bank of the Flats in downtown Cleveland. New restaurants have already opened along the riverfront boardwalk, and plans are under way to build a theater, hotel, and microbrewery within walking distance of these new establishments.

"We're proud of being born and raised in Cleveland," says Bert, chairman emeritus of DDR.

A REAL ESTATE INVESTMENT TRUST

*E*stablished in 1965, Developers Diversified Realty Corporation is today a fully integrated real estate company that has been publicly traded since its initial stock offering in 1993. DDR was recently recognized as one of the fastest-growing REITs in America. In fact, with dividend reinvestment, an investor's total return from the initial stock offering through the end of 1996 would have been nearly 118 percent.

The company consistently posts numbers that are envied throughout the industry. In 1996, for example, DDR developed five projects and opened more than 1.2 million square feet of space, including close to 600,000 square feet in Cleveland and Akron/Canton.

The company continues to move aggressively toward improving its leadership position in the

PRESIDENT AND CEO SCOTT A. WOLSTEIN AND CHAIRMAN EMERITUS BERT L. WOLSTEIN HAVE BUSINESS ROOTS IN CLEVELAND THAT EXTEND BACK TO 1950 (TOP).

BARRINGTON GOLF COURSE, LOCATED IN AURORA, OHIO, IS A JACK NICKLAUS-DESIGNED COURSE AND PLANNED COMMUNITY DEVELOPED BY THE WOLSTEINS (BOTTOM).

leasing, expansion, acquisition, and development of commercial real estate. In 1996, for example, construction increased DDR's total retail holdings to more than 20 million square feet. Its total building area of both retail and business centers exceeds 24 million square feet, and by year end 1996, DDR had quadrupled its market capitalization to $1.5 billion.

In 1995, the company acquired the Homart Community Center division of Sears, Roebuck & Co. and its $500 million, 4.3 million-square-foot portfolio, including 10 power-strip centers located in or

near the country's fastest-growing areas. In June 1996, the trade publication *Chain Store Age* ranked DDR third among companies acquiring shopping centers and fifth among the fastest-growing developers in the country.

THE FUTURE

DDR employs a four-pronged approach to business known as LEAD, an acronym representing the company's emphasis on integrated growth through leasing, expansion, acquisition, and development.

"This company is part of a

revolutionary trend in the ownership and operation of real estate," Scott says. "As Americans increasingly turn to large mass-merchandising stores for their shopping, this company will be at the forefront of that trend."

Scott adds that, as one of the nation's fastest-growing REITs, Developers Diversified Realty is able to take advantage of its unique versatility and broad expertise. "We're manufacturers. We develop from the ground up," he says. "As a result, we can earn higher returns for our shareholders."

DDR MANAGES A STRING OF PRIVATE BUSINESS VENTURES ENGAGED IN COMMERCIAL AND RESIDENTIAL DEVELOPMENT ACROSS THE COUNTRY, INCLUDING (CLOCKWISE FROM TOP LEFT) CARMEL MOUNTAIN PLAZA IN SAN DIEGO; GLENMOOR COUNTRY CLUB IN CANTON, OHIO; WOODFIELD VILLAGE GREEN IN SCHAUMBURG, ILLINOIS; AND FAIRFAX TOWNE CENTER IN FAIRFAX, VIRGINIA.

1968

1968
   CLEVELAND-CUYAHOGA COUNTY PORT
   AUTHORITY

1968
   A.T. KEARNEY, INC.

1969
   KRAFTMAID CABINETRY, INC.

1970
   KINETICO, INCORPORATED

1972
   CSM INDUSTRIES

1972
   HEALTH O METER, INC./MR. COFFEE INC.

1972
   NORTHEAST OHIO REGIONAL SEWER DISTRICT

1973
   MAXUS INVESTMENT GROUP

1974
   STAFFING SOLUTIONS ENTERPRISES

1975
   GREATER CLEVELAND REGIONAL TRANSIT
   AUTHORITY

1979
   CHRISTIAN & TIMBERS INC.

1979
   CLARION HOTEL AND CONFERENCE CENTER

1981
   YORK INTERNATIONAL CORPORATION

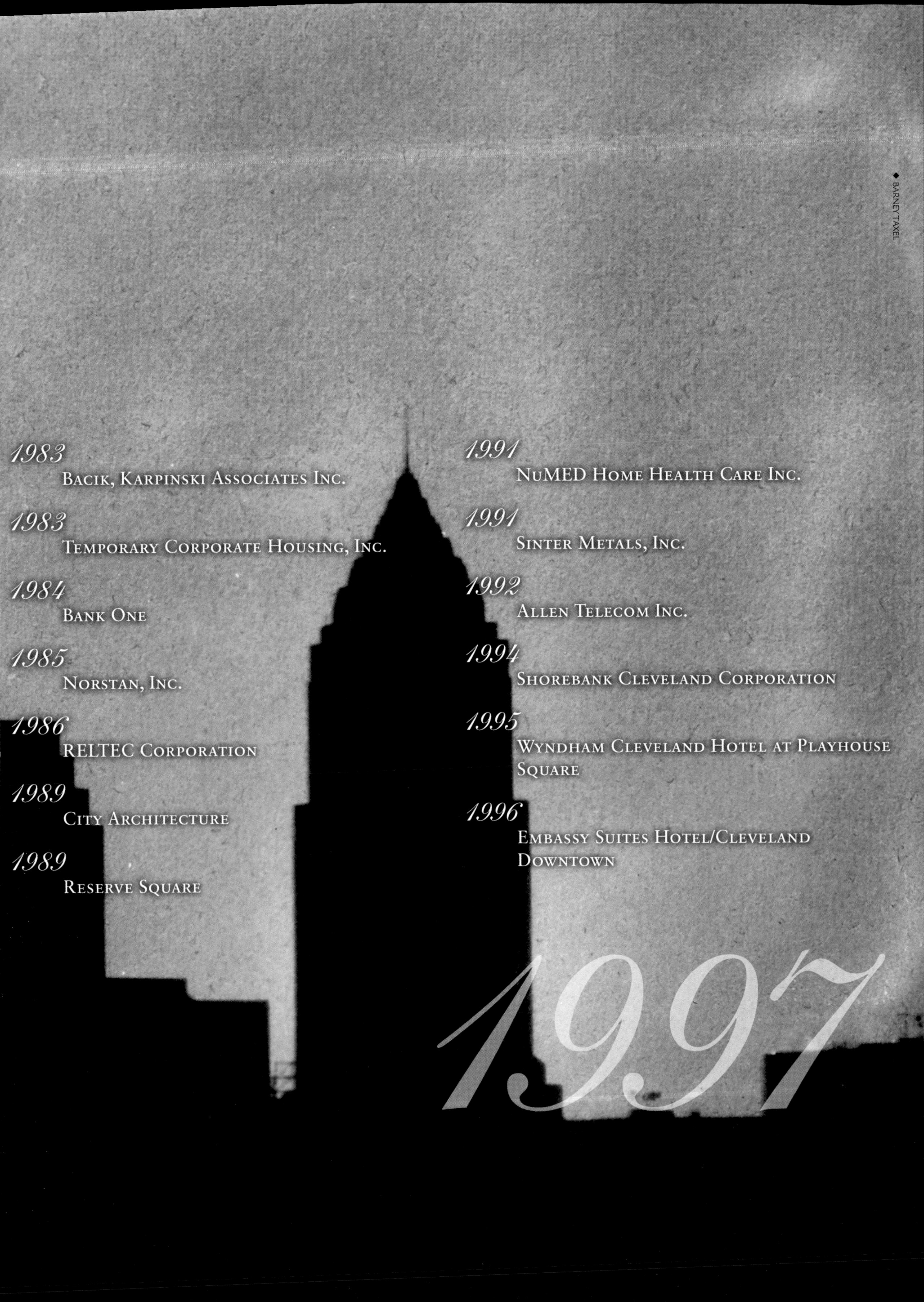

BARNEY TAXEL

1983
BACIK, KARPINSKI ASSOCIATES INC.

1983
TEMPORARY CORPORATE HOUSING, INC.

1984
BANK ONE

1985
NORSTAN, INC.

1986
RELTEC CORPORATION

1989
CITY ARCHITECTURE

1989
RESERVE SQUARE

1991
NUMED HOME HEALTH CARE INC.

1991
SINTER METALS, INC.

1992
ALLEN TELECOM INC.

1994
SHOREBANK CLEVELAND CORPORATION

1995
WYNDHAM CLEVELAND HOTEL AT PLAYHOUSE SQUARE

1996
EMBASSY SUITES HOTEL/CLEVELAND DOWNTOWN

1997

THE MANAGEMENT CONSULTING HISTORY OF A.T. KEARNEY IN Cleveland mirrors the development of business in the 20th century. The firm and its founder, Andrew Thomas Kearney, supported clients' early strategic progress as the country moved toward industrial

leadership. As business continued to grow, so did A.T. Kearney—in size, strength, and scope. Today, A.T. Kearney stands as one of the few global, multidisciplined, value-added general management consulting practices. In business for more than 70 years, the firm continues to help shape the history of companies in northeast Ohio, America, and worldwide.

CLEVELAND—A GREAT OPPORTUNITY

Cleveland was at an economic crossroads in the 1960s. Its heavy industries—steel, autos, manufactured components, and chemicals—had come of age as industry pacesetters. New production technologies were on the horizon, encouraged by pressures to be more efficient and quality conscious as competition grew. Concurrently, a new class of companies—in fields such as insurance, financial services, retailing, and business services—was sprouting in northeast Ohio. Indeed, Cleveland was coming of age as "The

Best Location in the Nation." A.T. Kearney, well established since 1926 as one of the premier management consulting firms in the country, began to hear the call from Cleveland companies looking for strategic counsel and planning acumen to navigate the exciting, yet challenging, postmodern era of commerce. The firm took advantage of the opportunity and opened its Cleveland office in 1968.

THE GLOBALIZATION OF THE HEARTLAND

Since 1968, the growth strategies of the Cleveland area's businesses have changed drastically. No longer is the focus one of regional or national growth. Cleveland companies now serve worldwide markets. This globalization of the heartland has brought a new set of questions. A.T. Kearney has positioned itself to provide the answers.

A.T. Kearney has worked for clients in more than 90 nations, including both mature and newly market-oriented economies. In 1980, the firm generated less than 10 percent of its revenue overseas. By 1992, more than half of its revenue was generated outside the United States, and that figure is expected to grow.

This international growth is the result of A.T. Kearney's commitment to foster a global orientation and culture among its staff by encouraging their active participation in such venues as global boards, international exchange programs, and worldwide professional development programs. They deliver a global perspective through a well-established network of offices in North America, Europe, and Asia. The practice continues to expand in these areas, as well as in Central and South America.

The firm also uses the latest technological tools in helping to assist clients in global management. One of these is Stages of Global Development, a diagnostic program designed to help a company analyze and plan its evolution from opportunistic exporter to fully global organization.

During the 1990s, A.T. Kearney has consistently strengthened its

ANDREW GREEN SERVES AS VICE PRESIDENT AND HEAD OF A.T. KEARNEY'S CLEVELAND OPERATIONS.

THE FIRM'S OFFICE, LOCATED AT EAST 6TH STREET AND SUPERIOR AVENUE IN DOWNTOWN CLEVELAND, PROVIDES COMPANIES WITH LOCAL ACCESS TO GLOBAL INDUSTRY PRACTICES.

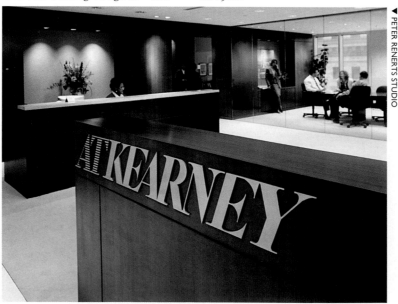

◄ PETER RENERTS STUDIO

capabilities across diverse industries including automotive, telecommunications, financial services, utilities, and retail. And its expertise and service offerings have more than kept pace. The firm's most significant change occurred in 1995 when it joined forces with information services powerhouse Electronic Data Systems (EDS). The merger has added an unsurpassed range of skills and capacity in information management. As a result, A.T. Kearney now offers a wider breadth of information resources than virtually any other consulting organization.

ENABLING POWERFUL CONTRIBUTIONS

*I*n maintaining its leadership role in management consulting, A.T. Kearney focuses on three critical factors: superior people, superior products, and superior performance. The key to making these elements work together successfully is found in the firm's philosophy.

In every engagement, A.T. Kearney focuses on making the most of an opportunity—an obsession with gaining what it calls "the most powerful contributions" for a business. Simply put, a powerful contribution is one that delivers a deep yet mea-

surable improvement in any or all of a client's economics, products and services, and customer and supplier relationships. Key to success in this philosophy is the translation of top-level strategies to action on the front lines of a business.

According to Andrew Green, vice president and head of the firm's Cleveland office, "The most powerful statement about A.T. Kearney comes from our clients. They tell us that our firm is unique in its ability to make change happen in powerful and sustainable ways."

This philosophy is at the heart of everything A.T. Kearney does: its approach to consulting, its value proposition, its analytical frameworks, and the way it measures performance.

CONTRIBUTIONS TO THE COMMUNITY

*T*he firm's powerful contributions philosophy also applies to its commitment to the communities where it is located. A.T. Kearney upholds the principle of community involvement by actively supporting such organizations as Cleveland Ballet, Great Lakes Science Center, and Playhouse Square, and by offering pro bono services to such civic groups as the Cleveland Center for Con-

temporary Art, Governor's Commission for Economic Choice, and Business Volunteerism Council. The A.T. Kearney commitment to Cleveland is strong and growing—much like the firm itself and the marketplace it serves.

AHEAD TO THE 21ST CENTURY

*S*ince 1926, A.T. Kearney's primary objective has remained unwavering—to exceed client expectations by delivering more than anticipated. In Cleveland and elsewhere, the future shines brightly for A.T. Kearney, a firm with a singular ability to combine excellence, strategy, and information technology to create a definitive advantage through management consulting in the 21st century.

A.T. KEARNEY USES SUPERIOR PEOPLE PROVIDING SUPERIOR PERFORMANCE WITH SUPERIOR PRODUCTS TO GAIN "THE MOST POWERFUL CONTRIBUTIONS" FOR ITS CLIENTS.

THE FIRM'S MERGER WITH INFORMATION POWERHOUSE EDS HAS BROUGHT AN UNSURPASSED WEALTH OF INFORMATION RESOURCES TO HELP CLIENTS WITH ACCESS TO INTERNATIONAL MARKETS.

A KEY PLAYER IN CLEVELAND'S RENAISSANCE AS AN INTERNATIONAL city, the Port of Cleveland is a vital resource for world trade, jobs growth, economic development, and even tourism. As the governing body of the port, the Cleveland-Cuyahoga County Port Authority is making waves as it guides the port's maritime and economic development operations to a position of leadership that extends far beyond the docks.

MARITIME OPERATIONS ARE ONE IN A MILLION

The Port of Cleveland is helping northeast Ohio chart its course in world markets, moving a record-breaking 1.1 million tons of international cargo during 1996. Total cargo moved through the port, including inter-lake shipments, exceeds 16 million tons a year. Port of Cleveland activities have created more than 4,700 jobs in northeast Ohio, generated more than $425 million in spending, and increased household earnings in northeast Ohio by more than $150 million.

While nearly 90 percent of the port's international cargo is steel, the Port Authority also provides superior handling for a variety of break bulk, dry bulk, and container cargoes. The port offers its customers the key advantage of easy access and ideal location at the hub of the nation's largest concentration of industrial and consumer markets. The Port of Cleveland is a full day's travel time closer to Europe than other key lake ports and, because of the St. Lawrence Seaway, is 300 miles closer to Europe than most East Coast seaports.

MAKING WAVES IN ECONOMIC DEVELOPMENT

The Port Authority not only oversees the port's busy maritime operations, but also is taking an increasingly higher profile in nonmaritime activities. Namely, the Port Authority is impacting regional economic growth, corporate jobs retention, and a multiuse waterfront designed to capture tourism dollars for the area economy.

The Port Authority has a vision of the waterfront as an accessible community asset. That vision reflects the romance of a working port operating alongside popular recreational attractions—ultimately positioning Greater Cleveland among the ranks of renowned port cities such as San Francisco, Osaka, and Antwerp.

It is through the building of public-private partnerships that the Port Authority is helping turn this vision into reality. Given the authority to exercise a variety of financing programs under Ohio law, the Port Authority became a key funding partner by issuing $39 million in revenue bonds to build the $92 million Rock and Roll Hall of Fame and Museum. The Port Authority was also an important player in another public-private funding partnership when it issued more than $18 million in revenue bonds to help finance Applied Industrial Technologies' $37 million head-quarters, located in Cleveland's MidTown Corridor. This project helped retain more than 300 jobs and millions of dollars in tax revenue for Cleveland.

This bonding financing capability has also been channeled into a unique funding program, the port's Common Bond Fund Program, which provides long-term, fixed-interest-rate financing of $1 million to $6 million to credit-worthy small and medium-sized businesses for industrial and commercial projects.

From crucial bond financing to record-breaking cargo handling, the Cleveland-Cuyahoga County Port Authority and the Port of Cleveland are making waves as an important regional force in Greater Cleveland.

CLOCKWISE FROM TOP: A LONGSHOREMAN AT THE PORT OF CLEVELAND UNHOOKS THE CABLES USED TO UNLOAD A STEEL COIL DESTINED FOR LOCAL MANUFACTURERS.

THE PORT SHARES THE LAKEFRONT WITH SUCH NORTH COAST HARBOR ATTRACTIONS AS THE ROCK AND ROLL HALL OF FAME AND MUSEUM, THE GREAT LAKES SCIENCE CENTER, THE *Goodtime III* TOUR BOAT, AND THE MUSEUM SHIP *William G. Mather*.

THE MV *Island Gem*, OF GREEK REGISTRY, UNLOADS STEEL AT THE PORT AUTHORITY DOCKS.

ROGER MASTROIANNI

ROGER MASTROIANNI

IN THE EARLY 1970S, CARMELLA CALTA HAD A DREAM OF PROVIDING qualified office staff to businesses needing temporary help. And over the more than 20 years that she has been in business in Cleveland, Calta has turned that dream into a reality by building one of the

city's largest and most highly respected full-service staffing companies.

Founded in 1974, Staffing Solutions Enterprises is today the umbrella name for TempsPlus temporary services, interim-to-hire and direct placement, payrolling, on-line recruiting, and PC training through JPC Computer Learning Centers. In all, Staffing Solutions has six recruiting offices and three computer learning centers in Greater Cleveland and Akron, serving all of northeast Ohio. The company specializes in placing computer-skilled office administration and professional level candidates.

"Staffing and technology are the two largest expense items of most companies, and making good choices around these items is crucial to their success," says Calta, now the company's CEO. "Our core business is focused on matching the right person with the right skill set to the right position. We place a great deal of emphasis on who we hire."

The company's growth and success have not gone unrecognized. In 1992, the Weatherhead School of Business at Case Western Reserve University ranked TempsPlus/Staffing Solutions as the third-fastest-growing company in northeast Ohio for its Weatherhead 100 awards. The company was also honored as Service Company of the Year. In 1996, Calta was chosen as one of the Top 20 Women Business Owners by the National Association of Women Business Owners.

SOPHISTICATED SERVICE

Peter Tuttle, president of Staffing Solutions Enterprises, says the firm's success has not come without its share of challenges: "The marketing of our services and the services themselves are becoming increasingly more sophisticated. The constant evolution of technology, as well as the advent of the Internet as a recruiting tool, has led Staffing Solutions to invest in the development of new services and training programs designed to help clients maximize the capabilities of available technology." In response to this rapid expansion of technology in business, the company opened three JPC Computer Learning Centers in 1995 and 1996, and began its OnLine Recruiting service in 1996.

The learning centers are state-licensed proprietary schools offering individualized, on-demand training for the latest business software and the Internet. JPC is open to the general public and corporate clients of Staffing Solutions, but was developed specifically to provide accessible, job-ready training for Staffing Solutions assignment employees. JPC has become the only training facility in northeast Ohio that can claim guaranteed results and has gained national recognition by the U.S. Department of Labor.

OnLine Recruiting is Staffing Solutions' latest venture, offering Internet recruiting, consulting, and custom tele-recruiting. This service enables companies to take advantage of today's recruiting technology without the up-front investment in equipment and software.

Staffing Solutions sees its future growth coming not only from the exploding on-line services arena, but also from the need to provide continuous training and

PRESIDENT PETER TUTTLE AND FOUNDER/CEO CARMELLA CALTA OVERSEE THE SUCCESS OF STAFFING SOLUTIONS ENTERPRISES (TOP).

THE COMPANY SPECIALIZES IN THE STAFFING OF PROFESSIONAL INDIVIDUALS WITH OFFICE AUTOMATION SKILLS (BOTTOM).

support for existing business clients. If its track record is any indication, the company will keep its finger on the pulse of the needs of Cleveland-area employers long into the 21st century.

KraftMaid Cabinetry, Inc.

KraftMaid Cabinetry, Inc., a full-service cabinetry company, was started in 1969 by company President Richard Moodie. In 1990, KraftMaid merged with the Masco Corporation of Taylor, Michigan, a Fortune 500 company that specializes in consumer

products for the home and the family and is listed on the New York Stock Exchange. Today, KraftMaid, the largest built-to-order cabinetry manufacturer in the United States, offers more than 85 door styles in six wood species and a large selection of laminates, as well as more than 100 optional convenience features. KraftMaid has dealers and distributors throughout the United States, Japan, Mexico, and other countries. In 1995, the 26-year-old company posted record annual sales of $250 million.

The company's continued growth, through product innovation and aggressive marketing concepts, has made KraftMaid an industry leader. Moodie's business philosophy of "a total commitment to KraftMaid customers" is a prime factor for the company's success and rapid growth. It is that commitment to customers that claims priority throughout the organization. Under Moodie's leadership, the company has become one of the greatest success stories in the history of the cabinetry industry.

Middlefield, Ohio, is the home of KraftMaid's factory and corporate headquarters. More than 2,000 people are employed by the company worldwide. Approximately three-quarters of them work in Middlefield, making KraftMaid the largest nongovernment employer in Geauga County. KraftMaid's manufacturing facility covers more than 1.25 million square feet and produces more than 7,000 cabinets, or 600 kitchens, per day. State-of-the-art equipment and production techniques are frequently fine-tuned, updated, and integrated with a strong tradition of Amish craftsmanship to consistently produce quality products.

PRODUCTS AND FEATURES TO MEET DIVERSE CONSUMER NEEDS

KraftMaid has a cabinetry style for all tastes and budgets. The company's semi-custom, built-to-order cabinetry is comprised of the Traditional and Euro 6 lines, featuring wood species in oak, maple, cherry, hickory, birch, and pine. Up to nine

rich colors and finishes are available, as are a number of stylish laminates.

Traditional-style cabinetry features solid hardwood, full-front frames. Rich hardwoods give a timeless, warm appearance. KraftMaid's Euro 6 European-style cabinetry (frameless construction) features a selection of solid wood doors and high-tech laminates for a sleek, contemporary look.

KraftMaid also offers two fully assembled, ready-for-installation stocked lines of cabinetry, KraftLine and KraftBath. KraftLine cabinetry is designed to satisfy the most discriminating tastes and discerning budgets, offering more for less in a large assortment of hardwood and laminate door styles. When price is important and quality a must, consumers can turn to KraftLine by KraftMaid.

The company's unique KraftBath Right Height Vanities are taller and deeper than conventional vanity bases, providing more comfort and storage. They have passed several tough tests for quality and structural integrity and contain wipe-clean interiors, smooth-action self-closing drawers

KraftMaid's Traditional line features oak, maple, cherry, hickory, birch, and pine in up to nine rich colors and finishes. The company's maple cabinetry, shown here in a natural finish, creates a simple gracefulness in this kitchen (top).

KraftBath Right Height Vanities are taller and deeper than conventional vanity bases, providing more comfort and storage. Solid oak cabinetry in KraftMaid's honey spice finish features a tall vanity linen cabinet topped with classic crown and rope molding (bottom).

and hinges, and solid hardwood-framed construction.

Custom craftsmanship and long-lasting durability are trademarks of all KraftMaid products. The company continues its commitment to product excellence by incorporating many specialty features as standard items on all cabinetry. Included is KraftMaid's exclusive, environmentally safe 14-step DuraKraft furniture finish, the finest in the industry, exceeding all specifications set by the Kitchen Cabinet Manufacturers Association (KCMA).

KraftMaid cabinetry is built within a one-week production cycle, the first one-week shipping program in the semicustom cabinetry industry. The company offers a quick-ship program from six distribution centers placed strategically throughout the United States. KraftMaid's large trucking fleet guarantees that orders arrive complete and on time—every time.

The first cabinetry manufacturer to offer a line of cabinetry exclusively for universal design, KraftMaid introduced the Passport Series to meet the needs of all kinds of consumers, from those with physical limitations to multi-generational households. Integrating these specialty cabinets with KraftMaid's other lines multiplies the possibilities and ensures a kitchen that will be as functional as it is fashionable for years to come.

Consumers are encouraged to personalize their kitchens by adding molding applications to enhance the room, decorative hardware to give character to the cabinets, and leaded glass and mullion doors to display fine china and family heirlooms. A seemingly endless list of optional convenience features makes kitchen life more livable, including lazy Susans, multistorage pantries, wine racks, microwave shelves, and cutlery dividers.

Cabinetry isn't just for the kitchen or bath anymore. With KraftMaid products, it's easy to create home furnishings for every room and to build entertainment centers, hutches, bedroom furniture, home offices, and more.

GETTING THE MESSAGE TO THE MARKET

KraftMaid's in-house advertising agency resides at the Hanna Building in the heart of Cleveland's theater district. The department is responsible for servicing the company's advertising, public and media relations, special events, premium program, and promotional needs. Intense marketing strategies have earned KraftMaid brand awareness and a reputation for quality. National and international trade and consumer magazine advertising and television commercials presell KraftMaid to the public, bringing customers into dealer locations. KraftMaid has been called the only company in the industry to simultaneously and successfully sell to both the kitchen and bath dealer and the home center markets, notoriously known for aggressive competition.

The World Wide Web offers

consumers the newest opportunity to receive the KraftMaid message. The company's site on the Web, www.kraftmaid.com, can be accessed at any time from anywhere in the world to view KraftMaid's products in full color.

KraftMaid builds some of America's finest cabinetry and Americans make it theirs. KraftMaid Cabinetry is a company built on people and ideas. It's a powerful combination, the result of which makes it easy to understand why KraftMaid considers itself America's cabinet choice.

KRAFTMAID DELIVERS CUSTOM CABINETRY, WITHOUT THE CUSTOM PRICE. THE COMPANY'S ENTERTAINMENT CENTERS FEATURE CUSTOM-DESIGNED ACOUSTICAL MATERIAL, WHICH HIDES THE SPEAKERS AND MEDIA EQUIPMENT.

KRAFTMAID OFFERS MORE THAN 85 DOOR STYLES AND MORE THAN 100 OPTIONAL CONVENIENCE FEATURES, INCLUDING A BASE DRAWER BUFFET, WHICH CONTAINS A CUTLERY DIVIDER, CUTTING BOARD, AND BREAD BOX.

ENTREPRENEURSHIP AND A KNACK FOR PIONEERING NEW TECHNOLOGY have made Newbury, Ohio-based Kinetico Incorporated a global leader in the manufacture of water treatment equipment. And because of its remarkable engineering achievements, the company has helped

more than 1 million people in more than 60 countries experience the benefits of better water through its residential, commercial, industrial, and community water systems.

Kinetico's president, William C. Prior, maintains that even with all of the company's success, he never envisioned a career in water treatment. After working as an engineer for an industrial equipment manufacturing firm, Prior was commissioned by a local water tank manufacturer to design a valve for its water softening equipment. With no background or knowledge of water treatment, Prior went to work on the valve, which became the foundation for Kinetico.

Prior was later joined by fellow engineer James W. Kewley, now executive vice president, and the two formed Kinetico Incorporated in 1970. Their business has grown tremendously from its humble beginnings in a rented, 1,600-square-foot garage. Today, Kinetico occupies a 175,000-

square-foot headquarters facility and has more than 500 dealers in the United States and abroad.

WATER CONDITIONERS AND MORE

Kinetico's success can be attributed to its innovative, almost radical system of softening water. The company's water conditioning systems are the only products of their kind that operate non-electrically, by the power of moving water. Kinetico systems are demand operated, using no clocks or timers, and feature twin tanks for an uninterrupted supply of soft water. This technology is what made Kinetico different from the beginning and has allowed it to go unmatched in the industry. The company holds more than 20 patents on its line of water treatment technologies.

Kinetico's commitment to designing water treatment products of superior quality, requiring

low maintenance and low operating costs, continued with the introduction of its first reverse osmosis drinking water system in the mid-1980s. The unique system produces high-quality drinking water on demand, and features the patented EverClean Rinse™ to help protect the life of the system and ensure the best-quality drinking water. Another exclusive feature is the patented MACguard Filter™, which lets the user know when the cartridges should be changed.

Kinetico's Consumer Products Division manufactures a diverse line of water conditioners, reverse osmosis systems, backwash filters, aeration systems, iron filters, neutralizers, and carbon filters, among others.

SERVING A DIVERSE MARKETPLACE

In the beginning, Kinetico only manufactured water conditioners for residential customers. Its success in this area led the

KINETICO INCORPORATED HAS HELPED MORE THAN 1 MILLION PEOPLE IN MORE THAN 60 COUNTRIES EXPERIENCE THE BENEFITS OF BETTER WATER. THE COMPANY'S INTERNATIONAL HEADQUARTERS IS LOCATED IN NEWBURY, OHIO (BOTTOM).

company to meet the growing demand for water treatment in commercial, industrial, and municipal applications. Kinetico has evolved into a global enterprise, offering water treatment solutions to a variety of customers, from hotel and restaurant chains to major manufacturers throughout the world.

Kinetico's Engineered Systems Division offers high-purity water production, wastewater treatment, and water recycling to its industrial customers. Because of stricter environmental regulations and new technology pioneered by Kinetico, this area has become a major source of growth for the company.

Kinetico's newest division, Community Water Systems, customizes treatment for municipalities. The division primarily benefits small communities that need to comply with federal and state drinking water standards. Kinetico's community water systems utilize Macrolite®, an exclusive ceramic filtration product developed in cooperation with 3M.

A REPUTATION FOR QUALITY

*Q*uality assurance is a top priority at every level of Kinetico's operations. Every product is individually tested for performance and undergoes a thorough manual inspection. As a way of maintaining the flow of innovative ideas that have long kept the company in the forefront of technology, Kinetico invests heavily in research and development. Its R&D staff operates two state-of-the-art laboratories where products are developed and tested, and certified water quality professionals analyze commercial, municipal, and residential water samples from all over the world.

Kinetico's water treatment products have consistently earned high marks for quality. Kinetico systems are certified by NSF International and the Water Quality

Association to perform as claimed. Select systems have also earned *Consumers Digest*'s prestigious Best Buy ranking and are recommended by the Good Housekeeping Institute.

WHERE THE WORLD TURNS FOR WATER

*K*inetico has recently begun a campaign designed to educate consumers and generate more awareness of its name in the marketplace. The company also has established a Web site at http://www.kinetico.com and a consumer water hot line, 800-944-WATER, through which consumers can request free information and answers to questions about water quality. And Dean Johnson and Robin Hartl, hosts of the popular home improvement television series *Hometime*®, have recently become spokespeople for the company.

As awareness of health and environmental issues increases

EXECUTIVE VICE PRESIDENT JAMES W. KEWLEY AND PRESIDENT WILLIAM C. PRIOR ARE COMMITTED TO PROVIDING THE MOST INNOVATIVE WATER TREATMENT PRODUCTS IN THE INDUSTRY (TOP).

KINETICO'S WATER CONDITIONING SYSTEMS ARE THE ONLY PRODUCTS OF THEIR KIND THAT OPERATE NONELECTRICALLY, BY THE POWER OF MOVING WATER (BOTTOM).

into the next century, Kinetico Incorporated will be there to improve the quality of one of life's basic necessities, offering the most innovative water treatment products in the industry.

HEN IT COMES TO REFRACTORY METALS, CUSTOMERS HAVE BEEN turning to Cleveland and CSM Industries since the company began its local operations in 1972. This Cleveland-based producer of specialized metal products, which has served the area for 25 years, is a major local presence—maintaining four plants worldwide, employing 300 people, and exceeding $80 million in annual sales.

Previously a division of Cyprus Amax Minerals Company, CSM was purchased in 1995 by Key Equity Capital, an investment arm of KeyCorp. The ownership change not only abbreviated the company's name from Climax Specialty Metals, but also unleashed the entrepreneurial spirit of its employees.

Located in Euclid, a suburb east of Cleveland, CSM's headquarters facility was built in 1961 to roll tungsten sheets and was purchased from General Electric by Amax, Inc. in 1972. Today, 35 sales, operating, and staff managers plan for the future and handle current business at the Euclid plant, while 70 employees produce hot and cold rolled plate, sheet, and foil from a range of refractory and specialty metals.

Three other facilities complete CSM's holdings. Built in 1958, the Coldwater, Michigan, plant employs 120 people and produces

powders, mill products, fabrications, and extrusions. Forty-four employees in the Brentwood, England, plant produce special metal fabrications and machined parts, and staff the company's European service center. Specialty metal products are further processed by 25 employees in the Latrobe, Pennsylvania, facility, which doubled in size to 25,000 square feet in 1996.

"Our intention is to increase the size and scope of our business," says William H. Steinbrink, president and chief executive officer, "and to become a publicly owned company based in Cleveland."

MOLYBDENUM IN ITS MANY FORMS

CSM processes refractory metals, including molybdenum, tungsten, tantalum, niobium, rhenium, and combinations formed into special alloys. The foundation of its business, however, is molybdenum, a metal with a list of re-

CLOCKWISE FROM TOP:
USING MORE THAN 3 MILLION POUNDS OF SEPARATING PRESSURE, CSM MILLS ROLL MOLYBDENUM AND TUNGSTEN INGOTS AT TEMPERATURES EXCEEDING 3,000 DEGREES FAHRENHEIT, CREATING MOLYBDENUM AND TUNGSTEN FLAT-ROLL PRODUCTS FOR A VARIETY OF APPLICATIONS.

WITH THE FOCUS ON PRODUCT DEVELOPMENT FOR NEW APPLICATIONS, CSM CONTINUES A COMMITMENT TO PARTNERSHIP, AS CUSTOMERS CREATE MORE USES FOR THE COMPANY'S VERSATILE PROCESS MATERIALS.

ROLLED PLATE, SHEET, AND FOIL—RANGING IN THICKNESS FROM TWO INCHES DOWN TO 0.0003 INCH—ARE PRODUCED FOR CSM CUSTOMERS THROUGHOUT THE WORLD.

markable properties that make it the material of choice in a wide variety of applications.

Molybdenum resists melting up to 4,730 degrees Fahrenheit—more than 20 times the temperature required to boil water. Also, it is highly resistant to corrosion and possesses high electrical and thermal conductivity. Molybdenum wears extremely slowly and resists abrasion. As a result, CSM products are used in heat-intense environments.

FROM SPACE TRAVEL TO LIVING ROOM LIGHTS

*M*olybdenum and its alloys can be found in electrical and electronic devices, materials processing, glass manufacturing, high-temperature furnaces and equipment, and aerospace and defense applications.

The wire used in the manufacture of lamp filaments is made from molybdenum, as are the leads and support structures in lighting and electronic tubes. Molybdenum powder is used in special circuit inks, and sheet is used in the tooling that applies those inks to multilayered circuit boards. Additionally, molybdenum is used in the internal components of microwave devices, high-performance electronic packaging, and heat sinks for solid-state power sources.

High-performance circuit boards and silicon wafers also benefit from molybdenum's thermal properties.

CSM products are used in medical equipment that requires special materials for performance. X-ray tubes and X-ray detectors, for example, feature parts made from molybdenum and tungsten metals and alloys.

Fashioned into electrodes, molybdenum is used to melt glass in high-temperature furnaces. This versatile material outperforms other specialty metals in glass handling equipment and tooling.

As a consequence of its strength and stability at high temperatures, molybdenum is often utilized in vacuum furnaces, fixtures, and tooling. It is the material of choice in construction of vacuum furnaces used to treat critical titanium components in the aerospace industry. These qualities also make the metal ideal for use in processing nuclear fuel and other specialty ceramics.

FROM THE DEPTHS OF THE EARTH TO THE REALMS OF SPACE

*C*SM Industries also manufactures plate and sheet metal from MP35N, an alloy of nickel, cobalt, chromium, and molybdenum. This material has

unique properties that make it ideal for applications requiring high toughness at low temperatures, high spring rates, and resistance to the effects of sulfurous gases. CSM's material is used in the severe environments found in deep-hole oil and sour gas wells. It has the greatest resistance to sulfide stress cracking of any material yet developed. It also has been selected as the construction material for a critical seal in the alternate liquid hydrogen turbopump for the space shuttle's main engine. The process used to manufacture the plate for this seal requires CSM to roll four-inch-thick material to 1.5 inches thick, with a strength exceeding 220,000 pounds per square inch. The finished plate is machined by a contractor to a thickness of 0.015 inch. CSM thus brings its specialized production skills to demanding applications for unique metals.

Buoyed by Key Equity's multimillion-dollar investment, CSM Industries stands poised to fashion a bright future from its work with molybdenum and other refractory metals. While improving its position in existing markets, the company expects to find new applications for its products and expertise, and to seek other opportunities in related markets.

PRODUCTS ARE SHIPPED WORLDWIDE FROM CSM'S LOCATION IN EUCLID, WHERE 105 EMPLOYEES SERVE MORE THAN 2,000 CUSTOMERS (LEFT).

CAREFUL QUALITY CONTROL OF PROCESSES AND MATERIALS ASSURES CUSTOMERS THAT CSM'S FLAT-ROLLED PRODUCTS MEET THEIR EXPECTATIONS (RIGHT).

IN THE PAST 25 YEARS, CLEVELAND HAS TRANSFORMED ITSELF INTO A national comeback story and a popular tourist destination. The efforts of the Northeast Ohio Regional Sewer District have contributed greatly to this transformation. ❖ Established in 1972, the District has led the

CLOCKWISE FROM TOP:
THE WESTERLY WASTEWATER TREATMENT PLANT, NEAR EDGEWATER BEACH, DISCHARGES INTO LAKE ERIE.

THE DISTRICT HAS BUILT A NUMBER OF MASSIVE INTERCEPTOR SEWER SYSTEMS AS PART OF ITS CAPITAL IMPROVEMENT PROGRAM, INCLUDING THE BIG CREEK INTERCEPTOR.

Discover the World beneath Your Feet WAS PRESENTED AT EARTHFEST AT THE CLEVELAND METROPARKS ZOO.

clean water initiatives that allowed the city to plan a bicentennial celebration along the Cuyahoga River and Lake Erie. It also has helped restore Cleveland's waterfront to a vital center of recreational and commercial opportunities.

By continuing its current efforts, Executive Director Erwin J. Odeal believes the District will contribute further to the city's rebirth. "The future of Cleveland's water resources is in the hands of its residents and its clean-water utility, the Northeast Ohio Regional Sewer District. By working cooperatively, we can continue to positively shape the city's destiny," Odeal says.

CLEANING UP CLEVELAND'S WATER

A city built on manufacturing and industry, Cleveland can trace its water quality problems back nearly 100 years, when local sewers emptied into nearby streams, the river, and Lake Erie. Suburban growth, the lack of industrial discharge regulation, and inadequate older combined sewers exacerbated the problem. Water was considered unsafe for recreational use, discouraging the development of river and lakefront projects.

In 1972, in reaction to nationwide water quality problems, Congress enacted the Clean Water Act and, by court order, the Northeast Ohio Regional Sewer District was created. Today, the District has 650 employees who serve more than 1 million people living in Cleveland and 52 suburban communities. This region encompasses more than 295 square miles.

The District operates three wastewater treatment facilities. The Southerly and Easterly plants have received national awards for meeting permit limits set under the National Pollutant Discharge Elimination System (NPDES). Improvements completed at the Westerly plant in 1996 now enable it to meet all NPDES permit limits.

As part of its effort to control industrial waste, the District monitors and samples discharges from more than 1,000 industrial and commercial users. It also analyzes more than 600,000 samples of water, wastewater, and industrial waste in one of the state's largest laboratories.

The District has built a number of massive interceptor sewer systems as part of its capital improvement program. Wastewater from overburdened sewer systems that had previously drained into the region's streams and lake now feeds into these interceptors. The District built the Northwest Interceptor in the early 1980s and completed the 22-mile-long Cuyahoga Valley Interceptor in

1984. The Cuyahoga River Valley is now a national recreational area, attracting thousands of outdoors enthusiasts annually.

At a cost of nearly $350 million, the Southwest and Heights/Hilltop interceptors also relieve overburdened sewer systems. Completed in 1995, the Southwest Interceptor transports wastewater from Cleveland's southwest suburbs to the Southerly Plant. Upon completion in 2000, the Heights/Hilltop Interceptor will serve about 252,000 residents in the eastern suburbs and transport flow to the Easterly Plant. These interceptors alleviate overflows to the environment, provide additional capacity to community or county sanitary sewer systems, and eliminate the need for smaller plants and pumping stations.

ENVIRONMENTAL ACTION AND EDUCATION

The District has initiated several projects to improve water quality in Greater Cleveland. One such program is the Mill Creek Project, which will encourage public contact with the historic Mill Creek region. This project is the first of several planned to control combined sewer overflows.

To teach citizens the importance of the environment, the District has developed educational programs. For example, the Student Teacher Enrichment Program arranges field trips to public works agencies to educate junior high school students. The District also organizes tours for the public and participates in community events to teach the importance of clean water.

To help local businesses grow and thrive, the District encourages participation in its capital improvement projects. In addition, the District has received national recognition for providing business opportunities to minority- and

women-owned businesses.

The District is one of 34 agencies involved in the Cuyahoga River Remedial Action Plan (RAP). RAP is an initiative to reduce pollution along 10 miles of Lake Erie shoreline and 45 miles of the Cuyahoga River. These riverfront areas run from Cleveland to Akron along the Ohio and Erie Canal Towpath Trail.

FLOWING INTO THE FUTURE

As the District enters the 21st century, the largest challenge it will face will be to further control water pollution caused by overflows from combined sewer systems during heavy rainstorms. These discharges can trigger high levels of bacteria that hamper the ecosystem, carry debris such as bottles and cans into the waterways, and create potential health hazards. As part of the solution, the District operates a computerized system of more than 25 dams and gates to store overflows. Once a storm has passed, overflows are routed to the nearest wastewater treatment plant.

Though improved wastewater treatment and new sewer construction have largely revitalized Cleveland's river and lake, the District still has work to do. Combined and wet-weather sewer overflows, as well as polluted

storm water, continue to impact water quality in local streams that are tributary to the Cuyahoga River and Lake Erie. Since all costs are paid by District sewer users, the ongoing challenge is to cost-effectively address pollution sources. By continuing to work cooperatively with businesses, industry, and citizens, the Northeast Ohio Regional Sewer District can positively help shape the future of the city's waterways and continue to protect Greater Cleveland's clean water investment.

CHEMICAL ANALYSES AT THE DISTRICT'S LABORATORY ARE SHOWN TO JUNIOR HIGH SCHOOL STUDENTS AS PART OF AN EDUCATIONAL PROGRAM SPONSORED BY THE DISTRICT (TOP).

THE DISTRICT INTENDS TO CONTINUE SHAPING THE FUTURE OF THE CITY'S WATERWAYS, PROTECTING GREATER CLEVELAND'S CLEAN WATER INVESTMENT (BOTTOM).

FOUNDED IN CHICAGO IN 1921, HEALTH O METER HAS ESTABLISHED a long-standing reputation for producing commercial-quality thermometers; high-quality electronic and mechanical physician, neonatal/pediatric, wheelchair, ramp, platform, chair, and stretcher/

lifter scales; and the Pelouze brand of electronic and mechanical parcel post, general utility, postal, portion control, and receiving scales. The company achieved $14.6 million in net sales in 1984, and by 1993, had reached the $67.6 million mark.

Not willing to slow down with that success, Health o meter's 1994 acquisition of Cleveland-based Mr. Coffee Inc. provided a boost in revenue of 286 percent—from $69.4 million for the nine

months following the acquisition to $267.9 million in 1995. Soon after the transaction, Health o meter named Peter C. McC. Howell to the post of chairman and CEO and relocated its corporate headquarters to the Bedford Heights offices of Mr. Coffee.

Joining three high-recognition brand names under one umbrella—Mr. Coffee, Health o meter, and Pelouze, each of which occupied the number one market position within its own category—

has allowed the company to pursue further growth from a position of strength. The combined impact of these brand names and the advertising support behind them ensure powerful consumer demand for the company's products and enable it to compete with larger and better capitalized manufacturers.

THE HISTORY OF MR. COFFEE

Founded in Cleveland in 1972, Mr. Coffee revolutionized an entire industry when it introduced the first home automatic drip coffeemaker to an upscale market. By offering superior-tasting coffee brewed faster, the product blasted the percolator out of the market, helped create the $400 million home coffeemaker industry, and put Mr. Coffee's products in more than 70 million U.S. homes. By 1976, the company had captured a 55 percent share of the market.

Within the next decade, Mr. Coffee's creative development dropped off and its market share slipped to 27 percent. Company founders decided to sell the business in 1987 at the height of the leveraged buyout (LBO) craze, and permanent financing was completed in February 1988.

Mr. Coffee went public in 1990, and began to recapture a more substantial share of the market by introducing new products, such as the Iced Tea Pot; the Water Filter Pitcher; and the Potato Perfect Quick Potato Baker, its first nonbeverage product. In 1993, the company retired its $86.5 million LBO debt and opened its Appliance Innovations division to more aggressively pursue expansion through new products. Mr. Coffee went on to generate more than $160

A NEW PRODUCT IN 1997, THE HANDSOME MR. COFFEE® THERMAL GOURMET® THERMAL CARAFE COFFEEMAKER RETAINS A JUST-BREWED FLAVOR FOR UP TO FOUR HOURS, THANKS TO DOUBLE-WALL INSULATION.

million in sales, making it a prosperous corporation at the time of its acquisition by Health o meter.

PROFESSIONALS AND CONSUMERS

*I*n a key strategic move following the acquisition, Health o meter determined that it would operate and manage its business in two distinct groups: professional and consumer. By approaching the business in this way, the company emphasized growing the professional group, which also provides product development and quality reputation benefits to the consumer group.

The professional group, which includes Health o meter's medical distribution, office products, food services, commercial coffeemaker, and international businesses, experienced strong growth right away. This success was primarily due to an increase in the company's office products business and an impressive new product introduced in 1995: an advanced postal and shipping scale featuring a programmable rate calculator.

The consumer business, which is built around the Mr. Coffee and Health o meter product lines, initially experienced modest growth, due mainly to a difficult retail environment. However, investment in new product development was rewarded with several innovative additions to the company's offerings, including the new Big Foot scales and the Mrs. Tea by Mr. Coffee automatic hot tea maker. Additionally, Health o meter remains the leader in its core categories of brewers, tea makers, branded filters, replacement decanters, and scales.

HEALTH, WELLNESS, AND SAFETY

*F*ocused on refining and enhancing its core strengths, Health o meter has continued to build on its medical

heritage and to solidify its reputation as America's health, wellness, and safety company. Health o meter has also realized further growth in light of the increasing importance of home health care and personal weight management as an important aspect of preventive health care. Fully aware of the exceptional consumer confidence in its products, Health o meter incorporated the technology from its medical scales into home health care non-invasive measuring devices, and introduced products to assist the health-conscious consumer. Also, in 1996, the company entered the veterinary market with the broadest line of scales available in the industry.

Perhaps most important, though, is Health o meter's ongoing development of partnering

THE MRS. TEA™ HOT TEA MAKER BREWS DELICIOUS TEA IN A BEAUTIFULLY CRAFTED CERAMIC POT THAT IS PERFECT FOR TEA LOVERS.

EXTENDED FOOT ROOM AND A WONDERFULLY EASY-TO-READ DIAL MAKE THE HEALTH O METER® TOP-END PROFESSIONAL SCALE A STANDOUT.

relationships with major retailers. In today's retail environment, mass merchandising and supplier consolidation are currently shaping the future of the retail industry. The successful integration of the best components of Health o meter and its newly acquired Mr. Coffee has positioned the company to benefit from this dynamic retailing arena, setting the stage for exciting growth for years to come.

FINANCIAL SECURITY, INTEGRITY, SERVICE, PEACE OF MIND—THIS HAS been the philosophy behind Maxus Investment Group since it opened its doors in 1973. Maxus Investment Group is considered one of the oldest investment firms in the Cleveland area to focus on asset

management and equity research. The company was established by Richard A. Barone during a time of significant change in the investment industry. Maxus began in a stock market environment that was tentative at best, and, to most, it appeared practically impossible to survive in any corner of the investment industry, let alone begin a new business. "When I left the regional broker where I had worked for seven years, many of my previous partners told me that I would not survive," recalls Barone, who currently serves as the firm's chairman and CEO. "Looking back, I could not have picked a better time to begin to develop a track record as a money manager."

Maxus was instantly successful in its early years. Barone's vision, and the one compelling reason that prompted him to establish Maxus in the first place, was that he believed successful and thoughtful businesspeople would be more willing to pay for investment advice if the advice could be separate from the com-

mission on each transaction. Those advisers who provided the best advice would attract the most money to manage. Those brokers who provided the best and least expensive execution would attract the most stock transactions. Smaller investors would be able to pool their accounts in such vehicles as partnerships or smaller, highly managed mutual funds, so that everyone could reap the benefits of a more efficient marketplace.

If this sounds familiar today, it was no more than a figment of the imagination in 1973. Nevertheless, Barone believed that, by 1980, private investment, discount brokerage, and mutual funds would comprise the three great channels through which private individuals and institutions would invest their funds. It made sense to him to position Maxus to take advantage of each.

VISION BECOMES REALITY
*M*axus was successful in those early years. In terms of investment performance alone, by 1984, Maxus had achieved what the national media characterized as an exceptional

investment record. Client portfolios were based upon a value-oriented investment style. Value investing during the years after the firm's founding produced results far superior to the traditional growth style of investing.

Barone spent some time considering where the firm might be going in the future. The eight or nine individuals who made up the marketing and support team at the time were banking their careers not only on whether he made the right investment decisions, but on whether or not he was committed to growing the company. Based upon experience, including the investment house failures in the 1970s, it made a great deal of sense to avoid high overhead in this extremely cyclical industry. On the other hand, providing meaningful careers and opportunity for the people in the organization, as well as moving to the leading edge within the Cleveland investment management community, required a substantial investment in people, infrastructure, marketing, product development, and technology. Since Barone still believed in his original vision of some 10 years earlier, he decided

FOUNDED IN 1973, MAXUS INVESTMENT GROUP HAS ALWAYS BEEN FIRMLY COMMITTED TO THE CLEVELAND COMMUNITY (TOP).

FINANCIAL SECURITY, INTEGRITY, SERVICE, AND PEACE OF MIND COMPRISE THE PHILOSOPHY BEHIND MAXUS INVESTMENT GROUP (BOTTOM).

to bite the bullet and move the company forward.

In 1985, the firm made its first commitment to the mutual fund industry with the introduction of the Maxus Income Fund. In 1989, a second mutual fund, the Maxus Equity Fund, was introduced. Both the Maxus Income and the Maxus Equity funds were performing well and growing in total assets when, in 1993, Maxus introduced its third mutual fund, the Maxus Laureate Fund.

By 1992, Maxus moved to expand its senior management team, another indication of Barone's strong commitment to growing the company. Today, he oversees 50 employees and, in terms of investment transaction revenues produced by nonbank, Cleveland-based companies, Maxus ranks second in size. Currently, the firm manages $1.2 billion and transacts nearly 1 million shares daily on the various exchanges for clients, other broker/dealers, and money managers. Maxus also holds a minority interest in the Midwest Research/Maxus Group, which is focused

on researching publicly traded companies in the Midwest, and continues to hold minority interests in various publicly and privately traded companies.

Maxus Investment Group has always been firmly committed to the Cleveland community, but, in 1994, that commitment was enhanced by the creation of the Maxus Foundation. Sharing good fortune, advancing causes worth believing in, and leaving a positive mark on the future are what the Maxus Foundation is all about. The foundation helps to make philanthropy simple and more effective through flexibility in the timing of charitable gifts, administrative ease, and immediate tax benefits. Many organizations have benefited greatly from Maxus' generosity through the establishment of scholarships and donor-advised funds. In addition, the Maxus Foundation has contributed significantly to many educational programs, including the Educational Endowment Fund at one of Cleveland's premier attractions—the Rock and Roll Hall of Fame and Museum.

INFORMATION TECHNOLOGY GUIDES FUTURE GROWTH

*I*n the future, information technology will further enhance the ability of individual investors to pick and choose among a variety of investment choices and investment managers. "The whole concept of controlling your own transaction is a key component to the future of the investment industry and central to its entire infrastructure," according to Barone.

Today, Maxus Investment Group offers one of the most comprehensive and performance-driven investment services available. The company's people, programs, and performance are focused exclusively on the building of wealth and security for its clients. With three mutual funds, various proprietary partnerships, private portfolio management, on-line brokerage, and a core of investment advisers and investment consultants, Maxus is exceptionally well equipped to face the challenges of the 21st century.

RICHARD A. BARONE, CHAIRMAN AND CEO, FOUNDED MAXUS WITH THE BELIEF THAT SUCCESSFUL AND THOUGHTFUL BUSINESSPEOPLE WOULD BE MORE WILLING TO PAY FOR INVESTMENT ADVICE IF THE ADVICE COULD BE SEPARATE FROM THE COMMISSION ON EACH TRANSACTION.

THE GREATER CLEVELAND REGIONAL TRANSIT AUTHORITY (RTA) IS driving the city's renaissance, transporting residents and visitors wherever they need to go. Since its inception in 1975, RTA has served the needs of riders within a territory that now totals 459 square miles and encompasses 59 cities populated by 1.6 million people. In 1996 alone, RTA carried 58.7 million riders by bus or rail.

Using the system's heavy-rail line, riders can travel from Cleveland Hopkins International Airport to a string of west-side stops, and continue on to the Tower City Station downtown or east as far as Windermere station, which is currently undergoing a $12.7 million face-lift. Additionally, RTA's light-rail system provides easy access to Shaker Square and downtown Cleveland from many east-side communities, including Shaker Heights, Beachwood, and University Heights.

From any stop along the way, riders have the option of transferring to buses that can put them within walking distance of virtually any destination in Greater Cleveland. Whether looking for a ride to work or to the ballet, residents can depend on RTA to get them there.

Tourists enjoying the city's various attractions will quickly become acquainted with the new Waterfront Line, a $55 million rail project that transports riders from the Tower City stop to the Rock and Roll Hall of Fame and Museum, the Great Lakes Science Center, and the Flats entertainment district.

RTA also provides special service to events downtown, including baseball at Jacobs Field, the Cleveland Grand Prix, and the National Air Show, and to summertime fun at such destinations as the Metroparks RainForest and Zoo, Sea World, and Geauga Lake. Celebrants of the city's bicentennial in 1996 enjoyed services tailored to the many events that were planned throughout the year across Greater Cleveland.

Beyond its transportation role, RTA has forged partnerships with governments across the region, joining municipal leaders to complete a long list of projects, including the Walkway to Gateway from Tower City. Central to RTA's initiatives is its commitment to becoming a total quality organization focused foremost on serving customers.

PLANNING FOR 2010 AND BEYOND

In 1996, RTA invested $6 million in a new headquarters facility. Located in the Root-McBride Building in the historic Warehouse District, RTA is now close to its Waterfront Line and the center of Cleveland's urban renaissance. In conjunction with the opening of its Harvard Garage in 1995, RTA added 65 buses powered by compressed natural gas, especially appealing to those concerned about the environment, as well as to riders who appreciate a quiet, smooth ride. Eventually, RTA plans to replace its fleet of 600 diesel coaches with buses running on this environmentally friendly fuel.

In other future plans, RTA envisions 40 major bus and rail projects. The $200 million Euclid Corridor Improvement Project will establish dedicated bus lanes along Euclid Avenue from Public Square to University Circle. The development of transit centers at strategic locations throughout Greater Cleveland will simplify bus transfers where multiple bus lines intersect. Smaller vehicles will provide transportation to popular destinations in the Lee-Harvard and St. Clair-Superior neighborhoods.

Among the expansions on the drawing board is the extension of rail service to Berea, located southwest of the airport. In coming years, the Regional Transit Authority will also begin providing rail service connecting Cleveland, Akron, and Canton, furthering its mission of improving the mobility of area residents, as well as responding to the needs of the area's growing tourism market.

PART OF THE THRILL OF GETTING TO CLEVELAND'S NEWEST AND MOST POPULAR ATTRACTIONS IS RIDING RTA. SPECIAL SERVICE PROVIDED FOR THE 1995 OPENING OF THE ROCK AND ROLL HALL OF FAME CARRIED APPROXIMATELY 500,000 RIDERS. IN 1996, THE WATERFRONT LINE BEGAN PROVIDING RAIL SERVICE TO THE FLATS AND NORTH COAST HARBOR AREAS, LINKING SUCH ATTRACTIONS AS THE GUND ARENA, JACOBS FIELD, AND TOWER CITY WITH THE GREAT LAKES SCIENCE CENTER AND THE ROCK AND ROLL HALL OF FAME.

BANK ONE

ORN IN THE NEIGHBORHOODS AND SMALL COMMUNITIES THAT COM-
prise northeast Ohio, Bank One has never forgotten its roots. Formed
from the merger of three community institutions—Chardon
Savings Bank, Euclid National Bank, and Lake National Bank—the

Cleveland arm of Columbus-based BANC ONE CORPORATION today has nearly 60 offices in a five-county market, boasts $2.7 billion in assets, and serves as the regional headquarters for the bank's northeast Ohio operations.

Despite its growing presence across the region, Bank One has remained close to the people, businesses, and nonprofit organizations that it serves.

One of the hallmarks of the bank's community outreach initiative has been its desire to make banking responsive to neighborhood needs. For example, in 1994, the bank opened a branch at the Karamu House complex in Cleveland's Fairfax neighborhood. The office provides discounted money orders, check cashing for non-account holders, and extended banking hours.

Similarly, in 1995, Bank One opened community banking centers in the Gordon Square Arcade in the Detroit-Shoreway neighborhood, at a shopping center on Ridge Road, and in the Glenville community. The latter office was visited by Vice President Al Gore in 1996, who lavished praise on it as a national model for community reinvestment. An ongoing dialogue is held with community advisory councils in Ashtabula, Cuyahoga, Geauga, Lake, and Lorain counties so as to apprise the bank of the area's most pressing financial needs.

Bank One is at the vanguard of efforts to add affordable housing stock to the community while preserving Cleveland's architectural heritage. The bank's indirect home improvement program helps

residents of designated low- and moderate-income areas by processing their loan applications directly through home improvement dealers. In partnership with the

Diocese of Cleveland, the bank financed Ascension Village, a west side apartment complex for elderly people on fixed incomes; and in 1997, on the near west side, it put up financing for three different occupant-owned housing projects.

On a related front, new life is being breathed into efforts to revitalize housing and preserve historic buildings, in large part due to the bank's long-running support of the Cleveland Restoration Society, Cleveland Action to Support Housing, Living in Cleveland Center, Habitat for Humanity, and Lutheran Housing Corp.

Bank One has been a trailblazer in helping small businesses grow. In 1996, the bank ranked fourth nationally in small-business lending and topped the list of statewide SBA lenders. Its revolving credit lines continue to make working capital available at reasonable interest rates, and its

participation in Cleveland's microloan program assists entrepreneurs who have well-conceived business plans, but who are unable to secure conventional sources of credit. Through other programs, the bank reaches out to veterans in the small-business community, and its sponsorship of the Weatherhead 100 gives recognition to the area's fastest-growing companies.

As new opportunities to make a difference present themselves, the bank responds. Recently, Bank One became a founder of Cleveland's new football stadium, a project that will generate new jobs and a steady stream of tax revenues.

Through its business lending practices, charitable contributions, and understanding of the neighborhoods that are its roots, Bank One remains a vital part of Greater Cleveland's economic and spiritual renaissance.

BANK ONE CENTER IS LOCATED AT 600 SUPERIOR AVENUE IN DOWNTOWN CLEVELAND (LEFT).

IN 1994, THE BANK OPENED A BRANCH AT THE KARAMU HOUSE COMPLEX IN CLEVELAND'S FAIRFAX NEIGHBORHOOD. THE OFFICE PROVIDES DISCOUNTED MONEY ORDERS, CHECK CASHING FOR NON-ACCOUNT HOLDERS, AND EXTENDED BANKING HOURS (RIGHT).

CHRISTIAN & TIMBERS INC.

CHRISTIAN & TIMBERS IS THE NATION'S FASTEST-GROWING RETAINED executive search firm and ranks among the top 20 executive search firms in the country. The company was founded in 1979 and now has full-service offices in Boston; Cupertino, California; New York City; and Washington, D.C., in addition to its Cleveland headquarters.

Christian & Timbers specializes in senior search execution, focusing on CEO, general manager, vice president level, and board positions. The company executes search assignments for established Fortune 500 companies as well as hard-charging emerging-growth companies worldwide. Christian & Timbers' practice areas have expanded to include information technology, health care, manufacturing, consumer products, environmental services, and financial services.

The company works with corporations like Nestlé, Xerox, Black & Decker, Compuserve, Dell Computer, GoJo Industries, Kaiser Aluminum, Lucent Technologies, Picker International, Universal Electronics, America On-Line, KeyBank, Allen Bradley, IBM, AT&T, Welch Foods, Microsoft, Disney, McDonald's, Apple Computer, and Pillsbury. Working across this breadth of companies has given Christian & Timbers insight into the people who effectively drive managerial success. As a result, Christian & Timbers is the world's leading search firm when it comes to placing key executives at Internet companies.

The firm is also known for building management teams for emerging-growth companies. Christian & Timbers was a significant player in staffing Dental Research, the company that invented Interplak, the toothbrush that was eventually sold to Bausch & Lomb.

And, today, the company is building entire management teams for several Internet companies. Christian & Timbers has recently helped AT&T, Borland International, Disney On-Line, Hewlett-Packard, Open Market, and PictureTel in this regard.

Christian & Timbers is small enough to provide the personal attention that its clients expect. Being client focused, no matter what the size of the client, is a hallmark of Christian & Timbers' search execution.

Research is a core function of the firm. Christian & Timbers' highly resourced, internal research does the original raw research for each new assignment.

As a result, Christian & Timbers has developed two proprietary research methods that enhance the search process— Universe 100 and People Asset Management—both groundbreaking methodologies in the recruitment field.

Universe 100 has proved to be the definitive method for identifying the most complete pool of top executive talent. In addition, the company has developed People Asset Management, a diagnostic tool that enables companies to focus on critical paths to strengthen their management teams. It is a method that predicts organizational fit and team cohesion.

In fact, Christian & Timbers' goal is to have the highest ratio of researchers to search executives of any firm. Through the People

CHRISTIAN & TIMBERS ASSOCIATES BRING EACH OTHER UP TO DATE WITH A NEW INTERNET SEARCH REQUEST.

Asset Management approach, each senior partner serves three to four corporations, diagnosing their management strengths and establishing a basis when the time comes to hire new employees. Each client receives guidance on such issues as compensation, relocation, diversity staffing, organizational dynamics, transitions, succession planning, management development, and management assessment and audits.

Rather than relying on outdated information, the firm's trademark Universe 100 process utilizes extensive computer-aided research done by in-house specialists to provide clients with the latest information on viable candidates.

These research techniques have allowed Christian & Timbers to discover talent for corporate America. The firm's research has been instrumental in the success of every one of its searches, whether it be filling the post of a CEO, a board director, or any position in executive management, across functional disciplines.

AT CHRISTIAN & TIMBERS, CONSULTANTS MEET DAILY TO DISCUSS HOT ISSUES IN EXECUTIVE RECRUITING.

In 1994, Christian & Timbers established a business model that places the greatest emphasis on client satisfaction. As a result, company specialists know the unique needs of clients and the intricacies and nuances of their various lines of business. Christian & Timbers continues to provide clients with assistance after a search, helping during offer negotiations and when a candidate tenders his or her resignation. With the firm involved in this way, managers have more time to concentrate on running their businesses.

The company has rapid growth plans that include several more domestic offices and at least two international offices. Christian & Timbers has also established a presence on the Internet at http://www.ctnet.com.

ACCORDING TO DICTIONARY DEFINITIONS, A CLARION IS A LOUD, CLEAR sound resembling a trumpet's call. Perhaps that's why the name of the Clarion Hotel and Conference Center seems so fitting. As a hotel with one of the largest conference areas on Cleveland's east side, the

Clarion seems to beckon business and pleasure travelers with its elegance, amenities, and quality service.

MAINTAINING A COMMITMENT TO THE CORPORATE CUSTOMER

The Clarion Hotel and Conference Center has 115 guest rooms and 12,446 square feet of meeting space, as well as six parlor suites, a pool, an exercise and fitness area, and a sauna. Mantel's, a full-service restaurant, is open for breakfast, lunch, and dinner. The hotel's flexible ballroom space can accommodate up to 400 people, or it can be reconfigured for a small, intimate luncheon. The Clarion's

versatile ballroom is often used for weddings, family gatherings, and business and organizational banquets.

While the hotel caters to visitors requiring an array of services, it has not forgotten its roots in serving the corporate customer in fine style. To that end the Clarion offers a complete conference center as well as services for individual business travelers. Its 15 classrooms can accommodate from 10 to 150 people each, and its auditorium can seat up to 600. The Clarion's conference center provides such audiovisual services as slide projectors, video projectors and screens, satellite hookups, and even a photography and tele-

vision studio for its guests. A business center, which includes computers, fax machines, and secretarial services, is also available for corporate clients.

The hotel has separate dining areas for those attending business meetings and offers private memberships to a corporate luncheon club. Regardless of the setting, the Clarion is equipped to handle all the details of a business meeting, fulfilling whatever needs may arise. As a result, the hotel has been able to generate and maintain the loyalty of many corporate customers in the Cleveland area.

Another sign of the Clarion's commitment to corporate customers is the close relationship

THE CLARION'S FIVE-STORY GUEST-ROOM BUILDING IS JOINED TO THE CONFERENCE CENTER THROUGH THE LOBBY AREA.

THE BALLROOM IS SUITED FOR
UP TO 400 PEOPLE FOR DINNER
OR 600 FOR A CONFERENCE.

the hotel has maintained with Reliance Electric Co. An anchor tenant of the Clarion property since it opened, the motors and computerized drives company leases 25,000 square feet of space from the hotel.

The Clarion also places great emphasis on a philosophy of appreciation and consideration—to both its customers and its employees. The results are satisfied customers who come back time and again, as well as happy employees who will remain loyal to the Clarion far into the future.

SERVING THE COMMUNITY

*T*he Clarion is committed to the community in which it does business. Hotel managers hold active memberships in the Lake County Convention Bureau, the Eastlake Chamber of Commerce, the Greater Cleveland Hotel and Motel Association, and the Cleveland Convention and Visitors Bureau. In addition, the Clarion's 120 year-round employees regularly support local Red Cross blood drives.

MANTEL'S IS A FAVORITE WITH
LOCAL CLIENTELE, AS WELL AS
HOTEL GUESTS.

Located at the intersection of Routes 2 and 91, and easily accessible from Route 90, the Clarion is a 15-minute drive from Cleveland and such attractions as Jacobs Field, Great Lakes Science Center, Rock and Roll Hall of Fame and Museum, Playhouse Square, and the museums at University Circle. The hotel is also close to entertainment opportunities in the eastern suburbs, such as Sea World, Geauga Lake amusement park, Mentor Headlands lakefront park,

and several eastern Metroparks. And the Clarion's Lake County location makes the hotel part of a bustling new growth area in metropolitan Cleveland, which is home to booming corporate and residential developments.

Whether serving the business customer, the leisure traveler, or the Greater Cleveland community, the Clarion represents a refreshing lodging alternative. And its call to provide friendly, quality service is being heard far and wide.

THE NATION'S LARGEST INDEPENDENT SUPPLIER OF HEATING, ventilation, air-conditioning, and refrigeration equipment has had a major presence in northeast Ohio since 1981. York International Corporation's influence can be felt around the world.

The air cooling the English Channel Tunnel, the World Trade Center towers, the U.S. Navy's submarine fleet, and the world's tallest twin towers in Kuala Lumpur is generated by York technology. The company has also contributed its ingenuity, innovation, and quality to the English Parliament building, the Russian Kremlin, the Pentagon, the Hong Kong skyline, and the Grand Mosque in Mecca.

From its headquarters in York, Pennsylvania, the company manufactures, sells, and services heating, ventilation, and air-conditioning systems, and compressors for residential and commercial markets; gas compression equipment for industrial processing; industrial and commercial refrigeration equipment; and compressors for air-conditioning and refrigeration.

York offers innovative solutions in response to technological improvements, environmental mandates, cost savings, and quality assurance; completes strategic acquisitions, joint ventures, and alliances; and moves aggressively into commercial and residential markets for new and aftermarket services in heating, air-conditioning, ventilation, cooling, and refrigeration. These abilities have generated positive results: In 1995, York set new annual financial records, increasing its gross revenues by 21 percent to $2.93 billion and improving its international revenues by 25 percent.

GLOBAL PRESENCE

Since 1874, York has been meeting the needs of its customers worldwide. The company operates 300 service offices and 19 manufacturing facilities around the world—in Australia, England, France, Germany, Mexico, the United States, and Uruguay. Through joint ventures, York has also extended its manufacturing operations to Egypt, Malaysia, and Taiwan.

In response to the clamor for energy efficiency, York has brought to market low-energy, high-performance chillers; refrigeration; and unitary air-conditioning products, allowing customers to enjoy utility rebates and other demand-side management benefits.

When the industry called for alternatives to traditional refrigerants, York responded with designs that allow customers to choose between water- and ammonia-based refrigerants. Indoor air-quality needs are met by York products that use the latest in air-handling technology to purge the air of environmental hazards. Likewise, York food refrigeration designs have eliminated gaps where food particles and dirt can become trapped, thereby compromising the quality of the contents.

AN OLYMPIC SPONSOR

York has also established a global presence by contributing to many memorable Olympic competitions. Since its debut at the 1960 Winter Games, when it was responsible for the smooth ice on which skaters competed at Squaw Valley, California, the company has designed the innovative bobsled track used at the 1988 Winter Games in Calgary as well as the facilities for the bobsled, figure skating, and speed skating competitions during the 1994 games in Lillehammer. In addition, York snowmaking machines covered the slopes for the 1992 Winter Games in Albertville. At the 1992 Barcelona and 1996 Atlanta Summer Games, York air-conditioning cooled indoor athletic competitions, and in the year 2000 the company will cool the

"OUR FOCUS ON QUALITY IS FOUNDED IN THE BELIEF THAT PEOPLE WANT TO DO A GOOD JOB AND WANT TO BE INVOLVED IN THEIR COMPANY," SAYS ROGER FISHER, DIRECTOR OF YORK'S ELYRIA OPERATIONS.

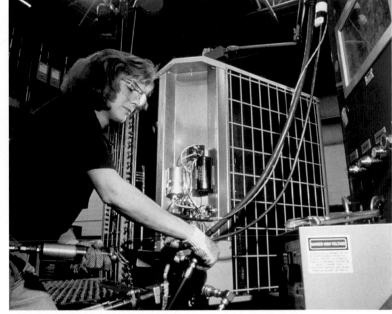

Indoor Aquatic Center for the Olympic Games in Sydney.

The company provides continued technical expertise to practice facilities used by American Olympic athletes, including the York International Luge Training Complex in Lake Placid, New York, the world's most technologically advanced indoor luge facility. And the company sponsors the York Team Advantage, a group of prominent Olympic athletes—including Bruce Jenner, Bonnie Blair, Bill Toomey, and Pablo Morales—who appear at major sporting events nationwide.

Much like the Olympic athletes it supports, York depends on teamwork in meeting the needs of commercial and residential customers who demand the finest in heating, air-conditioning, ventilation, and refrigeration equipment. In this way, York International can continue to improve the quality of life for all generations.

ELYRIA—GLOBALLY COMPETITIVE

*B*uilt in the late 1800s and acquired by York in 1981, the company's facility in Elyria, Ohio, has undergone several expansions. Originally a stove-casting operation, the plant now manufactures furnaces, air conditioners, air handling equipment, and condensing coils. This manufacturing complex covers approximately 800,000 square feet and employs approximately 1,200 associates.

To help Elyria better compete globally, York began a re-engineering program at the site in 1994. The "factory within a factory" approach was implemented throughout the plant. This concept involves smaller assembly areas called cells, where employees can view all stages of product assembly from inception to completion. This transformation emphasized flexibility within the workforce as well as a "craftsmanship" focus on quality and service to the customer. To support the assembly operations, fabrication and material storage areas were located near assembly areas. Extensive capital investments were incorporated to allow for state-of-the-art manufacturing to support the reengineering program.

To ensure that the concept was properly implemented, however, the central element of the site needed to be its people. "Our focus on quality is founded in the belief that people want to do a good job and want to be involved in their company," says Roger Fisher, director of York's Elyria operations. "We need to let people know where we want to be and what we need to do, soliciting their involvement and keeping them advised of the progress we're making."

The implementation of this concept has resulted in several major changes at the site. Product development teams consisting of engineers, assemblers, and other specialists now track products, sharing knowledge and expertise at each stage of the operation. Through the involvement of these various levels of the organization, teams are able to identify potential problems within the process and thus emphasize craftsmanship, quality, and teamwork as priorities.

In summarizing Elyria's approach, Fisher says, "Just as athletes train to reach Olympic status, manufacturers must pursue world-class status. The York Elyria team is striving to reach that pinnacle in much the same way our U.S. Olympic team does. The keys to success are focus on performance goals, involve all team members, and establish an ongoing pattern of do-measure-improve-do again."

THE ELYRIA PLANT DESIGNS AND PRODUCES WORLD-CLASS RESIDENTIAL HEATING AND COOLING PRODUCTS (LEFT).

ALL YORK PRODUCTS ARE THOROUGHLY TESTED PRIOR TO SHIPPING (RIGHT).

*J*N 1989, BACIK, KARPINSKI ASSOCIATES INC. USED A HELICOPTER TO set pieces of a new climate control system onto the roof of the Huntington National Bank building on an otherwise quiet Sunday morning. Since then, Huntington has saved $850,000 a year in utility

costs at its historic downtown banking offices.

Under the watchful eye of the Federal Aviation Administration, Bacik, Karpinski also engineered the $2.3 million expansion of the electrical system at Cleveland Hopkins International Airport. A tunnel was snaked 1.2 miles beneath the facility and an active taxiway to an expanded cargo terminal—all while planes zoomed in and out of the airport.

Bacik, Karpinski has provided creative solutions and technical expertise for a growing string of new buildings and renovations associated with Cleveland and its renaissance. The firm has put its trademark of engineering excellence on numerous health care, educational, and governmental

facilities, as well as commercial and industrial buildings.

"We serve many clients in the downtown area," says President Dale A. Bacik. "We're an organization that's on the move. We bring fresh ideas to the engineering community."

THE FIRM AND ITS PHILOSOPHY

*A*t any given time, Bacik, Karpinski Associates is providing the mechanical and electrical engineering for approximately 20 projects. The firm is managed by four principals, who, with more than a century of experience between them, are registered as engineers in more than half the states in the United States.

A Cleveland State University graduate, Bacik is a past president

of the Cleveland Consulting Engineers Association and past board member of the Cleveland Engineering Society. Dennis J. Wessel, another Cleveland State graduate, has served as chairman and vice chairman of technical committees and handbook committees of the American Society of Heating, Refrigerating and Air-Conditioning Engineers. M. James Karpinski, the firm's director of engineering, brings 30 years of experience to the company, while C. Anthony Bledsoe, director of operations, adds another 20 years.

The principals are committed to a system that allows them and the other staff members to work with the same clients on various projects, bringing their background knowledge to bear while building a level of familiarity and professional relations that will stand the test of time. "Our staff builds strong relationships with our clients," Bacik says. "When they call, they know who to ask for."

Joining the principals is a staff of bright, energetic engineers who are ready to accept all challenges and apply creative solutions to projects requiring heating, ventilation, and air-conditioning; plumbing and piping systems; power distribution and lighting systems; communications systems; and energy use analysis. "We rely on the expertise of our engineers," Bacik says. "They're very energetic and progressive in their thinking."

The latest developments in computer technologies are applied. Drawings are prepared on a special AutoCAD system, while customized software assists engineers in determining the optimal solutions to energy conservation opportuni-

BACIK, KARPINSKI ASSOCIATES ASSUMED THE LEAD ROLE IN THE ELECTRICAL DESIGN FOR THE VOLVO GM HEAVY TRUCK ASSEMBLY PLANT.

◀ MORT TUCKER

▶ CHARLES HUDSON

▶ GERALDINE W. KIEFER

ties. "We're not afraid to explore new technologies and new methods of putting a building together," Bacik says.

PREPARED FOR FUTURE CHALLENGES

Bacik, Karpinski engineered the first system in Ohio that met new indoor air quality standards: the striking Ohio Aerospace Institute in the Cleveland suburb of Brook Park. The company also has provided drawings for fast-track construction projects and worked as a consultant under architects, building owners, and project managers.

In coming years, the firm expects to provide services for traditional construction projects as well as the design-build process—a new process in which the building owner hires a building contractor to manage design and construction. "Regardless of the market conditions, regardless of the pace at which a certain owner wants to go forth, we offer a service that fits," Wessel says.

From offices on Euclid Avenue in downtown Cleveland, Bacik, Karpinski continues to make significant contributions across its professional communities. Wessel's article on the work done at the historic Huntington National Bank building was featured in the *ASHRAE Journal*, the magazine of the American Society of Heating, Refrigerating and Air-Conditioning Engineers. In addition, the firm's innovative work on an ice storage system that cools a massive data center was profiled in *Heating • Piping • Air Conditioning*, a trade magazine that serves the mechanical systems engineering profession. Over the past two decades, its engineers have received awards for technical achievement and excellence. "This helps advance our profession, while improving our professional expertise," Wessel says. "We're also giving something back to the profession."

In coming years, Bacik, Karpinski's contributions will continue to take shape on Cleveland's skyline in the form of the Law Library and College of Business and Urban Affairs at Cleveland State University; the Rainbow Babies and Childrens Hospital for University Hospitals of Cleveland; the Cleveland Clinic Cancer Center; and the new facility for the Cuyahoga County Coroner at University Circle. These important edifices will stand alongside such landmarks as the Old Post Office Building, now the M.K. Ferguson Plaza; the North Point Tower; the renovation of the north and main clinics at the Cleveland Clinic complex; Sherwin-Williams' new technical research center; and the complete renovation of the Cleveland Renaissance Hotel, one of the jewels that decorates the downtown square.

While actively working elsewhere in the country, Bacik, Karpinski remains inextricably linked to developments that will carry the city and all of northeast Ohio into the 21st century. "We are absolutely committed to the City of Cleveland," Bacik concludes.

CLOCKWISE FROM TOP LEFT: BACIK, KARPINSKI HELPED THE OHIO AEROSPACE INSTITUTE FACILITY BECOME THE FIRST IN OHIO TO INCORPORATE MECHANICAL SYSTEMS TO MEET FUTURE INDOOR AIR QUALITY STANDARDS.

THE FIRM IS INVOLVED IN A NUMBER OF CORPORATE HEADQUARTERS FACILITIES FOR SUCH ORGANIZATIONS AS PIERRE'S FRENCH ICE CREAM CO.

BACIK, KARPINSKI'S INTERIOR ENGINEERING WORK INCLUDES THE NEW ATRIUM IN THE AMBULATORY SERVICES WING AT MERIDIA HILLCREST HOSPITAL MEDICAL CENTER.

WHERE CAN TRAVELERS GO WHO TIRE OF THE SAMENESS OF THE hotel/motel lifestyle, or executives who must move to a new city and cannot afford to spare the time to find short-term housing? What about businesspeople who are living in a strange city while on

assignment or while attending training seminars? People yearning for the comforts of home when they are out of town can faithfully turn to Temporary Corporate Housing, Inc. to satisfy their needs.

Whether seeking overnight accommodations or a home for several months, travelers can find an exhaustive array of standard comforts at every company location in Cleveland, as well as in Columbus, Cincinnati, and Pittsburgh. In addition, Temporary Corporate Housing tailors packages to satisfy its customers' individual wants and desires. Yet tenants pay surprisingly affordable rates for lodging in either the heart of downtown or a quiet outlying suburb—and all without the hassles of a long search or lease restrictions required to find a traditional rental unit.

TEMPORARY HOMES FOR VARIOUS TASTES

When visiting Cleveland, customers can select from 14 first-class accommodations across the city. Kitchens are

fully equipped, and washers and dryers are available inside most suites. In addition, housekeeping services are provided, and valet dry-cleaning services are an option. Wood-burning fireplaces contribute to a quaintness and a comfort level normally associated with home. At the same time, guests will find modern luxuries, such as exercise facilities, Jacuzzis, tennis courts, and swimming pools.

While offering many of the same amenities, each Cleveland-

area residence is unique in its own way. Locations in downtown's Warehouse District are near coffeehouses and eclectic shopping, and are only a short walk from the Flats and Public Square. These urban apartments feature loft bedrooms and 12-foot ceilings.

Downtown, near Playhouse Square, guests can enjoy an on-site grocery, a restaurant, a hair salon, laundry facilities, and a bank machine, as well as ready access to nearby theaters, restaurants, and shops. An indoor park-

WHETHER SEEKING OVERNIGHT ACCOMMODATIONS OR A HOME FOR SEVERAL MONTHS, TRAVELERS CAN FIND AN EXHAUSTIVE ARRAY OF STANDARD COMFORTS AT EVERY TEMPORARY CORPORATE HOUSING LOCATION. SEVERAL CLEVELAND-AREA COMPLEXES PROVIDE SUCH LUXURIES AS A JACUZZI, SWIMMING POOL, AND FITNESS CENTER.

ing garage offers direct access to guest apartments, an amenity that combines both convenience and security.

The Westlake apartments, located near Interstate 90, provide such luxuries as a Jacuzzi, swimming pool, and fitness center. Families staying in Westlake, North Royalton, Mentor-on-the-Lake, or Mayfield Heights/Beachwood can take advantage of the highly touted school systems in these areas. Guests lodging in North Olmsted are minutes from shopping at Great Northern Mall and a short drive from NASA Lewis Research Center and Cleveland Hopkins International Airport.

In Solon, guests are only a short drive from Sea World and Geauga Lake amusement parks, while Mayfield Heights/Beachwood guests can enjoy wooded grounds and fine shopping at Beachwood Place. The Mentor-on-the-Lake apartments offer quick access to beaches and Lake Erie. Other apartment locations and condominiums may also be available throughout Greater Cleveland.

Complementing its diversity of lodging styles and locations, Temporary Corporate Housing strives to meet the individual needs of each guest. For example, bedrooms can be converted to offices. Sight-seeing tours and limousine

service can be arranged, as can preferred rates on rental cars. Private phone service is standard in all units, and voice mail is an option. Additional items to enhance guests' working or leisure environment are available on request.

As the largest and most established temporary housing service in the Midwest, the company can also assist guests in finding lodging at their next stop, whether at other Temporary Corporate Housing facilities or elsewhere in the United States, through affiliates in the National Interim Housing Network.

AMBASSADORS FOR CLEVELAND

Begun in Columbus in 1972, Temporary Corporate Housing has been serving guests in Greater Cleveland since 1983. A professional staff is available around the clock to meet guests' every need.

The company is committed to promoting Cleveland and its ongoing renaissance. Each guest is provided a detailed directory with information about local attractions, restaurants, and entertainment, as well as listings of cable television programming options. "Temporary Corporate Housing sees its role as ambassador to the city," says General Manager Michael Screptock. "We are proud to be part of

every major promotional organization in town."

For more than a decade, Temporary Corporate Housing has been providing homes away from home for such film and stage stars as Tony Randall, Hal Holbrook, and Lynn Redgrave, as well as thousands of other people who find themselves living temporarily in Cleveland. "Our commitment is to treat every guest as a star—whether it's for a night, a week, a month, or more," says Screptock. Whether they are relocating to Cleveland or simply in town for a short stay, guests can expect to receive a rare combination of value, quality, and personalized service at Temporary Corporate Housing, leaving them to concentrate on business, pleasure, or both.

CLOCKWISE FROM TOP LEFT: KITCHENS ARE FULLY EQUIPPED, AND WASHERS AND DRYERS ARE AVAILABLE INSIDE MOST SUITES.

SEPARATE DINING ROOMS PROVIDE SPACE FOR A QUIET DINNER OR ENTERTAINING CLIENTS.

WOOD-BURNING FIREPLACES CONTRIBUTE TO A QUAINTNESS AND A COMFORT LEVEL NORMALLY ASSOCIATED WITH HOME.

N o r s t a n , I n c .

N 1973, GETTING ACCESS TO A LONG-DISTANCE LINE WAS A time-consuming experience for many corporate employees, but today, businesspeople have come to expect easy access to voice mail, teleconferencing, call centers, and interactive voice processing.

Before long, videoconferencing and the integration of telephone and computer networks will be commonplace. How can a corporation keep abreast of the ever changing and increasingly complex communication technologies available? The simple answer is Norstan.

Based in Minneapolis, Norstan is a full-range provider of integrated voice, video, and data communication solutions. In 1985, the firm expanded into northeast Ohio, acquiring the assets of Solsound Industries, Inc., including the Cleveland-based Electronic Engineering Co.

NORSTAN IS A MINNEAPOLIS-BASED, FULL-RANGE PROVIDER OF INTE- GRATED VOICE, VIDEO, AND DATA COMMUNICATION SOLUTIONS (TOP).

NORSTAN OFFERS THE BREADTH OF TECHNOLOGIES, EXPERTISE, AND EXPERIENCE NEEDED TO HARNESS THE POWER OF THIS NEW AGE. THE COMPANY'S CAPABILITIES ENCOM- PASS THE FULL COMMUNICATIONS AND INFORMATION TECHNOLOGY SPECTRUM (BOTTOM).

THE BEST PRODUCTS AND SERVICES

Norstan is unique in that it doesn't maintain its own network or manufacture anything. Rather, the company develops strategic partnerships with the best technological companies in the telecommunications industry. As a result, Norstan is able to choose which vendors' products to represent and then create the best telecommunications system to match a customer's needs. The company is also free to replace products if they are no longer competitive. As new products become available, Norstan adds them to the company's list of offerings, guaranteeing customers access to the most advanced communication products on the market.

More than a product distribution company, Norstan is a service company, providing communication systems integration services and full turnkey communication management outsourcing. Currently, 45 percent of Norstan's revenues come from services and 55 percent from product sales. "The convergence of voice, video, and data communication systems isn't simply the coming together of the historically disparate modes of communication delivery—telephony, data, video," says CEO Paul Baszucki. "It is also the integration of those technologies in the workplace. We want to be the single source for the full range of our customers' communication needs."

Breadth

To deliver the full breadth of its capabilities, Norstan is organized around five businesses. The first group, Communication Systems, which includes the Cleveland office, is responsible for providing customers with the full range of communication equipment, systems, and services drawn from strategic partnerships with leading communication systems and equipment manufacturers.

Customer Services provides Norstan customers with systems maintenance, moves, adds and changes, troubleshooting, and repair. It also supports the service requirements of the systems management teams for customers who choose to outsource their communication systems.

The third group, Integration Services, offers the in-depth analysis, consultation and systems design, Internet services, and cabling services customers need to merge their voice, video, and data communication into fully integrated systems. This group has developed important strategic partnerships with the industry's hardware and software leaders.

Financial Services offers Norstan customers a comprehensive array of custom-tailored, highly flexible financing programs for communication equipment and systems. And Resale Services offers previously owned, reconditioned, and fully warranted communication equipment. At the heart of the Resale Services group is Rolm Resale Systems, a partnership between Siemens Rolm and Norstan—the only authorized North American reseller of previously owned Siemens Rolm systems and equipment.

LEGENDARY SERVICE

Through its 64 offices, Norstan extends the full range of its services to more than 13,000 customers throughout the United States and Canada. Products and services sold to Norstan customers annually total more than $320 million in revenues.

Baszucki attributes this impressive growth to the company's commitment to providing "legendary service," which works on two levels: offering responsive delivery of products and solutions to problems, and seeking out the best possible communication solutions, regardless of the products or technologies involved.

"We recognize in our mission statement that to be successful we must provide solutions that satisfy both today's and tomorrow's needs," says Baszucki. "That means listening to our customers' concerns and building long-term customer relationships based on integrity and our ability to deliver on our commitments.

"Our success comes not only from what we provide," he continues, "but from how we provide it—through ethical, responsible, and profitable actions, and by providing a fulfilling work environment for our employees, legendary service for our customers, enhanced value for our shareholders, and a spirit of shared responsibility with our community. The greatest measure of our success is our ability to translate those values into strong, profitable business relationships."

To reflect its commitment to ethical, responsive, and profitable actions, the company has created the Norstan Values Cycle, in which the company develops these values among its employees. Says Baszucki, "The successive concentric circles represent the company's commitment to personify these values in its actions with customers, shareholders, and respective communities. Our values-based approach to management is the cornerstone of what Norstan is, and we believe it will continue

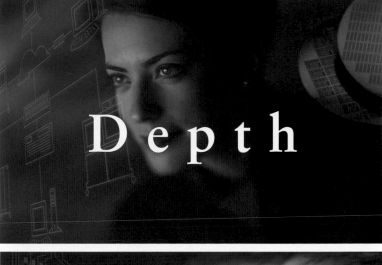

to provide returns for our shareholder groups."

LOOKING TO THE FUTURE

Norstan's path to continued growth is well laid out. Customers are rapidly increasing their demand for specialized communication solutions. As their desires exceed their ability to manage, they will come to depend on the one-stop source that promises legendary service: Norstan. "As the telecommunications industry continues to change and adapt, we believe Norstan will be the model that proves most effective," says Baszucki. "As a result, Norstan will be a premier integrator of telecommunications products and services long into the future."

NORSTAN HELPS ORGANIZATIONS MEET THE CHALLENGE OF BUSINESS COMMUNICATIONS WITH THE DEPTH OF EXPERIENCE AND TECHNICAL KNOW-HOW REQUIRED TO INTEGRATE COMMUNICATION SYSTEMS (TOP).

WITH AN EYE FOR DETAIL, THE COMPANY'S FIVE MAJOR BUSINESS UNITS WORK IN TANDEM TO SERVICE ITS CUSTOMERS, WORKING FROM 64 OFFICES THROUGHOUT THE UNITED STATES AND CANADA (BOTTOM).

FOR CLOSE TO A CENTURY, THE BUSINESSES THAT NOW COMPRISE the RELTEC Corporation have parlayed their talents for innovation and performance into products and services with a reputation for excellence in the communications industry. Today, as the world finds

STATE-OF-THE-ART POWER PRODUCTS ARE PRODUCED IN RELTEC'S LORAIN, OHIO, FACILITY, ONE OF THE LARGEST EMPLOYERS IN LORAIN COUNTY (LEFT).

LORAIN® POWER PRODUCTS HELP RELTEC CUSTOMERS RUN THEIR WIRELINE AND WIRELESS NETWORKS FOR VOICE, VIDEO, AND DATA SERVICES AROUND THE WORLD (RIGHT).

itself in the midst of a communications revolution, RELTEC's broad solutions offerings, sought by the world's leading service providers, will meet the technological challenges and demands of the dynamic information age.

Based in Cleveland, RELTEC provides stand-alone and integrated solutions to meet the communications needs of the world's leading wireless and wireline network providers and other equipment suppliers for these industries. The RELTEC offering includes Lorain® power products and systems; Rainford® and Reliable Electric® connection, protection, and enclosure products; advanced

transmission systems, loop electronic products, and loop test systems; and worldwide service solutions including engineering, furnishing, installation, and training services and support.

"The company's heritage in the Cleveland area dates back to 1936," says Dudley P. Sheffler, president and chief operating officer of RELTEC. "We have grown and evolved with the area and with our industry as both have dramatically changed over these many years. Today, RELTEC is a major industry supplier that ranks among the top 250 privately held companies in America."

BUILDING A STRONG, FOCUSED FUTURE

An independent firm, RELTEC came into being in August 1995, when an affiliate of the New York investment firm Kohlberg Kravis Roberts & Co. and RELTEC's management purchased what was then known as Reliance Comm/Tec from Rockwell International's Cleve-

land-based Reliance Electric. The company was renamed RELTEC Corporation and its focus directed entirely on the worldwide communications industry.

Sheffler elaborates: "RELTEC concentrates on the segment of the industry where wireline and wireless network providers are competing and converging—the local loop. This is where the service providers connect their residential, industrial, or commercial customers to the global communications networks. It is also where tremendous network investment is now being made in expanding and upgrading capabilities to provide new and better voice, data, and video services worldwide."

With more than 4,400 employees; manufacturing plants in the United States, United Kingdom, Canada, and Mexico; and joint ventures in the United States, Japan, and China, RELTEC stands poised to capitalize on the changes that promise to dramatically transform how the world communicates. Head-

quartered east of Cleveland in Mayfield Heights, the company maintains a strong presence in northeast Ohio, where about one-third of its employees live and work. Since 1936, RELTEC's power business has been a major employer in Lorain, located about 20 miles west of Cleveland. In addition, its service business has now become an important part of the North Ridgeville business community, about 15 miles west of Cleveland.

For more than six decades, Lorain power products have provided industry-leading solutions in applications at the very heart of the networks involved for everything from DC power systems to ringing and signaling products to battery chargers and modular power systems. Through its Outside Plant businesses in Chicago, Milwaukee, Georgia, Mississippi, and Coventry, England, RELTEC brings to bear more than 90 years of experience in producing some 3,000 products for cable, copper, and fiber-optic systems. Since 1965, RELTEC's Transmissions Products business in the Dallas-Fort Worth area has pioneered local loop transmission and test solutions, and continues to produce a variety of digital, fiber-optic, and electronic products shaping tomorrow's

communications networks. Rounding out the RELTEC offering is the services business, which provides engineering, installation, and technical support for company products and other network infrastructure equipment and systems.

A KEY PLAYER IN THE GLOBAL COMMUNICATIONS REVOLUTION

*H*eading into the 21st century, RELTEC offers a range of complementary products and services tailored to suit companies' growing needs for high-tech communications. Through its operations and sales/ service offices around the world, RELTEC will continue to serve a diverse list of wireless and wireline communications customers. This includes telephone network providers, long-distance carriers, cable television system operators, cellular and PCS companies, and various competitive access providers. It also includes a network of industry distributors and the companies manufacturing equipment for these networks.

RELTEC's goal is to serve these markets with best total value, while maintaining its focus on the local loop and helping to connect individuals and businesses to an evolving offering of network

services with its broad range of sought-after product, systems, and service solutions.

"As we go forward, RELTEC will continue to demonstrate its commitment to excellence in serving customers, suppliers, employees, shareholders, and the communities in which we operate," Sheffler says. "We will add to our investments in new technology and introduce a continuous stream of new offerings to meet the dynamic needs of our customer base. We have what it takes to make our vision of the future a reality—industry-leading customers, solid product solutions, quality services, the right technology investments, strong financial support, and an experienced, capable team of skilled and dedicated employees worldwide. Moreover, we are proud of our commitment to Cleveland and our employees who call this city home."

RELTEC'S INTEGRATED SOLUTIONS COMBINE ITS POWER, ENCLOSURE, AND SOPHISTICATED TRANSMISSION CAPABILITIES FOR LEADING-EDGE FIBER-OPTIC SYSTEMS DRIVING TOMORROW'S INFORMATION AGE (LEFT).

RELTEC PRODUCTS AND SERVICE SOLUTIONS ARE HELPING TELEPHONE, CABLE TV, CELLULAR, PCS, AND OTHER COMPANIES BRING A WORLD OF NEW SERVICES TO RESIDENTIAL AND BUSINESS CUSTOMERS (RIGHT).

ESTABLISHED IN 1988, RESERVE SQUARE HAS BEEN HOME TO thousands of Clevelanders who have chosen an exciting downtown lifestyle without sacrificing any of the comforts of home. ❖ Those who come home to Reserve Square are offered every amenity

imaginable, only minutes away from most office buildings, fine downtown restaurants, theaters, nightlife, and shopping. Many residents can't fathom living anywhere else. "This is the life of the city," says Kathy Kuhn, manager of the apartment community.

Located at East 12th Street and Superior Avenue, Reserve Square is downtown Cleveland's largest mixed-use building, with 1.7 million square feet. The complex consists of two 23-story towers set at the east and west ends of a four-story, 1,000-car parking garage. Reserve Square's apartment units boast 10 different floor plans. All units have bright, airy interiors with large expanses of glass, spacious closets, eat-in kitchens, and bathrooms complete with ceramic-tiled floors and generous dimensions.

A CITY WITHIN A CITY

The 709-suite complex includes an inside retail mall on the street level designed to provide convenient amenities for urban dwellers. The thriving "city within a city" includes a deli and grocery store, a restaurant, a dry cleaners, an ATM, laundry facilities, flower and coffee shops, a hair salon, and doctors' and dentists' offices. In total, Reserve Square contains some 49,600 square feet of retail space organized around the sparkling Market Place at Reserve Square.

Above ground level, Reserve Square provides conference and meeting rooms; rooftop gardens; a fitness center, which includes showers and saunas, a lighted

LOCATED IN THE HEART OF DOWNTOWN CLEVELAND, RESERVE SQUARE OFFERS RESIDENTS THE BEST IN URBAN LIVING WITH ALL THE COMFORTS OF HOME.

tennis court, a 25-by-50-foot indoor lap pool, StairMaster and Nordic Track machines, speed bikes, treadmills, and other equipment; an aerobic exercise area; a sundeck; and a residents' lounge. The lounge area divides into a 78-seat conservatory area overlooking the rooftop gardens and a 12-seat library lounge for quieter conversation. The Reserve Square complex also has 24-hour door attendants, a 24-hour maintenance response team, 24-hour attended parking, concierge services, and valet service.

Designed for both permanent and short-term housing, Reserve Square includes 250 beautifully furnished and decorated corporate suites available to companies that are relocating executives, training managers, or housing employees in Cleveland for short-term projects. On all floors, the Preferred Corporate Housing Program is interspersed with units occupied by long-term leasers, allowing permanent residents a chance to mingle with out-of-towners, some of whom may be entertainers performing at nearby Playhouse Square.

In addition to magnificent views of downtown, air-conditioning, heat, and electricity are included in the rental price. Reserve Square apartments also provide maid service, wake-up services, plant and pet sitting services, and guest accommodations.

Like the microcosm of the city that it is, Reserve Square is home to people of all ages. Professional men and women, married couples and single individuals, business executives, and empty nesters all find the complex appealing.

FOCUS ON CONVENIENCE

For those who enjoy a homelike atmosphere while working, the Reserve Square complex also contains approximately 180,000 square feet of commercial office space divided into three areas: concourse level, street level, and gallery. On the third and fourth floors of the East Tower and the fourth floor of the West Tower are smaller, professional office suites. These office suites are ideal for small or start-up businesses wanting to get the downtown advantage.

Reserve Square is surrounded by other residential apartments, office buildings, and Chester Commons, a public park located directly across East 12th Street. Playhouse Square, the largest multiple performing arts theater complex in the Midwest, is situated just one block south. It is home to the Cleveland Ballet, the Great Lakes Shakespeare Festival, and the Cleveland Opera.

Residents of Reserve Square apartments can shop at the nearby Halle Building, Galleria at Erieview, and The Avenue at Tower City Center. Jacobs Field, home of the Cleveland Indians Major League Baseball team, is also just a few blocks away, as is Gund Arena, home of the NBA's Cleveland Cavaliers. Reserve Square offers easy access to Interstates 71 and 90. Burke Lakefront Airport is half a mile away, and Cleveland Hopkins International Airport is only a 20-minute ride by car or rapid transit.

As Cleveland continues to attract urban dwellers and as downtown apartment construction grows, the city can look to Reserve Square for a magnificent model of stylish living. With its vibrant mix of residents, an exciting location, and an abundance of amenities, it's easy to see why Reserve Square calls itself "an irresistible place to live." It's a place residents call home, right in the heart of downtown Cleveland.

THE 709-SUITE COMPLEX, A THRIVING "CITY WITHIN A CITY," FEATURES EVERYTHING FROM SHOPPING AND DINING TO A LIGHTED TENNIS COURT.

ESIGNING AWARD-WINNING BUILDINGS FOR CLEVELAND'S MAIN street—Euclid Avenue—represents a source of pride and accomplishment for the architects at City Architecture. From Ronald McDonald House to Beacon Place at Church Square to a new corporate office building and distribution center for Pierre's French Ice Cream Co., the firm's designs are reminiscent of the architectural splendor that once lined Millionaire's Row, maintaining historical integrity while enhancing the contemporary urban environment with exceptional designs.

"A key component of what we are as community architects is our absolute commitment to, and intensive involvement in, the urban design and planning of cities," says Paul J. Volpe, AIA, president of City Architecture. "We have established a reputation for weaving our work into the fabric of the city and making the whole better than the parts."

FROM THE GROUND UP

As Cleveland's commissioner of architecture for six years, Volpe, along with Mark A. Dodds, directed the planning, design, and construction of $150 million in municipal projects. In 1989, the two decided to form their own firm. Starting with three employees in the midst of a recession, they built City Architecture to its current size of 22, including 17 architects. Other principals include Kathleen Tark, Gary Neola, Christopher Auvil, Hong Beng Chew, and August Fluker.

All members of the firm contribute to the planning and design process. "We are a very interactive organization," says Dodds. "Everyone feels comfortable expressing themselves because they know their opinions are valued highly, and that enables us to solve problems, identify issues, and generate ideas together." This philosophy extends to the firm's clients, who participate in all phases of project development, which is critical to buildings that are responsive and creative.

DIVERSITY OF DESIGN/ ARCHITECTURE

City Architecture's mission is founded on three essential goals: to develop creative solutions that will result in a better place in which to work, live, or play; to provide clients with first-rate services focused on meeting

CLOCKWISE FROM TOP: CITY ARCHITECTURE'S THREE-STORY ADDITION OF NEW LUXURY CONDOS TO THE TOP OF A RESTAURANT/BREWERY IN A FORMER STREETCAR SUBSTATION OFFERS VIEWS OF CLEVELAND'S JACOBS FIELD.

THE RONALD MCDONALD HOUSE, A 35-GUEST-ROOM FACILITY, IS AN INVITING ENVIRONMENT FOR FAMILIES OF CRITICALLY ILL CHILDREN.

A NEW, 640-ACRE COMMUNITY PLANNED FOR CLEVELAND'S EASTERN SUBURBS IS INDICATIVE OF CITY ARCHITECTURE'S EXTENSIVE PLANNING CAPABILITIES.

their specific needs; and to design buildings of enduring quality for people that engender a sense of place. "Architects only get one chance with a building, so we have to understand the permanence of our work and the accompanying responsibility," Volpe says. This professional commitment has resulted in 32 awards and honors for architecture and urban design, craftsmanship in construction, and accessibility.

The work of City Architecture is varied in scope, complexity, and design. The firm has extensive experience in the design and construction of public and private projects for such clients as cities, nonprofit groups, corporations, industry, and a variety of developers. The firm's work includes municipal facilities, corporate offices, mixed-use retail developments, housing, town planning, industrial buildings, adaptive reuse, historic preservation, and a multitude of public and institutional projects.

The Pierre's French Ice Cream Co. headquarters is one example of the firm's unique portfolio of work. The award-winning corporate office building and ice cream distribution center is designed to intentionally engage the passerby. The giant cooler building and office facade subtly elicit the process of making ice cream, with stucco cylinders echoing raw material containers, windows and bands of brick, and white steel spires elegantly composed. Unusually landscaped with gardens, an entry court, and a curved wrought iron fence, the manufacturing campus creates an attractive presence in Cleveland's MidTown Corridor.

Other sizable projects include the rehabilitation of a 220,000-square-foot warehouse along the city's fast-growing waterfront into the Quay 55 mixed-use development. This new community features office space, restaurants, shops, loft apartments, and new town houses, as well as a lakeside park.

City Architecture has also achieved a reputation for successful projects on a neighborhood scale, such as the restoration of the landmark Centrum Theater into a restaurant and triplex movie house, reestablishing it as an anchor for the Cleveland Heights community.

In addition to its commercial work, City Architecture is creating beautiful homes that reflect the architectural character and pedestrian scale of traditional neighborhoods. Town houses and individual homes that foster neighborhood activity and interaction, as well as higher-density developments that boast a richness of detail and pleasant streetscapes, distinguish the firm's residential designs.

PLANNING CITIES AND TOWNS

*P*lanning and urban design are at the heart of City Architecture's practice. A deep commitment to the creation of great cities, communities, and public spaces is at the forefront of every design solution. The firm strives to balance the rational needs of development with the emotional needs of designing for people. In all the design efforts the firm undertakes, it seeks to create special places that people will identify with, care for, and remember.

City Architecture assists communities, commerce, institutions,

and industry in planning for the future. It may be designing a new neighborhood or business center where one does not exist, or it may be the revitalization of an older community or campus. The firm's considerable experience, combined with its unique approaches to problem solving and design, helps City Architecture to create implementable and strategic development plans. This unique process brings significant consensus building, which is critically important to the planning, design, and development process.

By weaving its distinctive designs into the fabric of Greater Cleveland's communities, City Architecture has grown far beyond its humble beginnings. The firm has become a positive force in shaping the architectural character and quality of life in Cleveland.

CLOCKWISE FROM TOP LEFT: A NEW MANUFACTURING PLANT AND DISTRIBUTION FACILITY, AS WELL AS NEW CORPORATE OFFICES AND RAIL SERVICE, WERE INCLUDED IN CITY ARCHITECTURE'S MASTER DEVELOPMENT PLAN FOR PIERRE'S FRENCH ICE CREAM CO.

THE FIRM'S DESIGN WORK INCLUDES THE RECEPTION AREA FOR THE RONALD McDONALD HOUSE.

QUAY 55, A FORMER WAREHOUSE ON THE SHORES OF LAKE ERIE, OFFERS OFFICE SPACE COMBINED WITH COMMERCIAL AND RESIDENTIAL UNITS IN A NEW WATERFRONT COMMUNITY.

HEN JUGAL TANEJA, A PETROLEUM ENGINEER WITH A MASTER'S DEGREE in business administration, attended a seminar emphasizing the potential for growth in the home health care industry, he never realized it would be the first step towards the creation of NuMED

Home Health Care Inc. At the seminar, Taneja learned that by the year 2000, Americans will spend $1.6 trillion annually—16 percent of the gross national product—on health care.

A first-generation emigrant from India, who also had served as senior vice president of Union Commerce and Huntington banks, Taneja recognized this prediction as an opportunity for financial growth. As a result, through a 1990 joint venture with Case Western Reserve University (CWRU), Taneja formed NuMED Technologies, a company designed to commercialize new technologies and research generated by CWRU scientists.

Through acquisitions and the creation of new businesses, the NuMED family of companies has experienced success in both the health care and financial communities. Today, it is comprised of eight firms and 1,100 employees, who collectively make 100,000 home health care visits to 300 private-duty patients each year. NuMED's companies deliver home health care and temporary nursing staffing services in Ohio, Pennsylvania, and Florida. In addition, its subsidiaries provide contract rehabilitation staffing of physical and occupational therapists, as well as speech/language pathologists, in Ohio, Pennsylvania, Illinois, Indiana, Kentucky, Maryland, and New Jersey.

During its relatively short history, NuMED's financial gains have been considerable. In fact, net revenues have grown approximately 525 percent, from $3.9 million in 1993 to $24.4 million in 1995. Heading into the 21st century, the company expects to experience continued substantial growth. "We are sharpening our focus on new business and growth, and look forward to new customer relationships and expanded services," Taneja says.

A HISTORY OF GROWTH AND COMPASSIONATE CARE

NuMED Home Health Care was created in 1991 to generate operating rev-

NuMED PROVIDES CONSISTENT, COMPASSIONATE HOME HEALTH CARE FOR A VARIETY OF PATIENT NEEDS, ALL WHILE KEEPING COSTS WELL WITHIN REACH OF THE AVERAGE AMERICAN FAMILY.

enues for NuMED Technologies. A year later, Taneja purchased a home health care company in Pennsylvania and named its manager, Susan Carmichael, the president of NuMED Home Health Care.

With Taneja handling financial matters and Carmichael devoted to operations, the NuMED family of companies began to grow. First, three more home health care agencies were purchased in Florida. Then, in 1992, NuMED successfully completed its first public stock offering. After a second public offering in 1995, the company acquired North American Rehabilitation Inc. and Care Management Services Inc., which helped NuMED's annual revenues grow from $1.2 million to more than $25 million in five years.

Traded on the New York Stock Exchange as NUMED and on the NASDAQ market system under the symbols NUMD and NUMDW, the company was recently ranked among the 10 biggest advancers among local stocks by *Crain's Cleveland Business*. Operating from headquarters in Clearwater, Florida, NuMED continues to maintain its corporate offices on Rockside Road in Independence, a suburb on the west side of Cleveland, as well as Ohio subsidiary offices in Youngstown, Conneaut, and Cincinnati.

Throughout its history, NuMED has managed to pair value with a record of high-quality, compassionate care. A comprehensive program of quality assurance measures guarantees adherence to a tradition of superior service. Meanwhile, managers are constantly instituting cost controls, which limit the growth of expenses and provide value for customers and shareholders alike. Through this strategy, NuMED plans to become the premier comprehensive provider of home health care services in each market it serves.

▶ WALTER E. DEPTULA

A FULL RANGE OF HOME HEALTH CARE OPTIONS

Community based, Medicare certified, and state licensed, NuMED agencies provide high-quality care to persons of all ages— seven days a week, 24 hours a day. The family of agencies includes NuMED Home Health Care, Total Professional Health Care, Florida Nursing Services, Countryside Health Services, PA Medical Concepts, and NuMED Rehabilitation Services.

In northeast Ohio, NuMED also operates Whole Person Home Health Care Inc. Since 1991, its employees have provided skilled nursing, home health aides, homemakers, physical therapy, speech therapy, and medical social work services.

Skilled nurses, acting on a physician's orders, provide a full range of care from initial evaluation, to the development of care plans, to administering medications. Physical therapists evaluate patients, develop care plans, and instruct patients and their families about exercise and care during rehabilitation from stroke, trauma, joint replacement, or other surgeries.

Speech therapists assist persons with difficulties in communication and swallowing, while medical social workers provide counseling and referrals. All of NuMED's home health care aides are state tested and work under the supervision of registered nurses.

In short, NuMED provides consistent, compassionate home health care for a variety of patient needs, all while keeping costs well within reach of the average American family. "We deliver cost efficiency and quality assurance," says Carmichael, a registered nurse with a master's degree in counseling/psychology. "Isn't that what health care is all about?"

NuMED HAS BEEN A PART OF THE GREATER CLEVELAND COMMUNITY SINCE 1991.

HEN THE SINTER METALS MANAGEMENT GROUP EXAMINED THE fragmented pressed powder metal (P/M) industry in 1991, it was clear that a well-capitalized and carefully implemented acquisition strategy would allow the company to assemble a world-class

organization able to assume the role of market leader. Over the following five years, the successful execution of its strategy vaulted Sinter to global leadership, with sales rising from about $51 million in 1991 to nearly $390 million by the end of 1996, including acquisitions completed in 1996 on a pro forma basis.

Sinter's strategy has enabled it to both diversify its individual product offerings (numbering 4,000 in early 1997) and complement internal growth with acquisitions that allow it to reach new customers and diversified markets. Between 1991 and 1995, the company acquired three domestic operations and entered the European market with an acquisition in Sweden, serving customers primarily in Scandinavia, such as Volvo, Saab/Scania, Electrolux, and Haldex. Sinter's acquisition strategy was in full flower during 1996 when it completed the acquisitions of SinterForm, Inc.; Delco Remy America, Inc.'s Powder Metal Forge unit; Powder Metal Hold-

ing, Inc., the nation's second-largest P/M producer; and Krebsöge Sinterholding GmbH, Germany's and Europe's largest P/M producer. With the latter acquisitions, Sinter became the world's largest global P/M supplier.

Sinter Metals takes its name from the heating process, called sintering, that is used to fuse powdered metal into solid components

without melting. It is an apt name because sintering is a creative process that forms new bonds among separate particles—similar to the company's acquisition program—as opposed to the destructive process of melting that breaks bonds in order to form new ones. Since the Stone Age, people have been using pressure and heat to shape objects from materials such as

TYPICAL P/M PARTS PRODUCED TO NEAR NET DIMENSIONAL REQUIREMENTS ARE SHOWN UNDERGOING A FINISHING PROCESS CALLED TUMBLING (TOP).

PARTS EVOLVE FROM COMPUTER-AIDED DESIGN CONCEPTS (BOTTOM LEFT) TO P/M MANUFACTURING PROCESSES, SUCH AS MOLDING OF THE POWDERED METAL UNDER EXTREME PRESSURE (BOTTOM RIGHT).

SCOTT PEASE PHOTOGRAPHY

clay. While the fundamentals are simple, the technology is sophisticated. P/M permits greater control over various properties of the finished product; the use of high-strength tungsten, stainless steel, and other metals with high melting points; and the production of porous metal objects. In the sintering process, metal powder is placed in a precision die and subjected to enormous pressures. The formed mass of powder is then ejected from the press and sent through a furnace that is heated to below melting point, but that has a controlled atmosphere to prevent oxidation.

P/M employs numerous types and combinations of metals to create even the most intricate components with specific strength and design characteristics. It also lowers unit costs because of its efficiency: Products with close tolerances can be manufactured with virtually no waste or extensive secondary machining. Moreover, powder metallurgy can create products that are impossible to make with conventional processes.

Because Sinter Metals provides the full range of P/M technologies and productive capacity, the company has become increasingly important to customers. Its

reputation for quality, advanced technology, and effective engineering assistance supports efforts to increase market penetration because companies are outsourcing more and more to capable partners such as Sinter. This is especially true in the automotive industry where quality is not only expected, but required. At the same time, Sinter makes sure that its product offerings evolve to avoid being a one product, one customer company. Of the 4,000 different parts produced by Sinter, no single product accounts for more than $5 million in sales, and Sinter is the sole source for 95 percent of its parts.

The outlook for Sinter Metals is bright. In 1987, the average family car produced in North America contained 20 pounds of pressed metal components, a figure that had risen to approximately 30 pounds by the end of 1996. This 50 percent increase has made pressed metal materials one of the fastest-growing segments of the North American automotive industry. In other sectors as well, from home appliances to power tools, pressed metal parts are rapidly replacing conventionally machined components.

The number of P/M parts used in typical cars is expected

to continue rising. For example, industry estimates are that P/M content in General Motors cars will rise 5 percent to 10 percent annually through 2001. This trend is being driven by demands to make vehicles lighter and to control costs by using the most efficient parts-producing technologies, areas in which pressed metals excel. Internationally, European and Japanese cars today contain substantially fewer pressed metal components than their U.S. counterparts, meaning good growth potential for the P/M industry. Sinter Metals supplies its components internationally and is aggressively pursuing opportunities worldwide.

The P/M industry is at a crossroads, with technology, quality, and reliability of supply separating first-tier companies such as Sinter from less capable competitors. Sinter is benefiting as well from structural change caused by customers' supplier consolidations and the need for suppliers to provide global support capabilities. A management team that has a strong track record in quickly integrating acquisitions, coupled with proven capabilities in anticipating and meeting customer needs, has enabled Sinter Metals to move to its dominant global leadership position.

SCOTT PEASE PHOTOGRAPHY

ALLEN TELECOM INC.

s ALLEN TELECOM APPROACHES THE 21ST CENTURY, THE COMPANY has literally transformed itself. For 60 years, the firm—known originally as Allen Electric and Equipment Co. and, until recently, as the Allen Group Inc.—had been an integral part of the automotive industry, bringing to market such products as diagnostic systems and rubber components for cars and trucks. But today, Allen Telecom is focused on providing products that power the wireless communications revolution, and is prepared to keep pace with the evolution of technologies in the information age.

The company's shift in emphasis began in 1988, when a new management team completed an internal analysis of the firm's operations. Based upon the success and outlook for Allen's Antenna Specialist Division (its only business in the wireless telecommunications industry), the company decided to make the gradual transition to a single-focus wireless telecommunications company. This was followed by a number of years of selling and spinning off the various automotive businesses to shareholders.

During that transition period, the organization acquired a number of companies compatible with its wireless telecommunications business, invested in a handful of start-up wireless businesses, and increased its research and development efforts to internally develop new and more technically sophisticated products. Allen also instituted a more decentralized management structure, reducing the corporate staff while transferring the operating authority and responsibility to the individual divisions.

"As with any company today, we like to think we are finished with transition," says Robert Paul, president and chief executive officer, "although there isn't a company today that won't find itself going through continual transition in one form or another."

THE YEARS OF CHANGE

s part of its transition, Allen Telecom relocated its home base in 1992 from Long Island to Beachwood, a suburb east of Cleveland. The move positioned the company's headquarters close to its telecommunications business in Solon, Ohio, and situated the corporate leadership in the Midwest, near most of Allen Telecom's remaining businesses.

"The six executives who have relocated to Beachwood formed the backbone of a new corporate staff with local hires in Greater Cleveland. I don't think we have missed a beat," says Paul, who has demonstrated his civic commitment as a member of the board of the Cleveland Play House.

To put its management team and employees on the same wavelength as shareholders, Allen Telecom has developed a program of equity-based incentives, whereby key executives are required to own significant amounts of company stock. Likewise, employees have been encouraged to take a more active role in corporate decisions. For example, workers in the company's manufacturing facilities set their own production schedules, while identifying their problems and obstacles, and arranging for solutions. Bonuses are tied to meeting or exceeding performance objectives.

BANKING ON THE FUTURE OF MOBILE COMMUNICATIONS

ith the passage of the Telecommunications Act of 1996, barriers were removed that had slowed the introduction

ALLEN TELECOM RELOCATED ITS HOME BASE IN 1992 FROM LONG ISLAND TO BEACHWOOD, A SUBURB EAST OF CLEVELAND. THE COMPANY'S MANAGEMENT TEAM INCLUDES (FROM LEFT) DARA FOLAN, VICE PRESIDENT AND GENERAL COUNSEL; JIM LEPORTE, VICE PRESIDENT AND TREASURER; BOB PAUL, PRESIDENT AND CHIEF EXECUTIVE OFFICER; ERIK VAN DER KAAY, EXECUTIVE VICE PRESIDENT; AND BOB YOUDELMAN, EXECUTIVE VICE PRESIDENT AND CHIEF FINANCIAL OFFICER.

of new mobile communications technologies. In the final years of the 20th century, Allen Telecom anticipates a burgeoning market for its products: two-way wireless communications systems, site management products, and antennas. American consumers are expected to become more comfortable with existing cellular systems, while embracing an emerging technology: personal communications systems (PCS) powered by a brand-new network.

In response, Allen Telecom has developed a range of new products, such as a hybrid wireless PBX system, which allows people to take calls on their cellular or office phones, regardless of which line the caller had dialed originally. A new generation of software has also been developed for the planning of cellular and personal communications systems.

"We think that people are getting more and more accustomed to the mobility of not being tied to something that's wired," says Paul. "We don't know why 10 to 15 years from now that's not going to be the norm."

In addition, foreign markets are expected to continue to develop and expand, resulting in growth opportunities for the company, which already does more than half of its business overseas. The international expansion was given a jump start with the acquisition of two significant European wireless equipment manufacturers. With offices in major markets around the world, Allen Telecom is positioned to participate in the worldwide wireless expansion. Such countries as India and China are using wireless telecommunications systems to enhance and expand their inadequate wired telephone networks because these systems are often less expensive and faster to install than the traditional wired phone infrastructure.

How far wireless technology can expand can be best seen in a country like Sweden, where 30 percent of the population are cellular phone subscribers. New technology is continually reducing the cost of wireless equipment, and large increases in the number of customers provide enhanced economies of scale. Both of these factors reduce cost to the customer, which makes wireless service affordable to more people. Prices are expected to continue to gradually decrease as acceptance of wireless technology becomes commonplace.

"There are a lot more wireless communications products that we cannot even envision today that are going to be a key part of our society over the next 10 years," Paul says.

Through its adroit management and research and development divisions, Allen Telecom expects to continue to make technological breakthroughs in the ever changing telecommunications industry. "Those kinds of strengths, plus our continued acquisition of additional technologies and products, will allow us to play an expanding role in providing the highest level of equipment and services to our customers for a very long time," Paul concludes.

ALLEN TELECOM IS FOCUSED ON PROVIDING PRODUCTS THAT POWER THE WIRELESS COMMUNICATIONS REVOLUTION, AND IS PREPARED TO KEEP PACE WITH THE EVOLUTION OF TECHNOLOGIES IN THE INFORMATION AGE.

MARGARET CLARK-MILLINGTON, PRESIDENT OF LACHAE COSMETICS, was offered a term loan by a conventional competitor. But, after meeting with Shorebank Enterprise agents Ken Patterson and Blaine Fairless, Clark-Millington chose to do business with the people at

Shorebank Cleveland Corporation. Patterson and Fairless provided an in-depth analysis of Clark-Millington's business that convinced her a smaller line of credit—instead of a larger term loan—would enable her to purchase inventory, set aside funds for working capital, and, most important, keep company debt manageable.

"I'm really interested in doing business with an institution that is interested in my business," Clark-Millington explains. "I learned more in that one meeting than I had in months."

INVESTING IN ALL ASPECTS OF THE COMMUNITY

Doing what it takes to create success for a customer is Shorebank Cleveland's specialty. Since being asked by city officials in 1994 to become Cleveland's community development bank, innovative approaches to commercial lending and development have drawn the interest of the entrepreneurial business community.

Intense concentration of real estate redevelopment, focused on the city's upper east side neighborhoods, is beginning to effect an increase in property values. The

three companies under the Shorebank Cleveland umbrella—ShoreBank, a commercial bank; Shorebank Enterprise, a nonprofit entity specializing in business development; and ShorePlace Development, a real estate developer—strategically combine knowledge and expertise to re-create housing markets, restore jobs, and provide community resources. Through its affiliates, Shorebank Cleveland aims to use a personal approach to trigger a chain reaction of reinvestment in local neighborhoods. Helping each customer create a success, whether buying a home or growing a business, adds to the success of the community.

"Our mission is to invest in underinvested neighborhoods with the hope that the three-pronged approach will have a positive impact on business, housing, and quality-of-life issues," says Shorebank Cleveland President Charles Rial. "Our role is to find ways of using our resources to create opportunities for owner-managed businesses, entrepreneurs, and the people who call our neighborhood home."

Located in a commercial park on East 105th Street in Cleveland's Glenville neighborhood, the affili-

ates and 29 other business occupants share common resources and easy access to downtown and interstates in a unique partnership that offers a variety of complimentary services within the complex.

From the Glenville headquarters, ShoreBank President A. Lamont Mackley directs the financing operation that focuses on lending to expanding, owner-managed businesses; entrepreneurs; and neighborhood home buyers. ShorePlace Development Corporation, headed by President Beth Hughes, purchases and renovates homes in Glenville, Hough, Buckeye-Shaker, Fairfax, Forest Hills, South Collinwood, St. Clair-Superior, and University Circle. Shorebank Enterprise, managed by Vice President Stephanie McHenry, offers loans, management assistance, and space in two enterprise centers to businesses, community development corporations, artists, and manufacturing companies.

CLEVELAND'S DEVELOPMENT BANK

At the invitation of Mayor Michael R. White, Cleveland Tomorrow, and the Cleveland and Gund foundations, Chicago's Shorebank Corporation opened the Shorebank Cleveland operations in 1994. These local institutions continue to support the bank's mission.

Results quickly followed the opening of ShoreBank. Since 1994, financing has been provided for 493 housing units in the eight target neighborhoods—placing ShoreBank as high as second among residential lenders in the area. Sixty prospective buyers have graduated from the Home-buyers College. Construction jobs have been created due to the bank's granting nearly $10 million in loans and lines of credit to neighborhood renovation companies. Property values have started to rise. Small, owner-managed busi-

nesses outside the target neighborhoods have benefited as well. At the close of 1996, a total of more than $16 million in development and other loans had been distributed in northeast Ohio.

Meanwhile, Shorebank Enterprise leased space to 29 tenants, employing 111 people in its commercial parks in Glenville and Collinwood. Seventeen African-American-owned businesses were among these tenants. Seven companies, collectively employing 46 people, have benefited from management assistance. Financing was secured for 25 entrepreneurial endeavors, 53 percent of which are headed by African-Americans.

In its first six months, ShorePlace began renovation or construction on 56 homes in Glenville, Fairfax, and Buckeye-Shaker. In 1997, another 175 remodeled homes and 200 apartments are slated for availability to former residents interested in renewing roots in their neighborhoods and for others ready to return to city living.

Anyone driving through the eight neighborhoods has noticed the trademark ShorePlace touch: Eye-catching trompe l'oeil boards, painted by Cleveland student artists, cover windows of houses still undergoing renovation. While discouraging graffiti, the artwork, completed under the direction of ShorePlace's project administrator—and Cleveland teacher/artist—has attracted prospective buyers. Inside, the homes feature fireplaces, carpeting, and designer kitchens and baths, as well as new mechanical systems.

All Shorebank Cleveland employees are active in churches, neighborhood schools, and PTAs—a business-school partnership with Cleveland Public Schools' Charles H. Lake Elementary highlights the collective educational effort. The organization supports showings by African-American artists at the Black Box Art Gallery, where

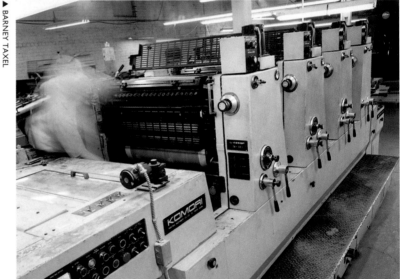

emerging artists can study art and dance. Employees exchange letters with student pen pals, have participated in fund-raisers and hunger drives, and hold leadership positions on various boards. Through the combination of these elements, Shorebank Cleveland participates in the rebirth of the upper east side.

While committed to the rejuvenation of these proud communities, Shorebank Cleveland expects its efforts to lead to financial success so it can continue working on its mission. "Ultimately, we are about the development of the community," Rial concludes. "If our neighborhoods and customers are successful, we're successful."

TOP: MURALS BEAUTIFY—AND IDENTIFY—SHOREPLACE HOUSES UNDER CONSTRUCTION. PROJECT ADMINISTRATOR DIANE COLLINS (FRONT) WORKS WITH ART STUDENT ARIANE TELL TO PUT THE SHOREPLACE SIGNATURE ON A TEMPORARY FRONT DOOR.

BOTTOM: WHETHER IT'S FINANCING EQUIPMENT OR SECURING A LINE OF CREDIT, OWNER-MANAGED BUSINESSES IN NORTHEAST OHIO, SUCH AS LAKE ERIE GRAPHICS, INC., GROW WITH SHOREBANK'S HIGHLY PERSONALIZED COMMERCIAL LENDING STRATEGIES.

A N IMPORTANT FACET OF CLEVELAND'S RENAISSANCE HAS BEEN THE dramatic development of the downtown area. New sporting facilities, museums, and hotels now make downtown Cleveland the destination of choice for thousands of tourists. Opened in 1995, the newest hotel to

cater to a growing legion of business and leisure travelers is the Wyndham Cleveland Hotel at Playhouse Square. Located in the heart of the city's theater and business districts, the Wyndham, with its distinctive curved design, is perfect for business travelers and for locals or visitors who wish to sample Cleveland's nightlife.

The management at the Wyndham Cleveland Hotel has gone to great lengths to make the property one of the city's premier lodging establishments, starting with the marble floors in the elegant lobby. The entire hotel maintains an art deco theater theme, honoring the heyday of Playhouse Square. The open-air terrace overlooking the square, coupled with a new park and promenade joining the Wyndham and the rejuvenated theater district, uniquely blends this modern hotel with the old-world charm of downtown Cleveland.

CONTINUOUS ELEGANCE

The elegant atmosphere of the Wyndham lobby is also present in the hotel's 205 guest rooms, which include 14 suites, a presidential suite, 77 double/doubles, and 113 king rooms. Each room is appointed with 18th-century-style mahogany furnishings, sheer and custom-color blackout draperies, and antique reproductions of artwork depicting European theaters. Each king room features a large writing desk and a recliner chair, an armoire, free color cable TV with remote control and in-room movie channel selections, a digital alarm clock radio, and a telephone with a 25-foot cord.

To provide guests with the comforts of home, all of the Wyndham's rooms contain coffee-makers, a complimentary supply of coffee and tea, removable hangers, feather pillows, hair dryers, and computer modem hookups. The bathrooms have extended vanity areas, decorative mirrors with gold braid frames, and shower massage heads. Complimentary toiletries include conditioning shampoo, lotion, mouthwash, bath gel, emery boards, shoe horns, shower caps, and shoe buffers.

FIRST-CLASS SERVICE AND ACCOMMODATIONS

In addition to its beautiful rooms, the Wyndham Cleveland Hotel offers its guests many amenities to serve their every need, including room service, business services, voice mail, laundry and dry cleaning services, and a daily newspaper. Guests can maintain their exercise regimens in the Wyndham's fitness facilities, which include an indoor lap pool and an exercise room.

Guests of the Wyndham Cleveland Hotel can also enjoy first-class dining at Winsor's. A full-service restaurant open for breakfast, lunch, and dinner, Winsor's offers an elegant, comfortable setting that features dramatic theatrical lighting, photos of movie stars on the walls, and reproductions of actual articles published by the *Cleveland Press* during the golden age of the theater district. There is also a stylishly appointed lounge for relaxing and socializing.

In addition to the four theaters and numerous sidewalk cafés of Playhouse Square, the Wyndham is within walking distance of such tourist attractions as Jacobs Field, home of Major League Baseball's Cleveland Indians, and Gund Arena, home of the Cleveland Cavaliers professional basketball team. Other downtown attractions near the Wyndham include the world-famous Rock and Roll Hall of Fame and Museum, the Cleveland Convention Center, the Cleveland State University Convocation Center, the trendy Warehouse District, and the popular Flats riverside entertainment district. For travelers whose itinerary includes shopping, the Tower City Center and Galleria at Erieview shopping complexes are also close at hand.

FRIEND TO THE BUSINESS TRAVELER

For business travelers, the Wyndham Cleveland Hotel's central location affords easy access to the city's business and financial districts. In addition, the Wyndham offers all of the facilities and services needed to conduct successful business meetings, including a service manager to coordinate meetings and food

functions, a 24-hour facsimile service, on-site audiovisual services, and a professional banquet staff.

Named for the legendary Palace, Allen, Hippodrome, and Hanna theaters, the Wyndham's meeting and banquet rooms provide two levels of versatile space totaling 14,000 square feet, including a 5,100-square-foot ballroom that is divisible into two separate rooms and can accommodate up to 500 people; eight

fixed-wall, state-of-the-art meeting and banquet rooms; and an executive boardroom.

As Cleveland continues its revival, the Wyndham Cleveland Hotel at Playhouse Square will play an integral role by helping to restore the city's theater district to its past glory. The addition of this hotel makes Cleveland an increasingly popular destination for business travelers and tourists, and adds an impressive new jewel to the downtown skyline.

EACH GUEST ROOM IS APPOINTED WITH 18TH-CENTURY-STYLE MAHOGANY FURNISHINGS, SHEER AND CUSTOM-COLOR BLACKOUT DRAPERIES, AND ANTIQUE REPRODUCTIONS OF ARTWORK DEPICTING EUROPEAN THEATERS (TOP).

A FULL-SERVICE RESTAURANT OPEN FOR BREAKFAST, LUNCH, AND DINNER, WINSOR'S OFFERS AN ELEGANT, COMFORTABLE SETTING THAT FEATURES DRAMATIC THEATRICAL LIGHTING, PHOTOS OF MOVIE STARS ON THE WALLS, AND REPRODUCTIONS OF ACTUAL ARTICLES PUBLISHED BY THE *Cleveland Press* DURING THE GOLDEN AGE OF THE THEATER DISTRICT (BOTTOM).

"TWICE THE HOTEL" IS THE MOTTO AND PHILOSOPHY OF DOWNTOWN Cleveland's Embassy Suites Hotel. Its managers and employees go the extra mile to ensure visitors have a double good stay: a high-class lodging experience with all the conveniences of home.

Embassy Suites has what it takes to be a premier hotel in the midst of downtown Cleveland's renaissance, including beautifully adorned rooms, proximity to businesses and tourist attractions, quality service, and abundant amenities. It's a great place to stay in the heart of a reborn city.

AN ABUNDANCE OF FIRST-CLASS AMENITIES

Formerly the Radisson Plaza, the hotel became part of the Embassy Suites chain of upscale, all-suite hotels in January 1996 when it was purchased by FelCor Suite Hotels Inc. of Irv-ing, Texas. FelCor has since been investing heavily in a renovation of the property, which has included a refurbishing of the guest rooms with new wallpaper and bedspreads and a new open atrium.

When the project is completed, some $2.5 million will have been spent on enhancing the hotel. The 268-suite property is managed by Promus Hotel Corp., a 650-hotel chain based in Memphis, Tennessee. Carla Gold, director of sales and marketing for the Cleveland property, says Embassy Suites employees work hard to fulfill their promise of "satisfying every guest every time." In fact, the hotel's policy promises guests who aren't 100 percent satisfied a full refund on their visit—a sure sign of commitment to service.

The Embassy Suites Hotel features an indoor swimming pool, the 100-seat Grill Restaurant, and more than 7,000 square feet of meeting space that can accommodate business groups of up to 225 people. The hotel boasts two executive boardrooms for smaller gatherings of about 12 each, as well as a large ballroom for parties or banquets. The Embassy Suites can also accommodate groups of up to 400 for cocktail parties and can seat 175 for dinner.

GUEST ACCOMMODATIONS AT THE EMBASSY SUITES INCLUDE SPACIOUS TWO-ROOM SUITES WITH SEPARATE LIVING AREAS. EACH UNIT TOTALS APPROXIMATELY 800 SQUARE FEET AND FEATURES A PRIVATE BEDROOM AND BATH, TWO TELEVISIONS, TWO TELEPHONES, A WET BAR, A COFFEE-MAKER, A REFRIGERATOR, AND A MICROWAVE OVEN.

Guest accommodations at the Embassy Suites include spacious two-room suites with separate living areas. Each unit totals approximately 800 square feet and features a private bedroom and bath, two televisions, two telephones, a wet bar, a coffeemaker, a refrigerator, and a microwave oven. The 10-floor hotel offers 42 king suites, 85 double suites, four two-bedroom suites, 14 Super Suites, 120 nonsmoking suites, and three suites for the physically challenged. Guests receive a complimentary cooked-to-order breakfast each morning and an evening managers reception, and children under 12 can stay in a suite with their parents for free.

Embassy Suites/Cleveland Downtown also offers a VIP club, similar to airline frequent flyer programs, in which frequent guests can accumulate points toward free accommodations, gift books, or savings bonds.

IN THE HEART OF DOWNTOWN CLEVELAND

As part of the Reserve Square retail and residential complex, the Embassy Suites Hotel is located across from a colorful downtown park and not far from the city's beautiful lakefront. Next door are the Reserve Square apartments, as well as an indoor mall that offers such amenities as restaurants, a grocery store, a travel agency, a gourmet coffee shop, a dry cleaner, a beauty salon, and a florist.

Also located just minutes away from the hotel are such popular tourist attractions as the Rock and Roll Hall of Fame and Museum; Playhouse Square; Jacobs Field; Gund Arena; the Great Lakes Science Center; the Galleria at Erieview; the Avenue at Tower City Center; and the Flats, Cleveland's center for entertainment and nightlife. Several restaurants, including the Ninth

Street Grill, Café Sausalito, and Hickerson's, are also nearby.

For the business traveler, the hotel is near the heart of the city's business districts—East 9th Street and Public Square—and its large corporations and institutions, which include Ernst & Young, Eaton Corporation, the Sherwin-Williams Company, Cleveland State University, the Federal Reserve Bank, the Cleveland Convention Center, the Cleveland Public Library, Cleveland City Hall, and the Justice Center.

The Embassy Suites Hotel is being reborn every day as it renovates, upgrades, and creates new services for its customers. For business guests, there's no place like it for downtown meetings with out-of-town clients. For the leisure traveler, the location and luxurious accommodations can't be beat. Like the city it calls home, Embassy Suites is truly experiencing a renaissance.

THE EMBASSY SUITES HOTEL OFFERS LUXURIOUS ACCOMMODATIONS IN AN EXCELLENT LOCATION NEAR THE HEART OF CLEVELAND'S BUSINESS DISTRICTS.

Photographers

Ian Adams is an Akron-based environmental photographer who has traveled throughout the eastern United States, documenting its natural, rural, and historical areas. He leads outdoor photography workshops, seminars, and photo tours. Adams' Ilfochrome color prints have been widely exhibited and are included in many corporate and private collections. His work has also been featured in *Avenues*, *Better Homes and Gardens*, and *Country*, and on 18 covers of *Ohio Magazine*, for which he is also a contributing editor.

Dennis L. Anderson, a native Clevelander, specializes in black-and-white photography of sports, special events, promotions, and people. He has studied at Karamu House, Cuyahoga Community College, and the Cleveland Photographic Society, as well as completing an internship at WVIZ-TV. Anderson's client list includes National City, United Way, American Red Cross, and Star Bank, to name a few, and his images have been featured in the *Plain Dealer*, *Northern Ohio Live*, and a coffee-table book on Cleveland titled *Images from the Heart: A Bicentennial Celebration of Cleveland and Its People*.

Donald Andreano is a freelance photographer from Brooklyn, Ohio. With a bachelor of arts degree from the University of Dayton, Andreano is interested in traveling the back roads of the United States by motorcycle.

Casey Batule is a product of the Cleveland environment, having lived within five miles of Public Square his entire life. He is the photographer for the Cleveland Metroparks and its zoo, and has operated a freelance commercial/industrial photography business since 1976. Batule's images have appeared in *Cleveland Magazine*, *Wildlife Conservation*, and *NaturEscape*.

Barbara Breen works for the Department of Veterans Affairs in her hometown of Cleveland. With an associate's degree in photography from the Ohio Institute of Photography and Technology in Dayton, Breen specializes in biomedical and fine art photography, as well as digital imaging. Her images have been published in *Images from the Heart: A Bicentennial Celebration of Cleveland and Its People* and are featured in the permanent collection of KeyCorp.

Janet Century has been producing black-and-white and color photography for a wide range of corporations, publications, agencies, and universities for more than 15 years. Her work has been published in *Images from the Heart: A Bicentennial Celebration of Cleveland and Its People*; *To Heal a Nation*, a book about the Vietnam Veterans Memorial; and *The Beacon* magazine, in a story about Vietnam veterans returning to Vietnam. The recipient of numerous industry awards, Century recently was commissioned to photograph workers for USS Kobe's *Steel Town Story*.

Marius A. Chira, a native of Romania, is an editorial and fine art photographer who is employed by Kira Photography. He has studied at the Cleveland Institute of Art and Liberty University. Chira's work has been published in *Cleveland Magazine*, *Northern Ohio Live*, *Forbes*, and *Images from the Heart: A Bicentennial Celebration of Cleveland and Its People*. He received the Best of Show award in the 1996 Faces of Cleveland contest, and has worked with Third Federal Bank and Progressive Insurance.

Beverly Conley, originally from San Francisco, specializes in documentary photography and is a member of the American Society of Media Photographers (ASMP) and the Media Photographers' Copyright Agency. Her photographs have appeared in numerous publications, including *Labor's Heritage*, *City Lore Annual Magazine*, and *Northern Ohio Live*, and in such books as *Cranberry Harvest* and *East Cambridge*. Conley's work has been exhibited in a number of shows and is part of several museum and library collections.

Lisa DeCesare, who originally hails from Rochester, New York, moved to the Cleveland area in 1994. A graduate of Kent State University with a degree in photo illustration, she was the studio manager at Barney Taxel & Co. until May 1997, at which time she began working for Andy Russetti. DeCesare specializes in fine art printing; images of food; and large-format, black-and-white landscape photography. She participated in a bicentennial project for the city and has taken photographs for a number of Web pages on the Internet.

Walter E. Deptula, a Chicago native, has photographed on a freelance basis since 1988. His photographs have been published in several Towery publications, including *Chicago: Second to None*, *Wichita: Visions from the Heartland*, *St. Louis: Home on the River*, *Cincinnati: Crowning Glory*, *Greater Detroit: Renewing the Dream*, and *Minneapolis-St. Paul: Linked to the Future*. Deptula is a frequent contributor to the Chicago Scenes and Events calendar published by Jeff Voelz of American City Calendars.

Dale Dong is a freelance photographer originally from southeast Michigan. With degrees from the University of Michigan (U of M) at Dearborn, Indiana University, and U of M at Ann Arbor, Dong specializes in fine art and architectural photography. He is particularly interested in photography as an art medium and in the way it has influenced emotions regarding the environment and humanity.

Barbara Durham enjoys nature images, multiple-exposure setups, and photographing any subject that reflects the essence of her hometown of Cleveland. A graduate of Cleveland State University, Durham has worked with such clients as Fairview General Hospital, Augsburg Fortress Publishers, and Hong Kong Museum of Science and Technology. Her images have appeared in such publications as *Cleveland: Shaping the Vision* and *Ohio: A Photographic Celebration*.

David Dvorak Jr., an employee of Cleveland Metroparks' Brecksville Nature Center, specializes in travel, nature, and outdoor photography. His work has been featured in such publications as *Bird Watcher's Digest*, *Sierra*, *Audubon*, the *New York Times*, and *Nature Conservancy Magazine*, as well as in books published by Simon & Schuster, Macmillan Publishing Co., and Lerner Publications. Dvorak is author and photographer of *A Sea of Grass: The Tall Grass Prairies*, and his scientific research has been published in the proceedings of both the Society of Ecological Restoration and the North American Prairie Conference.

Dan Gaines, a Cleveland native, specializes in wedding photography and portraits, as well as interior architectural photography. His images have appeared in local sporting magazines and railroad publications. A graduate of Winona International School of Professional Photography, Gaines enjoys nature photography in his spare time.

Bill Gance is a freelance photographer who specializes in photojournalism and architectural photography. Originally from Cleveland, Gance moved to West Salem, Ohio, in 1984. His work was published in *Images from the Heart: A Bicentennial Celebration of Cleveland and Its People*.

Stephen F. Harmon is a self-taught photographer whose areas of specialty include street scenes, pastoral images, and general natural light photography. A native of New York City, he attended both Queens College and Brooklyn College Law School. Harmon's work can be seen at the New York Historical Society, the

Museum of the City of New York, and the Brooklyn Museum, as well as in many corporate and private collections. Having married a Clevelander, Harmon has developed a love of the city and its people, and is proud to consider Cleveland his second home.

Heinz Juergen Hess, a native of Frankfurt, Germany, is a Cleveland-based freelance photographer who specializes in editorial photography. The son of a commercial photographer, Hess has had a lifelong interest in taking pictures, especially those of technical events, railroads, and trains. Some of his first images of Cleveland were featured in the Faces of Cleveland contest.

The Image Finders, founded by Jim Baron in 1986, is a stock photography company located in Cleveland. Its files cover a broad range of subjects, including agriculture, animals, butterflies, families, food, sports, travel, transportation, trees, and western states.

Jennie Jones has been a resident of Cleveland since 1978 and has made the city's renaissance a central theme in her work. A graduate of Northwestern University and the Layton School of Art in Milwaukee, Jones specializes in architectural and fine art photography, serving such clients as Forest City Enterprises, the Cleveland Clinic, and Ugrinov & Associates. Jones' images have been published in numerous books on Cleveland, and she is a recipient of the City of Cleveland Mayoral Award and the Birchfield Award from the Cleveland Institute of Art.

Veronica L. Koston is a native Clevelander who owns and operates VDK Imaging. Primarily a photojournalist, Koston also specializes in digital imaging and black-and-white photography. She is assistant editor of *Shooters News* magazine and mother of a young boy, who is her favorite subject to capture on film. Koston's images have been displayed at Cuyahoga Community College and Cleveland Hopkins International Airport.

Roger Mastroianni is a self-taught freelance photographer who has worked in the Midwest since the early 1980s. Currently, his corporate clients include many Fortune 500 companies, and he is a regular contributor to *Business Week, Fortune, Forbes, Newsweek,* the *New York Times,* and *Rolling Stone.* Mastroianni provides photography for many local theater companies, as well as the internationally renowned Cleveland Orchestra, the Cleveland Play House, and the Great Lakes Theater Festival.

Jim Metrisin began his career as a photographer in 1986, working as a lab technician at KSK Color Lab and as a staff photographer at Zena Photography. He now owns his own studio in Cleveland, and specializes in fashion and portrait photography for models and actors nationwide, as well as tabletop product photo illustration for local businesses. A member of ASMP, Metrisin cultivates his artistic side as president of EIO, an artist cooperative consisting of up to 15 members of all artistic disciplines.

Adam Misztal, originally from Germany, attended Cleveland State University. He specializes in fine art and documentary photography, and his images were published in *Images from the Heart: A Bicentennial Celebration of Cleveland and Its People.* A Vietnam veteran, Misztal is involved in an ongoing photographic documentary on other survivors of the Vietnam War.

Betsy Molnar is the owner and operator of Big Stills photography studio, which specializes in black-and-white and natural light photography. A graduate of the Cooper School of Art in Cleveland, as well as the Rochester Institute of Technol-

ogy in New York, Molnar is a recipient of the 1996 FaVa Architectural Award, second-place winner of the 1996 New American Talent contest at a SoHo gallery, and cowinner of the Faces of Cleveland contest in 1995.

Ian Naysmith is a native of Chicago who moved to Cleveland in 1987. Specializing in editorial, people, and architectural photography, Naysmith enjoys studying issues of social conscience. His images have appeared in *Northern Ohio Live* and *Cleveland Magazine.*

Deborah Phillips specializes in documentary photojournalism, emphasizing various ethnic groups and how they maintain their cultural identity. During her 20-year career in social services, Phillips developed visual communications skills and began producing public relations materials, including an award-winning videotape. She participated in the Cleveland Women's Bicentennial Photo Project, a result of which was the placement of four of her images in a time capsule to be opened in 2096.

Darryl Polk, originally from Nashville, discovered his passion for photography in high school. After studying fine art photography at Ohio University, he began his career in advertising product photography. Polk's client list includes Revco Drug Stores, Ohio Lottery, City of Cleveland, and KeyCorp. He has assisted on glamorous photography shoots in Key West and says that he also enjoys the rewards of portraying ordinary people with the dignity and respect that every individual deserves.

Kurt Shaffer is a self-taught photographer who specializes in nature and landscape photography, and people in natural surroundings. His work can be seen on the cover of *Praywell: A Holistic Guide to Health and Renewal,* in local publications, and in exhibits at galleries statewide. Shaffer is currently focused on his multimedia slide show, "Photohealing®: Healing the Human Spirit through Nature and Landscape Photography."

Carl J. Skalak Jr. is owner and operator of Skalak & Associates, which specializes in location photography for annual reports and brochures, as well as sports and recreation photography. A graduate of Bowling Green State University in Ohio, Skalak currently resides in Cleveland.

Ann Swider, a native of Regensburg, Germany, moved to Cleveland in 1950. A graduate of the Cleveland Institute of Art; the Folkwang School of Design in Essen, Germany; and Miami University, she specializes in black-and-white portraiture, magazine editorial photography, and home interiors and exteriors. Swider has worked with General Electric, the Cleveland Institute of Art, *Northern Ohio Live,* and *Cleveland Magazine,* among others, and she enjoys art, travel, horseback riding, yoga, poetry, and reading.

Al Teufen, originally from Pittsburgh, is a freelance photographer whose specialties include architectural, historical, and landscape photography. With a bachelor of science in photography from the Rochester Institute of Technology, Teufen is a member of ASMP and an affiliate member of the American Institute of Architects.

Other photographers and organizations that contributed to Cleveland: Continuing the Renaissance *include Herbert Ascherman Jr., Coventry Elementary School, Michael Evans, Mark E. Gibson, Neil Gloger, Steven Mastroianni, Mellott, Idris Salih, the Western Reserve Historical Society, and T. Williams.*

Index of Profiles

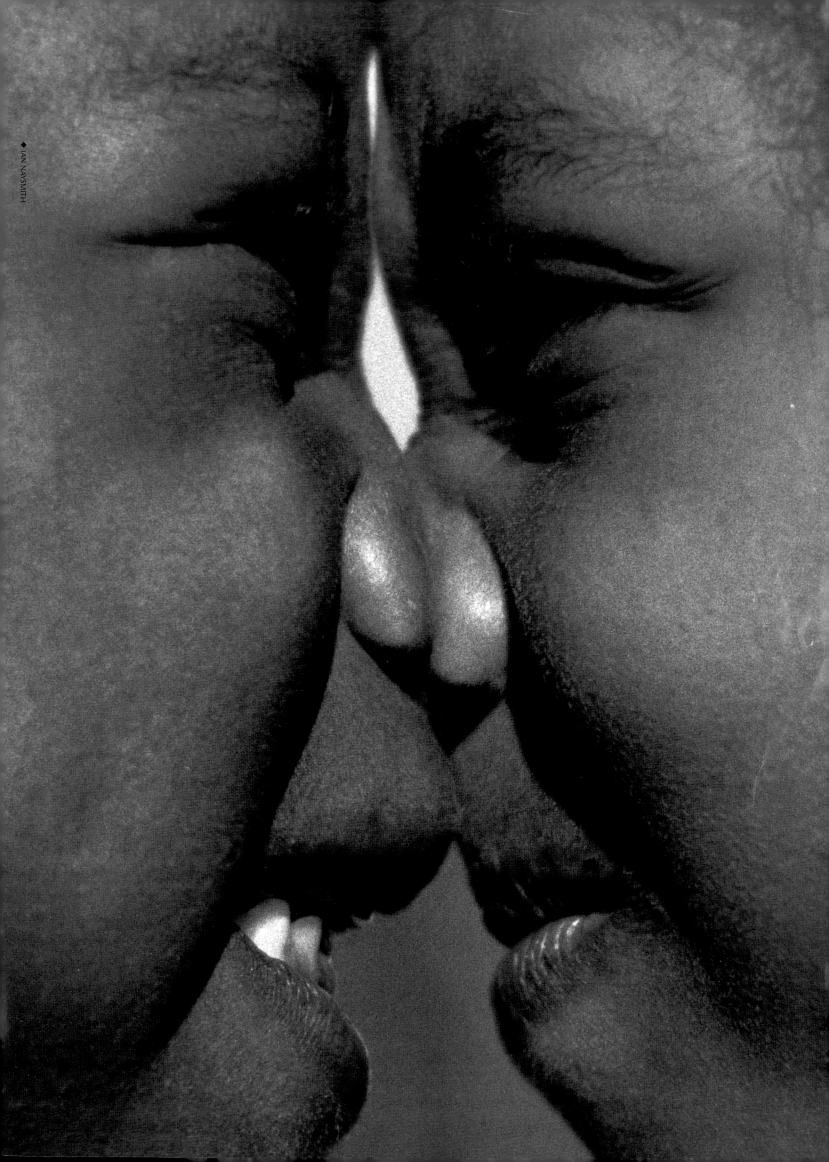